FAITHFUL WITNESS

❖

THE LIFE AND MISSION OF
WILLIAM CAREY

TIMOTHY GEORGE

New Hope
P. O. Box 12065
Birmingham, Alabama 35202-2065

Unless otherwise noted, Scripture quotations are from King James Version.

Scripture quotation indicated by NIV is from the Holy Bible, New International Version. Copyright ©1973, 1978, 1984 International Bible Society. Used by permission of Zondervan Bible Publishers.

Scripture quotation indicated by TEV is from the *Good News Bible*, Today's English Version—New Testament: Copyright © 1966, 1971, American Bible Society. Used by permission.

Scripture quotations indicated by NEB are from *The New English Bible*. Copyright © The Delegates of the Oxford University Press and the Syndics of the Cambridge University Press, 1961, 1970.

Dewey Decimal Classification: B
Subject Headings: CAREY, WILLIAM
                 MISSIONS—INDIA
                 MISSIONARIES—BIOGRAPHY

Maps of Carey's England and area of influence in India and Carey's family tree are adapted from *William Carey: A Biography* by Mary Drewery.

William Carey's *Enquiry* reprinted with permission of Criswell Publications, Dallas, Texas. Criswell edition edited by John L. Pretlove.

The cover photograph represents the three major aspects of Carey's life—his work as a shoemaker, his work as a missionary, and his lifetime interest in gardening. He would often keep his books on his workbench while making shoes.

Cover photo by John Cooper
Cover design by Janell E. Young
Items in cover photo courtesy of William A. Shoemaker
Photo credits: pp. 195-98, Dick Bodenhamer; pp. 199-200, Foreign Mission Board, SBC

N914102•0993•1.5M3
ISBN: 1-56309-025-2

For
Sam D. Sharp,
my boyhood pastor and lifelong friend,
who taught me to see the world
through the eyes of the
Saviour's love

Foreign Mission Board, SBC, photo

CONTENTS

WILLIAM CAREY AND HIS FAMILY

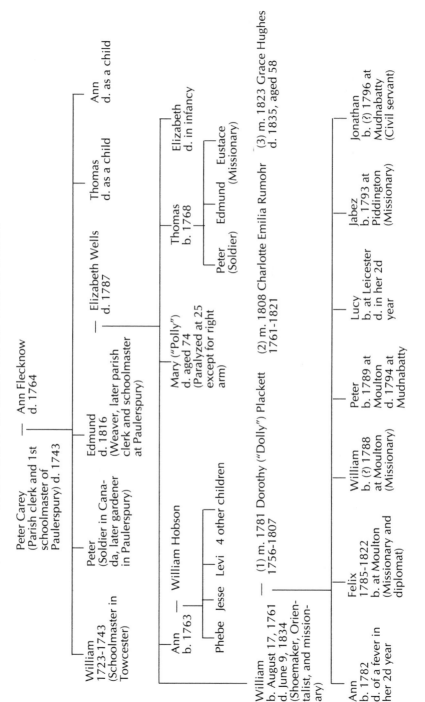

A CAST OF CHARACTERS

David Brainerd (1718-1747). Pioneer missionary to the Indians of North America. His *Journal* had a profound impact on Carey and many other missionaries.

Charlotte von Rumohr Carey (1761-1821). Carey's second wife. Daughter of a Danish count, she was devoted to Carey and the mission despite her debilitating illness.

Dorothy Plackett Carey (1756-1807). The first wife of Carey. Mother of his four surviving sons.

Edmund Carey (1736-1816). Village schoolmaster. Father of William Carey.

Grace Hughes Carey (1777-1835). Carey's third wife. Twice widowed before Carey married her in 1822, she outlived her famous husband by one year.

Alexander Duff (1806-1878). Scottish missionary to India. To him Carey remarked on his deathbed, "When I am gone, say nothing about Dr. Carey. Speak about Dr. Carey's Savior."

Jonathan Edwards (1703-1758). Leading theologian of the Great Awakening in America. His writings on human responsibility and divine sovereignty influenced the renewal of missionary theology in England.

John Eliot (1604-1690). New England pastor and Apostle to the Indians. Organized many Indian congregations and translated the Bible into the Algonquin dialect.

John Fountain (1767-1800). The first missionary sent by the Baptist Missionary Society to join Carey in India.

Andrew Fuller (1754-1815). Baptist pastor in Kettering. Leading theologian of the missionary movement. Author of numerous works, including *The Gospel Worthy of All Acceptation*.

Charles Grant (1746-1823). English businessman and high official in the East India Company. Evangelical Anglican and friend of missions.

Robert Hall, Sr. (1728-1791). Baptist pastor at Arnesby. One of Carey's mentors in ministry. Author of *Help to Zion's Travellers.*

Adoniram Judson (1788-1850). Baptist missionary to Burma. He and his wife, Ann, met Carey in Calcutta and were baptized there by William Ward.

Joshua Marshman (1768-1837). One of the Serampore Trio. He and his wife, Hannah, organized a boarding school at the mission which expanded into a large network of schools throughout India.

Henry Martyn (1781-1812). Anglican missionary to India. Trained at Cambridge under Charles Simeon who introduced him to Carey's journal.

John Newton (1725-1807). Anglican evangelical clergyman and hymn writer. Encouraged Carey's mission to India.

Clarke Nichols (d. 1777). Shoemaker of Piddington. Carey served as his apprentice.

Krishna Pal (d. 1822). Indian carpenter converted to Christ and baptized in 1800. The first Hindu convert under Carey's ministry.

Samuel Pearce (1766-1799). Pastor of Cannon Street Baptist Church in Birmingham. Devoted friend of Carey and tireless advocate for missions.

John Collett Ryland (1723-1792). Baptist pastor in Northampton. Rebuked Carey for his desire to send missionaries to faraway lands.

John Ryland, Jr. (1753-1825). Baptist pastor at Northampton and later at Bristol. Baptized Carey in 1783. Strong supporter of Baptist Missionary Society and Carey's mission to India.

Thomas Scott (1747-1821). Evangelical Calvinist theologian and Bible commentator. As a young man Carey was deeply moved by his preaching.

Charles Short (d. 1802). An official of the East India Company. Married Kitty Plackett, Carey's sister-in-law.

John Sutcliff (1752-1814). Baptist pastor at Olney. Studied at

Bristol College. Encouraged Carey's early efforts in ministry and inspired many other young missionaries.

John Thomas (1757-1800). Physician and pioneer missionary. Accompanied Carey and his family to India.

William Ward (1769-1823). The third of the famous Serampore Trio. A printer by trade, he oversaw the publication of Bible translations and other literature at the Baptist mission in India.

John Wesley (1703-1791). Founder of Methodism, leading figure in the Evangelical Awakening.

William Wilberforce (1759-1833). Slave-trade abolitionist and political leader in Parliament. A founder of the Church Missionary Society, he defended the right of Carey and other missionaries to carry the gospel to India.

HIGHLIGHTS OF CAREY'S LIFE

1761 William Carey born at Paulerspury in Northamptonshire, the eldest son of Edmund Carey, a weaver and village schoolmaster.

1775 Apprenticed to a shoemaker at Piddington where John Warr, a fellow cobbler, led him to faith in Christ.

1781 Married to Dorothy Plackett at Piddington.

1783 Baptized by John Ryland, Jr., in the river Nene at Northampton.

1785 Called as pastor of the Baptist chapel at Moulton.

1789 Began his ministry as pastor of the Baptist church in Harvey Lane, Leicester.

1792 Published *An Enquiry into the Obligations of Christians to Use Means for the Conversion of the Heathens.*

Preached "Expect great things. Attempt great things." sermon before the Northamptonshire Baptist Association meeting at Nottingham.

Present in Kettering at the founding of the Particular Baptist Society for Propagating the Gospel Among the Heathen.

1793 Commissioned along with John Thomas as a missionary to Bengal in India.

Sailed from Dover with his family on the Danish ship, *Kron Princessa Maria.*

1794 Settled first near Debhatta in the Sundarbans jungle.

Moved to Mudnabatty, near Malda, to work as an indigo planter.

His five-year-old son Peter died from dysentery; his wife grew progressively depressed and deranged.

1797 Completed first draft of his translation of the New Testament into Bengali.

1800 Moved to Serampore, organized missionary community, and began fruitful association with William Ward and Joshua and Hannah Marshman.

Baptized Krishna Pal, the first Hindu converted to Christ through his ministry.

1801 Appointed as professor in Fort William College in Calcutta.

First Bengali New Testament printed by the Serampore Press.

1807 Ordained his son Felix who was sent as a missionary to Burma.

Published Sanskrit New Testament.

Granted the doctor of divinity degree by Brown University.

1808 Married Charlotte Emilia Rumohr following Dorothy's death five months earlier.

1812 Serampore's printing presses destroyed in a fire.

1814 Ordained his son Jabez who was sent as a missionary to the Moluccan island of Amboyna.

1815 Mourned the death of Andrew Fuller. Tensions increased between the Baptist Missionary Society and the Serampore Mission.

1818 Serampore College founded.

1820 Organized the Agricultural Society of India.

1823 Married his third wife, Grace Hughes, following the death of beloved Charlotte in 1821.

Grieved over the death of William Ward.

1830 The Serampore Mission placed in financial jeopardy by the crash of the Calcutta banking houses.

1834 Died at Serampore. At his request, a simple tablet marked his grave, bearing the inscription: A wretched, poor, and helpless worm, on Thy kind arms I fall.

PREFACE

Two hundred years ago, on June 13, 1793, William Carey; his wife, Dorothy; and their four children, including a nursing infant, sailed from England on a Danish ship headed for India. At the time few people noticed their departure. Carey was a shoemaker by trade. With only a grammar-school education behind him, he had no credentials for missionary service except an inextinguishable conviction that God Almighty had called him to devote his life to "the conversion of the heathens." Moreover, he went to India as an illegal alien, having failed to secure the required immigration permit from the East India Company. He also lacked financial resources, apart from the meager funds he had scraped together. As the unknown pastor of a small-town church in the English Midlands, he had been able to muster the promise of support from only a handful of friends. The Baptist bigwigs felt the venture was too uncertain to commit their denomination to it.

Now, two centuries later, Carey is universally recognized as the father of modern missions. His name is synonymous with the heroic age of the Protestant missionary movement which began with his 40-year ministry in India and includes the saga of other notable figures such as Henry Martyn, John Wilson, Alexander Duff, Adoniram and Ann Judson, Robert Morrison, Lottie Moon, and David Livingstone, all of whom either knew Carey personally or were deeply influenced by his life and example. Thus in his history of Christian missions, W. O. Carver wrote of "Carey and the New Epoch."

This book was written to commemorate Carey's remarkable venture of faith and to encourage Christians in the last decade of the twentieth century to catch his vision for proclaiming the good news of Jesus Christ throughout the world. What Carey wrote about the fulfillment of the Great Commission 200 years ago is still valid, and even more compelling, today: "Some attempts are being made, but they are inconsiderable in comparison with what might be done if the whole body of Christians entered heartily into the spirit of the divine command on this subject." This study focuses on Carey's early life, his motivation and calling as a missionary, and his historic role in awakening the church of his day to the great challenge of world evangelization.

What kind of person was William Carey? What did he look like? Two portraits of Carey, both done during his lifetime, have come down to us. The first was drawn somewhat clumsily by a student artist shortly before Carey's departure from England. It shows the face of a plodder—brown eyes, firm lips, a determined brow smudged by the likeness of an ill-fitting wig, which Carey would throw overboard en route to India.

The second portrait was painted by the leading artist of Calcutta, Robert Horne, when Carey was in his 51st year. Here he sits at his desk dressed in the fine clothes of a scholar, busy with the work of translating the Scriptures. On the table before him is a copy of his Sanskrit New Testament showing a verse from Acts (2:11): "We do hear them speak in our tongues the wonderful works of God." His face is kindly and smooth shaven, his eyes piercing and alert, his jawbone no less determined than before. In 1826 two visitors from England described Carey, then 65, in this characteristic pose: "We found Dr. Carey in his study; and we were both much pleased with his primitive, and, we may say, apostolical appearance. He is short; his hair white; his countenance benevolent."

Since his death in 1834, some 50 biographies of Carey have been published in many languages of the world. Four of these stand out above all others and are foundational to this biographical study as well. The first biography of Carey was written by his nephew, Eustace Carey, and published in 1836 in both England and America. Eustace himself had spent more than 10 years as a missionary in India and was privy to his famous uncle's recollections and reminiscences about his early life. His *Memoir* is an invaluable resource although his interpretation of certain events is skewed due to the fact that he and his uncle took different sides in a painful dispute between the Serampore

Mission and Baptist Missionary Society.

John Clark Marshman was the son of Joshua and Hannah Marshman, fellow workers with Carey in the founding of the Serampore Mission. In 1859 he published a two-volume history entitled *The Life and Times of Carey, Marshman, and Ward*. It is both an apology for the Serampore Trio and a meticulous record of their achievements. He grew up at Serampore and had firsthand knowledge of many of the events he describes. Of Carey he said, "The basis of all his excellencies was deep and unaffected piety. . . . He was conspicuous for constancy, both in the pursuits of life and the associations of friendship."

In 1887 George Smith published his *Life of William Carey, Shoemaker and Missionary*. Smith had also gone to Serampore as a young man and was well acquainted with Carey's descendants and many Indian Christians who had been won to Christ through his ministry. In 1909 his classic study of Carey was included in Everyman's Library.

Drawing upon these published resources along with his own careful research, S. Pearce Carey, the great-grandson of William, published in 1923 what remains the standard biography of his revered forefather, *William Carey, D. D., Fellow of Linnaean Society*. His book is a lively and imaginative account, not likely to be superseded in its romantic casting and affectionate appraisal of the great missionary.

Carey was a prolific correspondent and also kept a journal for many years. However, he poured his tireless scholarly energies into translating the Bible into the many languages of India and the East rather than writing ponderous tomes of theology. His one original masterpiece, which became the manifesto of the entire missionary movement, was *An Enquiry into the Obligations of Christians to Use Means for the Conversion of the Heathens*. We have included this important work, first published in 1792, as an appendix to this volume. In many respects, the story of Carey's life is a commentary on this text. Many of Carey's letters, some recently discovered, were used in the research for this book.

Numerous individuals kindly helped me in the research and writing of this book. I am grateful to the librarians and staff of the following research facilities: the Southern Baptist Historical Commission; Woman's Missionary Union; the Southern Baptist Theological Seminary; Regent's Park College in Oxford; Dr.

Williams's Library in London; and the library of New College, Edinburgh. Elizabeth Wells and Shirley Hutchens of the Special Collections Department of the Samford University Library provided able and cheerful assistance in many ways. Donald MacKenzie and Ian Green, ministers of the Fuller Memorial Baptist Church in Kettering, received me cordially and took me to Carey sites in Northamptonshire. My friends B. R. White, Mark Dever, and Bruce Winter listened to my ideas and encouraged my interest in Carey. Cecile Glausier typed the manuscript of this book amidst her other pressing duties as administrative secretary of Beeson Divinity School.

My son Christian accompanied me to England and endured many long hours in musty libraries with a patience not common in eight-year-olds. My daughter Alyce Elizabeth shed new light on this study by sharing insights she learned in her Mission Friends group at church. My wife, Denise, embodies the graces of the Christian life in such a way that our marriage has been as blessed as that of William and Dorothy was vexed. If a happy home is but an early heaven, then I have been granted a foretaste of glory indeed!

This book is dedicated to Sam D. Sharp, fervent preacher, loving pastor, friend of missions. Like Carey, he too is a faithful witness.

Timothy George
Dean, Beeson Divinity School
Samford University

August 17, 1991
230th Anniversary of William Carey's Birth

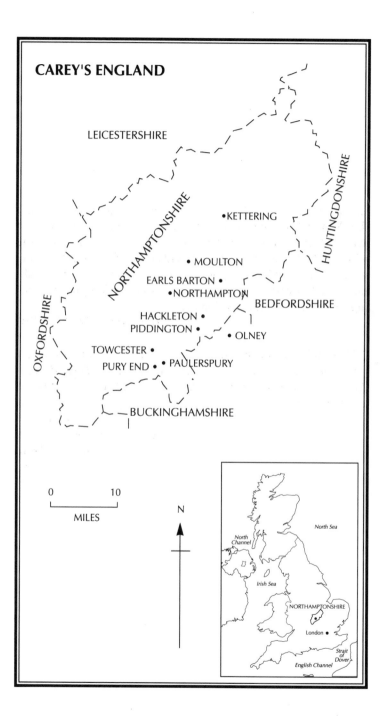

CAREY'S ENGLAND

LEICESTERSHIRE

NORTHAMPTONSHIRE

HUNTINGDONSHIRE

•KETTERING

• MOULTON

EARLS BARTON •
•NORTHAMPTON

BEDFORDSHIRE

OXFORDSHIRE

HACKLETON •
PIDDINGTON •
• OLNEY

TOWCESTER •
PURY END • • PAULERSPURY

BUCKINGHAMSHIRE

0   10
MILES

N

North Sea

North
Channel

Irish Sea

NORTHAMPTONSHIRE

London •

Strait
of
Dover

English Channel

MY brothers, think what sort of people you are, whom God has called. Few of you are men of wisdom, by any human standard; few are powerful or highly born. Yet, to shame the wise, God has chosen what the world counts folly, and to shame what is strong, God has chosen what the world counts weakness. He has chosen things low and contemptible, mere nothings, to overthrow the existing order.

1 Corinthians 1:26-29 (NEB)

THOSE who in that day sneered that England had sent a cobbler to convert the world were the direct lineal descendants of those who sneered in Palestine 2,000 years ago, "Is not this the carpenter?"

Frederick W. Farrar,
spoken in Westminster Abbey,
March 6, 1887

1

A Nest of Consecrated Cobblers

FOR three days in the summer of 1813 the House of Commons was embroiled in a fierce debate. Exactly 20 years earlier William Carey, a poor journeyman shoemaker turned Baptist preacher, had sailed to India, defying the East India Company's ban against the settlement of missionaries in territories under its control. Now a bill had been introduced to reverse that ban and the name of Carey was on everyone's lips.

Those leaders of Parliament who wished to keep the missionaries out of India (for fear that the company's investments would be jeopardized by their efforts to convert the nationals) blasted the humble origins of Carey and his friends— "apostates from the loom and anvil," "renegades from the lowest handicraft employments," vendors of a coarse theology who had crawled forth from "the holes and caverns of their original destinations."[1]

Such abuse was nothing new to the missionaries of Serampore. Earlier a leading churchman of the day had caricatured Carey and his associates as "a nest of consecrated cobblers."[2] In 1813, however, the friends of missions found a champion in the great abolitionist William Wilberforce, who defended Carey's "beneficent labors" in bringing Christianity to India. The work of the Baptists at Serampore, he said, was one of the chief glories of the British Empire. With the example of Carey before their eyes, and the arguments of Wilberforce ringing in their ears, the members of Parliament voted 89 to 36 to remove the legal sanctions against the sending of missionaries to British

India. A new era in the expansion of the church had begun. Carey was pleased the India Bill had passed, but he did not relish being cast in the role of missionary hero. When told of Wilberforce's high commendation of him in the Commons, he replied, "I wish people would let me die before they praise me."[3]

Throughout his life Carey resisted the lure of the personality cult. He resented the fact that some of his former acquaintances in England were beginning to collect relics from his youth and early life: a cup from which he had drunk, a pair of shoes he had made, a wooden board advertising his cobbler business. "The less said about me the better," he declared.[4]

When he lay dying in 1834, he summoned the Scottish missionary Alexander Duff to his side and whispered, "Mr. Duff! You have been speaking about Dr. Carey, Dr. Carey; when I am gone, say nothing about Dr. Carey. Speak about Dr. Carey's Savior."[5]

We would misunderstand Carey if we attributed such sentiments to a false modesty or a lack of proper self-esteem. Those who knew him best, including some who differed with him most, testified that his life was marked by childlike simplicity and utter transparency. Few persons in the history of the Christian faith have had a more profound sense of the grace of God. "If I ever get to heaven," he said, "it must be owing to divine grace from first to last."[6] He knew that feeling of absolute dependence which is at the core of all true religion. And yet, perhaps inevitably, Christians of later generations have indeed been interested in Carey, as well as his Saviour. The story of his life, retold scores of times, has inspired thousands of believers who have followed his missionary footsteps into all the world.

The Village Lad

William Carey first saw the light of day on August 17, 1761, in the obscure village of Paulerspury, in the county of Northamptonshire, in the Midland region of England. William Law, whose spiritual writings had awakened a new generation of evangelical believers (Charles Wesley once claimed that "Mr. Law was our John the Baptist"), died in the same year Carey was born. John Wesley was at the height of his powers, in his

58th year. George Whitfield, the greatest preacher of the century, was preparing to cross the Atlantic again for his sixth, and next to last, evangelistic tour of the American colonies. There he would inspire a Great Awakening among the churches of all denominations, a moving of the Spirit Jonathan Edwards called a "surprising work of God."

In Hanoverian England life was stately and measured. For 20 years fashionable Londoners had been crowding into Westminster Abbey to listen, enraptured, to Handel's *Messiah*. It was the age of Boswell and Dr. Johnson, of Jane Austen and Robert Burns, of Gibbon and Burke, of Wedgwood and Chippendale. It was also an age of violence and war. The American and French revolutions would both disrupt the peace of the world before Carey sailed for India. Six months before he was born, the last French outpost on the Indian subcontinent, Pondicherry, surrendered to the British fleet, assuring that the sun would not set on the Union Jack in that part of the world for almost another two centuries. In 1760 George III, aged 22, succeeded his grandfather to the throne of England, beginning a reign of 60 years, the longest of any monarch in the history of the realm until that of his remarkable granddaughter Victoria.

We can be sure these grand events had little impact on life in Paulerspury, whose 800 inhabitants were more concerned about the daily human drama of their own village, surrounded by forests and fields, subject to the whims of weather and seasons, shaped by stories of witches and ghosts and fairies no less than by the weekly routines of the parish church. Into this world William Carey came, the eldest of five children born to Edmund and Elizabeth Carey.

He was called William by his grandmother, Ann, the namesake of her own firstborn who had died prematurely many years before in 1743. That tragic loss had so pierced the heart of Ann's husband, Peter, that he too was buried within two weeks of his son's death, perhaps a victim of his own hand.[7] Little William's birth in 1761 brought old memories and new hopes.

Edmund Carey was only seven years old when the dark events of 1743 struck. Thinking of the future his mother had apprenticed him, while still a child, to a village weaver. He continued his labors at the loom (weaving a kind of woolen cloth known as tammy) until William was six years old when, like his father and deceased brother before him, Edmund was appointed master of the local charity school in the village.

This was not a major step up the social ladder since "elementary schoolteaching was far from being a respected profession at the time."[8] Charity schools, like the Sunday School movement founded by Robert Raikes in 1780, were designed to teach basic reading skills to children of the lowest classes of society. They carried all the negative connotations that the expression *living on charity* still holds today. Still, there were advantages too. Edmund had a larger house to accommodate his growing family and a little more income (he was also the parish clerk) with which to buy a few extra books and perhaps the weekly news sheets of the *Northampton Mercury.*

William was obviously a precocious child "having been accustomed," as he later recalled, "to read the Scriptures from my infancy." In 1815 his father remembered that "he was always attentive to learning when a boy." In addition to the Bible, he read books of adventure, science, and history. And, like Charles Spurgeon, his great admirer in the next century, he found a favorite in John Bunyan's *Pilgrim's Progress,* though he was first drawn to it merely as a "romance," and thus read it "to no purpose."[9] It was providential that Carey, whose interest in education would form a major part of his life's work, should begin his days as the son of a schoolmaster.

Knowledge of Carey's childhood is based largely on two letters he wrote from India, at the request of friends in England, together with the reminiscences of his favorite sister Mary, whom he affectionately called Polly. The two were extremely close. Polly recalled traipsing after her older brother as he scoured the fields and woods, the glens and coves, collecting flowers, plants, nests, and living creatures of every sort. "He often took me over the dirtiest roads to get at a plant or an insect," she remembered. These specimens he brought back to his tiny room at home which he had converted into a veritable laboratory of natural history, complete with a cage of birds Polly tended when William was at school or away on an errand.

Carey the naturalist was born in those countryside walks and boyhood experiments. It was a passion he never outlived. The miniature museum at Paulerspury was a beginning. In India he would amass a large collection of natural wonders from around the world, a botanical garden of international fame. His letters are filled with instructions like these he sent to his son Jabez and his daughter-in-law Eliza in 1815, soon after they had gone as missionaries to Amboyna: "I hope you will continue to send me curiosities of every sort. . . . Tell Eliza that I expect her to dry seeds for me and butterflies, also to pick up stones, shells, and crabs. Send them. But when you send seeds or dried birds—send me some stuffed birds—be careful to pack them very close, that no cockroaches can come at them. Send me bulbous roots and more parasitical plants. Send ugly shells as well as pretty ones."[10]

Edmund Carey was an honest man and a good provider for his family, but he was not one to fawn over his children. Polly says that his failure to show "any partiality for the abilities of his children" tended rather to discourage them. For this reason, the role of his uncle Peter in young William's life was all the more important.

As a young man Peter had joined the British army. For many years he was never heard from by his family, who assumed he had perished in some faraway land. But one day, like Rip Van Winkle, he returned to the village of his birth and settled down to tend his garden. Never a father himself, Peter found a surrogate son in William.

When the day's chores were done, and his schoolwork was finished, after Polly, Ann, and baby Tom had fallen asleep, William would listen to Uncle Peter's stories of adventure— sailing on the treacherous seas, fighting the French in Canada, tales of ships filled with slaves from Africa, of Indians and fur traders in the New World. Soon the children in his father's classroom had a new nickname for their robust companion in the schoolyard sports. They called him Columbus, for already he had glimpsed that wide, wide world which beckoned him forth. R. H. Lovell put it best. "Carey," he said, "felt the word *world*."[11]

Restless Cobbler

Given his love for plants and gardens, young William Carey seemed destined to a life in the outdoors as an agricultural laborer. At the age of 7, however, he developed severe allergies and a skin disease which was greatly irritated by long exposure to the sun. His parents, seeking a trade which would allow him to work indoors, found a shoemaker in the nearby town of Piddington who was looking for an apprentice. At age 14 Carey took up residence with Clarke Nichols and began to work with the awl and the last, learning the craft which would provide his basic income until he was 28 years old.

In the era before machines and factories, village shoemakers did play an important role in the leather works industry. They made shoes for their neighbors and friends, furnished supplies for shoe shops in the city, and even exported some of their stock to the colonies far away. Carey was an able workman and quickly mastered the trade, so much so that his employer once put a pair of shoes he had made on display in the window.

But his heart was not in it. In later life he was invited to a dinner party at the home of the governor of India. When another guest asked one of the servants whether Carey had not once been a shoemaker, Carey, who had overheard the question, stepped forward and said, "No, not even shoemaker, sir; just a cobbler!"[12]

How he would rather have cared for living animals than reshaped the dried skins of dead ones. How too he must have wondered about the destiny of the boots he carried to the shops of Northampton five miles away. What distant lands would they trample? What strange sights would their wearers behold? Did he wonder about his own destiny? Did he have an inkling that (as Adoniram Judson's biographer said of his great missionary subject) it would be "something connected with books and learning, something involving moving people's minds and hearts rather than grubby trade"?[13]

Carey had been baptized and brought up in the Church of England, as had Clarke Nichols; but his other apprentice, a lad named John Warr, came from a Dissenting family. During long hours in the workshop, conversation among the three of them often turned to matters religious. As parish clerk, Edmund Carey had required his children to attend church where they listened to the Psalms and lessons from the Book of Common Prayer. Although Carey never disparaged this religious training, it left him, as he put it, "wholly unacquainted with the scheme of salvation by Christ." Indeed, he confessed, "Of real experimental religion, I scarcely heard anything till I was fourteen years of age."[14]

John Warr, three years Carey's senior, was a persistent witness to his fellow apprentice. "He became importunate with me," Carey remembered, "lending me books (there were many such in his home) which gradually wrought a change in my thinking, and my inward uneasiness increased."[15] In the shoe-shop debates Carey nearly always had the last word, although he afterwards felt "stings of conscience" and wondered whether he had been right after all.

Carey's crisis of faith arose from a dual awareness: the gravity of his sinfulness and his inability to save himself. As a young teenager he was addicted to swearing, lying, and unchaste conversation, "which was heightened by the company of ringers, psalm-singers, foot-ball, players, the society of a blacksmith's shop, etc."[16] Polly tells us Carey was well liked by all his companions, and we might suppose he was a ringleader in such goings-on. In any event, like John Bunyan before him, for some years he gave little attention to his eternal destiny: "Heaven and hell were both out of sight and mind; and as for saving and damning, they were least in my thoughts."[17]

Stimulated no doubt by the hot-gospel pleadings of Warr, Carey did try to reform himself. He resolved to quit lying and swearing, but to no avail. Then one Christmas an incident occurred which marked a turning point in his spiritual struggle.

> I had been to Northampton, where I had made some purchases for myself, which amounted to about a shilling more than I was worth. But I had a counterfeit shilling, which Mr. Hall, the iron-monger, had given me as a Christmas-box. I knew it to be a bad shilling, but I was strongly inclined to assert to my master that it belonged to other money, with which he had intrusted me, to purchase things for him as this would clear my private account. I recollect the struggle I had all the way home, and I prayed to God to excuse my dishonesty and lying for this once; I would never repeat such action, but would break off with sin thenceforth. My wickedness prevailed, and I told the falsehood, and was detected by my master. A gracious God did not get me safe through. I soon concluded that my theft was known to the whole village. I concealed myself from all, as much as I could, and was so overwhelmed with shame that it was a considerable time before I went out.[18]

Through this event Carey was led "to see much more of myself than I had ever done before."[19] He realized nothing but an entire change of heart could remove his guilt and bring him peace with God. Through further struggles and studies and conversations with godly believers, he was brought "to depend on a crucified Savior for pardon and salvation; and to seek a system of doctrines in the Word of God."[20]

Soon after he was converted Carey began to press the claims of Christ upon others. He and Warr stood faithfully by the bedside of Clarke Nichols as he lay dying. As he slipped into eternity, he rejoiced in his newfound faith and admonished others "to flee to Jesus as the sinner's friend."[21]

Carey now became deeply concerned about his relatives. On visits back to Paulerspury he would ask permission to lead in family prayers. Sometimes his zeal outran his patience. Like Gideon he wanted to overthrow all the altars of Baal in one night! Even dear Polly resented his overeager efforts: "Often have I felt my pride rise while he was engaged in prayer, at the mention of those words in Isaiah 'that all our righteousness was like filthy rags.' I did not think he thought *his* so, but looked on me and the family as filthy, not himself and his party."[22]

Eventually, though, Carey's loving persistence won the day. Some ten years after his own conversion Carey addressed the following letter to his parents.

> Religion is far from being a dry and formal round [of] mere externals. When we pray, 'tis to the Almighty Governor of heaven and earth. When we hear a sermon it is for eternity. The solemn thought we are accountable immortals should on all occasions possess our minds. Probationers for an eternal world, how should we live! By nature children of wrath and under condemnation, how earnestly should we sue for mercy! . . . Repentance is absolutely necessary for salvation. . . . I hope all my dear relations know the truth of those observations by their own experience.[23]

For Carey evangelism was never an optional add-on to the gospel; it was the motivating force of every soul delivered out of darkness into the light of grace. The message of salvation which Carey would sound throughout India for 41 years he first proclaimed in the humble villages of his birth and youth.

Dissenter and Baptist

Sunday, February 10, 1779, was a day of national fasting and prayer, proclaimed by King George III in response to the British defeats in the war with the American colonies. On this occasion John Warr persuaded Carey to accompany him to the worship service led by Dissenters in the little meetinghouse at Hackelton, the sister village of Piddington.

These people were not strangers to Carey. Certain senior members of this fellowship, "some old Christians," Carey called them, had befriended him and encouraged him through his early struggles as a new believer. He had sometimes gone to prayer meetings at their church, but never before had he attended a Sunday service outside of the recognized parish assemblies of the Church of England.

The Dissenters of Hanoverian England had inherited a legacy of persecution and harassment. When the Act of Uniformity was passed in 1662, over 2,000 ministers were expelled from their posts because they refused to declare "unfeigned assent" to everything in the Book of Common Prayer and seek reordination from an Anglican bishop. Among these were some of the most able clergy in the land, including Samuel Annesley, John Wesley's maternal grandfather.

In those days the Clarendon Code imposed severe penalties on those who could not conform to the established religion: John Bunyan languishing for 12 years in the Bedford jail; George Fox locked up at Scarborough Castle in a cell which was open to the wind and rain of the North Sea, so that "the water came over my bed and ran about the room. . . . And when my clothes were wet I had no fire to dry them"; the Welsh evangelist Vavasor Powell dying in the Fleet prison in the 11th year of his incarceration there; sergeants disrupting services of worship; meetinghouses burned to the ground; properties confiscated; ruinous fines extracted. Such memories lingered long in the Nonconformist conscience.[24]

With the Glorious Revolution of 1688 and the Act of Toleration the following year, Dissenters were granted statutory freedom of worship. But this was a tenuous liberty which never extended to civil equality. Dissenters were generally held in scorn. One High Churchman blasted them as "miscreants begat in rebellion, born in sedition, and nursed in faction."[25]

In 1719 Parliament passed a bill forbidding anyone who attended a Dissenting meeting from teaching, with three months in jail as the penalty for its violation.[26] This may explain why Carey's schoolmaster father went so long without hearing his son preach publicly, finally sneaking in the back of the meeting-house one night unobserved.

Carey grew up sharing the common prejudice of his age against Dissenters. Before his conversion he even entertained the malicious thought of destroying single-handedly the very building where now he and John Warr sat listening to the sermon by Thomas Chater, the guest preacher from Olney.

It was a message on the cost of discipleship. It was necessary, said Chater, to follow Christ entirely. Carey listened entranced by his words, especially by the verse he repeatedly quoted to drive home his theme: "Let us go forth therefore unto him without the camp, bearing his reproach" (Heb. 13:13). It occurred to Carey that the "camp" in this text referred to the Church of England as established by law. Its "lifeless, carnal ministry" did not have to confront the scandal of the cross, protected as it was by privilege and status. The choice was clear. He felt he ought "to bear the reproach of Christ among the Dissenters; and accordingly I always afterwards attended divine worship among them."[27]

The name of Thomas Chater is never listed among the heroes of the Christian faith. Yet he had a decisive influence on Carey at a formative stage in his life. He took Carey under his wing and encouraged him to exercise his spiritual gifts.

In June 1782 he recommended his young friend to the Dissenters' meeting cottage at Earls Barton. This church, called the mat-shop after the rush-mat weavers who attended it, was so poor it could ill afford to supply the clothes and shoes Carey wore out walking to and from his preachings there. For several years he ministered to this little flock as a bivocational pastor, holding services for them every two weeks.

Chater was also involved in another event of seminal importance in Carey's career—his first experience with the Northamptonshire Baptist Association. In 1764 six Particular Baptist churches formed themselves into an association for mutual support and Christian service. By the 1780s the association had expanded to comprise many congregations throughout the Midlands, including churches in Bedfordshire, Hertfordshire, Nottinghamshire, and Lincolnshire. Its annual meetings were thronged by believers of like precious faith who gathered for prayer, powerful preaching, and close fellowship in the things of the Lord.

In the summer of 1782 the meeting was held at Olney. Carey attended, perhaps at the invitation of Chater who may have introduced his young friend to some of the luminaries whose lives were destined to be linked with his in a design greater than any of them could have foreseen at the time. There was John Collett Ryland, pastor of College Lane Church in Northampton, whose son Ryland, Jr., had just been ordained as copastor with him the previous year. There was John Sutcliff, host pastor at Olney, a Yorkshireman who had studied for three years at Bristol College, the first theological academy among the Baptists in England. Above all, there was Andrew Fuller, pastor at Soham near Cambridge, a man with "broad shoulders, thick eyebrows, and deep-set eyes, the visage of a village blacksmith," as William Wilberforce later described him, "though no less agile of mind and lips for that."

Fuller was the preacher of the hour and Carey listened to his message on the text, "Be Not Children in Understanding." Carey had walked over from Hackleton without a penny in his pocket. Too poor to purchase a meal, he fasted all day. Now, with the services over and the parting blessing given, Chater invited Carey to share a humble repast before the long walk back home.

Carey had embraced Dissent, but he was not yet sure about Baptist distinctives. The church which he joined at Hackleton in 1779 did not make one's baptismal preference a test of fellowship. They followed the policy expressed in the title of a pamphlet published by John Bunyan in 1673, "Differences in Judgment About Water-Baptism No Bar to Communion."

The Northamptonshire Association itself included among its members both Strict and Open Communionists. Fuller was an advocate of the former, while Robert Robinson of Cambridge agitated for the latter. Carey was confused about the whole matter. A sermon on the subject preached by a paedo-Baptist minister at the baptism of an infant left him unconvinced and drove him to further study. "Having so slight an acquaintance with ministers," he later recalled, "I was obliged to draw all from the Bible."[28]

His studies bore fruit and he became convinced of the necessity of believer's baptism by immersion. Acting on his newfound conviction, he applied for baptism himself at the hands of the senior John Ryland. Ryland gave him a pamphlet to read and turned him over to his son who did the actual baptizing. Ryland and three deacons from the College Lane Church met the eager candidate by the banks of the river Nene early one Sunday morning in October 1783.

Some 30 years later Ryland recalled this event and his impression of the man he baptized at Northampton that day.

> On October 5, 1783, I baptized in the Nene, just beyond Doddridge's meeting-house, a poor journeyman-shoemaker, little thinking that before nine years elapsed he would prove the first instrument of forming a Society for sending missionaries from England to the heathen world, and much less that later he would become professor of languages in an Oriental college, and the translator of the Scriptures into eleven different tongues.[29]

In the worship service that morning Ryland preached from the text, "But many that are first shall be last; and the last shall be first" (Matt. 19:30). Strange words from Jesus, which follow even stranger ones about forsaking houses, brothers, sisters, father, mother, wife, children, lands "for my name's sake."

I believe that God himself infused into the mind of Carey that solicitude for the salvation of the heathen which cannot be fairly traced to any other source.

John Ryland, Jr.

2

The Widening Vision

CAREY'S last 10 years in England, from his baptism in 1783 until his departure for India in 1793, were perhaps the most formative period of his entire life. During this decade the village shoemaker became a respected city pastor, the budding student a real scholar of promise. The zealous witness who sought to win his sisters to faith in Christ devised a strategy for world evangelization which would catapult the church into the era of modern missions.

Yet these were years of hardship and struggle, of sickness, bereavement, and (always) grinding poverty. On Sunday, June 10, 1781, William Carey and Dorothy Plackett were united in marriage at the church in Piddington. He was not quite 20, she 5 years his senior. Illiterate at the time, she marked the marriage license with an *X*.

Carey met Dolly, as she was sometimes called, through the auspices of Thomas Old, the shoemaker of Hackleton, to whom he had been apprenticed since Clarke Nichols's death. She was one of three sisters. The elder married Old; the younger, Katherine ("Kitty"), was destined to sail with the Careys to India. The law allowed girls to wed at 12 and boys at 14; both were seasoned for marriage by the custom of the times. No doubt the village gossips talked about how young Carey had rescued Dorothy from spinsterhood.

The shadow which was to fall with increasing darkness across the 26 years of their married life was present already in their newlywed days. Their firstborn child, a daughter named Ann after William's grandmother and sister, died of a fever in her second year. Some 40 years later Carey's other sister Polly lamented the loss of that precious little one, "How I did love that child!"[1] Carey himself nearly died of the same fever which left him bald for the rest of his life. He wore an ill-fitting wig for the remainder of his time in England.

When things were at their lowest ebb, Elizabeth Carey walked over from Paulerspury to care for her ailing son and his anguished wife. Perhaps she remembered a snippet of conversation with a woman of their home village who had heard Carey speak in a cottage prayer service. "What, do you think he will be a preacher?" she had asked. "Yes," her friend replied, "and a great one, I think, if spared."[2] No stranger to hard times herself, she was appalled at how little they had on which to survive.

Then, just as the sickness was easing, another blow struck: the death of Thomas Old, leaving Carey responsible for his wife's widowed sister and her four fatherless children. Hearing of his distress, his friends at Paulerspury collected an offering from their own meager resources; and his younger brother Thomas, still unmarried, sent along a generous gift out of his life savings.

Through all of these difficulties, Carey continued to read and study and preach. The one burning desire of his life was to know Jesus Christ and to make him known. To make ends meet he opened a night school for village children in his thatched cottage at Piddington. He traipsed the dirt roads and byways of Northamptonshire filling orders, selling shoes, eking out a living as best he could.

Discouraged he must have been, but quit he never could. He later remarked to his nephew Eustace, who became his first biographer: "If, after my removal, anyone should think it worth his while to write my life, I will give you a criterion by which you may judge of its correctness. If he gives me credit for being a plodder, he will describe me justly. Anything beyond this will be too much. I can plod. I can persevere in any definite pursuit. To this I owe everything."[3]

Ministry at Moulton

Although he had been duly baptized by John Ryland, and was preaching every other Sunday for the Dissenters at Earls Barton, Carey had not yet been set apart for the gospel ministry by any local congregation. This was a matter of concern to John

Sutcliff who remonstrated with his young friend about "the propriety of joining some respectable church, and being appointed to the ministry in a more regular way."[4] At this urging Carey decided to unite with Sutcliff's own church at Olney. He would seek its blessings on his labors for the Lord.

Olney was certainly respectable enough, as Baptist churches in the Midlands went. It traced its origins back to John Bunyan who in 1672 obtained an indulgence for a gospel meeting to be held in a barn owned by a certain Joseph Kent at Olney. From these humble beginnings the church grew and prospered. When Sutcliff became pastor in 1775, it could boast a sanctuary seating some 700 persons.

Even the parish church at Olney was a center of evangelical awakening. Here John Newton, the rough sea captain converted from slave trading to Christian service, was rector for 15 years. He and his friend William Cowper, also a resident of the town, produced the famous *Olney Hymns* which included "Amazing Grace," "Glorious Things of Thee Are Spoken," and "God Moves in a Mysterious Way."

When Newton moved to London, where Carey was later to meet him briefly, he was succeeded by Thomas Scott, a famous Bible scholar and commentator in the Scriptures. Scott first met Carey when he was still in the employ of Old. Scott sometimes stopped by the workshop on his pastoral visits. From the first he regarded Carey as "an extraordinary person." As a young Christian, Carey talked with the learned pastor about the deep things of God. He frequently walked over to Olney to hear him proclaim the gospel. Later he said, "If there be anything of the work of God in my soul, I owe much of it to Mr. Scott's preaching, when I first set out in the ways of the Lord."[5]

So Carey was no stranger to Olney. Here, of course, he had first heard Andrew Fuller preach at the association meeting in 1782. Now he awaited their verdict on his own fitness as a preacher. Sutcliff arranged for a trial sermon in the summer of 1785. We do not know his topic or text, but evidently things did not go well. Their response was that of the doubtful Athenians to the Apostle Paul, "We will hear thee again of this matter" (Acts 17:32).

The minute book of the church contains the following record of the event.

> W. Carey, in consequence of a request from the Church, preached this evening. After which it was resolved that he . . . should engage again on suitable occasion for sometime before us, in order that further trial may be made of his ministerial Gifts.[6]

How many young ministers bereft of formal training and lacking church endorsement would ever have recovered from such a snub? Yet Carey plodded on and soon found a "further trial" of his gifts in the call of the Baptist Christians of Moulton to come as their pastor.

Moulton has changed little in the 200 years since Carey moved there. One can still visit the cottage where Carey and his family lived next to the small Baptist church he faithfully served for 4 years. His salary was never more than 12 pounds per year, although he did receive an annual supplement of 5 pounds from the Particular Baptist Fund, a scholarship for young ministers jointly sponsored by several Calvinistic Baptist churches in London. Still, it was also necessary for him to make shoes and tend school as he had done in Piddington. Unable to buy a globe to teach his students geography, he sewed one together out of left-over leather, drawing the outline of countries on it with a marker. His great-grandson tells a story which, if true, must have puzzled the students in his class: The village schoolmaster pointing on the homemade globe to continents, islands, and peoples far away, sobbing all the while, "And these are pagans, pagans!"[7]

Meanwhile the church at Olney was observing the progress of their erstwhile ordinand. His reputation as a preacher was growing. Young converts, his "glory and crown" he called them, were crowding into the dilapidated meetinghouse at Moulton. Even Andrew Fuller, not one easily taken in by a showy performance, was deeply moved when he first heard Carey preach. He seized his hand and exclaimed, "We must know more of each other!"[8] On August 10, 1786, one year after he had been placed on probation, the Olney congregation recorded its "unanimous satisfaction" with his ministerial abilities and set him forth "to preach wherever God in his providence might call him."[9]

His formal ordination occurred the following summer, on August 1, 1787. Twenty ministers from the Northamptonshire Association joined the local villagers to celebrate the solemn setting apart of their pastor. His confession of faith was clear and convincing. Ryland, who had baptized him; Sutcliff, who had commissioned him; and Fuller, who had recognized in him a greatness yet unfulfilled, together inducted him by prayer, preaching, and laying on of hands into his new office. How little did any one of them realize that day how their lives would intertwine in an intimacy of love and commitment, the bond of a shared vision to carry the gospel into all the world.

Carey had a pastor's heart. In all his later labors as educator, linguist, evangelist, reformer, and missionary statesman, he never lost his love for people. In a letter to John Stanger, a Baptist pastor in Kent who had been present at his ordination, Carey set forth his ideal of the Christian ministry and the motive of his own pastoral work.

> [The minister] should keep up the character of a teacher, an overlooker, at all times; and in the chimney corner, as well as the pulpit. . . . The importance of those things that we have to do with, ought always to impress our minds, in our private studies, our addresses to God, and our labours in the pulpit. The word of God! What need to pray much and study closely, to give ourselves wholly to those great things, that we may not speak falsely of God. The word of truth! Every particle of it is infinitely precious. O that we may never trifle with so important things. The souls of men! Eternal things! All of the utmost moment, their value beyond estimation, their danger beyond conception, and their duration equal with eternity. These, my dear friend, we have to do with; these we must give account of. . . . Pray for me and God help me to pray for you.[10]

Life was hard in Moulton. Sometimes the Careys ate meatless meals for weeks at a time. Yet there was joy in the Baptist pastor's cottage too. Three little boys came to brighten the lives of William and Dorothy: Felix, William, and Peter. If ever there were a happy hiatus in Dorothy's married life, then it was at Moulton, despite the grinding poverty. Frequent visits from her sister Kitty, a loving congregation to lend prayers and support, the sounds of little feet on the cottage floor all helped to drown out the awful memories of a silent grave in Piddington. In October 1787 she submitted herself to believer's baptism by immersion at the hands of her pastor-husband. It was a definitive break with the paedo-Baptist upbringing she had received; a decisive casting of her lot with the man she had promised to love, cherish, and obey till death did them part.

Not everything went smoothly in the church at Moulton.

There were cases of discipline recorded in the church minute book in Carey's own meticulous hand: Elizabeth Britten censured for "tale bearing and tattling"; Edward Smith for receiving charity when he had adequate funds of his own; even a deacon and his wife for treating the poor unkindly.[11] But Carey loved his flock with the ardent love of a young pastor for his first church. When smallpox and fever ravaged the village, he visited the suffering and comforted the dying. Years later from India he wrote to his sisters back home, "Poor Moulton people, destitute and forlorn. I still love that people much, and hope God will provide for them."[12]

Expanding Horizons

In the very year that the Careys moved to Moulton the presses of London brought out the *Journal of Captain Cook's Last Voyage*. This best-selling book recounted the adventures of James Cook, Britain's pioneering navigator, who commanded three expeditions to the South Pacific mapping new islands and lands and discovering hitherto unheard-of peoples. He was killed by natives at Kealakekua Bay, Hawaii, in 1779. Carey later confessed that the reading of Cook's voyages "was the first thing that engaged my mind to think of missions."[13]

All of England was taken with Cook's exploits. His discoveries caught the imagination of a nation still smarting from defeat at the hands of American revolutionaries. Cook's journals revealed the Pacific to Europe as no other explorer had done. He also offered England what she wanted most at the moment: new lands to replace lost colonies. William Cowper, poet of Olney, caught the national mood of romantic yearning in his verse "Charity," published in 1781.

> When Cook—lamented, and with tears as just
> As ever mingled with heroic dust—
> Steered Britain's oak into a world unknown,
> And in his country's glory sought his own,
> Wherever he found man, to nature true,
> The rights of man were sacred in his view.[14]

Yet there was precious little about missions in all this. Cook was not himself a particularly religious man. Nor did he conceive his voyages as a prelude to world evangelization. He wrote concerning one of the South Sea islands he discovered: "No one would ever venture to introduce Christianity into Erromanga, because neither fame nor profit would offer the requisite inducement."[15]

Carey must have read those words with chagrin. It had already been said by another of the English who had settled in India that "the credit of a good bargain was the utmost scope of their ambition."[16] Where others looked for money and power, Carey saw men and women created in the image of God perishing without the knowledge of the Saviour. That is why he could not teach geography as a mere matter of fact. The burden of those who had never heard weighed heavy on his mind. What could be done? What could *he* do? His sister-in-law Kitty, who had come to Moulton to help with the little ones, says that "more than once [I] saw him stand motionless for an hour and more in his little garden, absorbed in his tense thoughts and prayers, till his neighbors judged him beside himself."[17]

He read not only Cook but everything else he could find about the distant lands and strange peoples— Guthrie's *Geographical Grammar,* John Entick's *The Present State of the British Empire,* the international news sections of the weekly *Northampton Mercury.* "From his cottage windows," one biographer wrote, "he looked out unto the uttermost parts of the earth."[18]

One day Andrew Fuller rode down from Kettering, where he had been pastor since 1782, to visit with Carey in Moulton. Entering his workshop, he saw a large map suspended on the wall above the trough filled with leather and the tools of the shoemaking trade. It was a large homemade map of the whole world pasted together of several sheets with the population, religion, and other facts about every country written on the map in Carey's own hand.

Over the years Carey had been collecting data for the book he was beginning to write. It would be published eventually in 1792 under the longsome title, *An Enquiry into the Obligations of Christians, to Use Means for the Conversion of the Heathens. In Which the Religious State of the Different Nations of the World, the Success of Former Undertakings, and the Practicability of Further Undertakings, Are Considered, By William Carey.* His "little piece," as Carey called it, would become the manifesto of the modern missionary movement. Its genesis was in the workshop and prayer garden at Moulton. John C. Marshman, who as a boy in India listened to Carey describe his early stirring, wrote this account of the scene which filled Fuller with wonder that day.

> While engaged in making or mending shoes, his eye was often raised from the last to the map, and his mind was employed in traversing the different regions of the globe, and musing on the condition of the various heathen tribes, and devising the means of evangelizing them.[19]

Carey did not—he could not—keep his concern to himself. His sermons, like those of Richard Baxter in an earlier generation, were the pleas of a "dying man preaching to dying men." One Sunday when Polly was visiting in Moulton, she heard her brother preach on the text, "For Zion's sake will I not hold my peace, and for Jerusalem's sake I will not rest" (Isa. 62:1). "It was a day to be remembered by me," she said, "a day set apart for prayer and fasting by the church."[20]

Slowly, steadily Carey was rousing his congregation, his family, his fellow ministers to the urgency that he felt like a fire burning within his bones. In the *Enquiry* he lamented the fact that "a vast proportion of the sons of Adam remain in the most deplorable state of heathen darkness . . . destitute of the knowledge of the gospel of Christ, or of any means of obtaining it."[21]

For Carey these "heathen" were not mere statistics, numbers he had gleaned from geographical surveys and news accounts. They were *persons,* eternal souls destined to live forever in the bliss of heaven or the darkness of hell. Somehow they must hear the good news of redemption through Jesus Christ. Carey pressed his case to Fuller and Sutcliff and Ryland until they too were convinced. "He would not give it up," Fuller recalled, "but talked with us one by one, till he had made some impression."[22]

When the first Baptist missionaries to Africa were being commissioned in 1795, John Ryland charged them to remember what Carey had made his constant theme a decade before: the infinite worth of a single soul.

> Think of the worth of a single soul—a soul delivered from eternal death, and made an heir of eternal bliss! Could you, brethren, at the present awful period, when the continent of Europe is deluged

with human blood, and the earth fattened with murdered corpses; could you still the madness of the people, and hush the insensate nations to peace; could you produce universal harmony and order, and revive trade and commerce in every country, now distracted by the wicked passions of men; and could you ensure all Europe, for a whole century, or for a thousand centuries, the inestimable blessing of peace; would not your names be recorded in history as the benefactors of mankind? Would you not be almost idolized as the temporary saviours of the world? Yet, all the sum of happiness that could be enjoyed on earth, by all the inhabitants of Europe in a thousand centuries, wherein the whole infernal art of war should be forgotten, and the most friendly intercourse should subsist between all its nations, and temporal prosperity bless every realm;—the whole sum of this happiness will be exceeded by the bliss of a single converted African, which he shall enjoy in a boundless and blessed eternity.[23]

While Carey never lost sight of this eternal dimension of his work, he was from the beginning also concerned with the "this worldly" aspect of the gospel. He was especially appalled by the horrors of the slave trade. He never prayed either in his church or with his family, his sister says, without remembering "those poor creatures."

By 1776 English traders had transported some 3 million slaves to America. As late as 1766 slaves were sold at public auction in Liverpool, as well as elsewhere in England.[24] It is to the credit of the evangelical Christians of the day that they were leaders in the movement which led to the abolition of the slave trade in 1807 and finally to the freeing of the slaves throughout the British Empire. The latter occurred one year before Carey's death. But from the early days of his vision for world missions, he opposed "the accursed Slave-Trade on the coasts of Africa." He also demonstrated his sympathy for the slaves by boycotting sugar from the West Indies produced through their labor, and encouraged others to do so as well.[25]

Along with gathering information on the climate, geography, population, and political life of distant lands and peoples, Carey also had an inordinate desire to learn their languages. When he was just a lad of 12 still living with his family at Paulerspury, he had taught himself Latin by studying an old textbook, Dyche's *Latin Vocabulary,* he chanced to find. Then, in Clarke Nichols's workshop, he had come across a commentary on the New Testament with part of the text printed in Greek. From a neighbor named Tom Jones he borrowed a Greek grammar and glossary. Soon he was on his way to unlocking one of the sacred languages of Holy Scripture. John Sutcliff, who had been trained in the biblical languages at the Baptist academy at Bristol, helped him to master Hebrew. On his own he acquired a reading knowledge of Dutch and then French.

Carey had a genius for learning new languages and was somewhat impatient with others who cited the linguistic barrier as an excuse for doing nothing about missions. "It is well known," he wrote, "to require no very extraordinary talents to learn, in the space of a year, or two at most, the language of any people upon earth, so much of it, at least, as to be able to convey any sentiments we wish to their understandings."[26] Eventually he would use his own "extraordinary" gift to preach the gospel in tongues he never dreamed of speaking as a village pastor in England and to translate the Scriptures into some 40 languages and dialects never before used for this holy purpose.

During his last year at Moulton, Carey's studies received a boon from two unexpected sources. Thomas Gotch, who was a deacon in Fuller's church, had contracted with the army to provide boots for its soldiers. Every other week Carey tramped the 12 miles from Moulton to Kettering with a supply of boots for Gotch, returning the same day with a new supply of leather.

One day after they had transacted their business, Gotch asked Carey how much he earned by his shoemaking. To which he replied, "About 9 or 10 shillings, sir." "Well," said Gotch, "you needn't spoil any more of my leather. I'll provide you 10 shillings a week from my private purse, so you can move on with your Latin, Hebrew, and Greek." Gotch, encouraged no doubt by his pastor, had glimpsed the potential greatness of the Moulton cobbler. Instead of laboring long hours to make shoes for others, his own feet could now be shod with "the preparation of the gospel of peace" (Eph. 6:15).

Another Baptist deacon who took an interest in Carey during this time was Thomas Potts. They met during a visit Carey made to Birmingham seeking to collect funds for the repair of the little Baptist meetinghouse at Moulton. Potts had been to America and had seen firsthand some of the horrors of the slave trade. Carey talked about his vision of a mission to the heathen, beginning perhaps with the South Sea Islands he had read about in Captain Cook's journals.

He mentioned the essay he was writing which he hoped would arouse a great interest in the subject. "Why don't you publish it?" asked Potts. "For the best of all reasons," said Carey. "I have not the means." So moved was Potts by Carey's conviction that he agreed to put up ten pounds of his own money toward the publication of the treatise.[27] Carey returned to Moulton buoyed by the encouragement of Potts but still unsure of what to do next.

Pastor in Leicester

The Moulton Church minutes contain the following entry for April 2, 1789: "Our Beloved Pastor who had been in considerable straits for want of Maintenance informed us that the Church at Leicester had given him an invitation to make trial with them, on which account we appointed to meet every Monday evening for prayers on that affair."[28] Actually the invitation had come two months earlier in February, for at that time we find him writing his father seeking his prayers. "I am exceedingly divided in my own mind," he declared. "If I only regarded worldly things, I should go without hesitation, but when I reflect upon the situation of things here, I know not what to do."[29]

Carey's reluctance to leave his little flock reflects not only a young pastor's love for his first church—the place where his three sons had been born and his wife baptized—but also a growing awareness of the serious character of his calling together with a sense of his own inadequacy. He felt acutely the urgency of Paul's question, "And who is sufficient for these things?" (2 Cor. 2:16). Nearly a year before the call from Leicester arrived, he wrote these lines to his father.

> I see more and more of my own insufficiency for the great work I am called to. The truths of God are amazingly profound, the souls of men infinitely precious, my own ignorance very great and all that I do is for God who knows my motives and my ends, my diligence or negligence. When I (in short) compare myself with my work, I sink into a point, a mere despicable nothing![30]

In Carey's assessment of himself, we see a spirituality strikingly similar to that of Francis of Assisi, whose profound humility was noted by everyone who knew him. What his biographer

Bonaventure said of Francis was also true of Carey: "In his own opinion, he was the greatest of sinners, and he believed that he was nothing more than a frail and worthless creature; yet, in reality, he was an example of holiness, chosen by God and shining by his manifold gifts of grace and virtue, and consecrated by the sanctity of his life."[31]

By May 7 the decision had been made and Carey announced his acceptance of the unanimous call from the Baptist church at Harvey Lane in Leicester. For the first time now Carey was a city pastor. His income was slightly larger than in Moulton, but Dorothy was pregnant again and so, again, Carey had to augment his living by making shoes and keeping school.

His friend Gardiner remembered the small house opposite the Harvey Lane Church where Carey moved with his expanding family in 1789. "I have seen him at work in his leathern apron, his books beside him, and his beautiful flowers in the windows."[32]

Soon after moving to Leicester Carey was drawn into an extraordinary group of scholars and activists whose wide-ranging interests matched his own deepening compassion for the sufferings of humanity. There was Dr. Arnold, a physician whose concern for the insane had led him to establish a special hospital for their care; and Robert Brewin, a friend of the prison reformer John Howard; and Richard Phillips, founder of Leicester's Philosophical Institute, a kind of scientific laboratory replete with telescopes and globes and even a lightning conductor. Carey was accepted as a respected member of this circle and spent many happy hours browsing through their libraries and discussing with them the urgent issues of the day, including the slave trade which they all opposed with a passion.

All the while Carey continued to study and preach and learn. On November 12, 1790, he wrote the following letter to his father back in Paulerspury, outlining his weekly activities.

> On Monday I confine myself to the study of the learned languages, and oblige myself to translate something. On Tuesday, to the study of science, history, composition, etc. On Wednesday I preach a lecture, and have been for more than twelve months on the book of Revelation. On Thursday I visit my friends. Friday and Saturday are spent in preparing for the Lord's day; and the Lord's day, in preaching the word of God. Once a fortnight I preach three times at home; and once a fortnight I go to a neighbouring village

in the evening. Once a month I go to another village on the Tuesday evening. My school begins at nine o'clock in the morning and continues till four o'clock in winter, and five in summer. I have acted for this twelve month as secretary to the committee of dissenters; and am now to be regularly appointed to that office, with a salary. Add to this, occasional journeys, ministers, meetings, etc.; and you will rather wonder that I have any time, than that I have so little.[33]

The ministry at Harvey Lane presented a unique challenge to the young pastor, only 28 when he accepted the charge. The unanimous call extended to Carey was a thin camouflage for serious troubles within the congregation. There is a hint of this in the opening sentence of the church's annual letter to the association, sent in the very month Carey agreed to become their pastor: "It is with a degree of pleasure we inform you that in the general we are at peace amongst ourselves."[34] In fact, the church had just gone through three pastors in as many years!

After an initial honeymoon under Carey's leadership, the old troubles broke out again. The membership sagged. The giving decreased. The next letter to the association meeting at Olney conveyed the ill tidings: "Far from enjoying harmony and peace, we are divided three against two, and two against three."[35] The disputes centered around antinomianism, the belief that the moral law is not binding on Christians in any sense. Ostensibly a doctrine which exalted the gospel (over law), this teaching actually was an abuse of true Christian freedom. It led the Leicester church to ignore and even countenance immoral behavior and undisciplined living among its members, including several of the deacons.

Congregational discipline as an essential mark of the true visible church was a hallmark of the Particular Baptist tradition. The London Confession of 1644 had declared bluntly that each congregation had power from Christ "to receive in and cast out, by way of excommunication, any member" (art. 42).[36] We have already seen Carey leading the Baptist congregation at Moulton to exercise this remedial discipline. At Harvey Lane the situation was so desperate Carey was driven to make a radical proposal. He decided that the best thing to do was for the congregation to dissolve its church relationship and start all over again! This they did, requiring all who wished to affiliate with the newly constituted body to sign publicly a declaration by which they promised "to keep up, in future, a strict and faithful discipline, according to the New Testament, let it affect whom it might."[37]

This crisis was a turning point in Carey's ministry at Leicester. Some of the "loose characters," not surprisingly, refused to go along with the new covenantal charter. Most, however, responded with repentance and renewed vigor to the challenge of a new beginning.

The church set aside days of fasting and prayer. A new gallery was added to the church to accommodate the crowds who now gathered to worship at Harvey Lane. The Anglican minister in Leicester, perhaps miffed at the declining numbers in his own flock, asked Carey whether he had been stealing the sheep of others. Carey replied that he had rather be the instrument of converting "a scavenger that sweeps the streets, than of merely proselyting the richest and best characters" in other men's congregations![38]

Carey sought for the "scavengers" not only in Leicester but also in the surrounding villages of Thurmaston, Syston, Sileby, Blaby, and Desford. In these places he conducted regular preaching missions and witnessed many conversions.

Carey's concern for the unevangelized heathen in distant lands did not slacken his zeal to share the good news of Jesus Christ with sinners at home. To his father he bared his heart. "The thought of a fellow creature perishing for ever should rouse all our activity and engage all our powers. . . . The matter is desperate. It calls for us to live and act alone for God. . . . [Let us work] with indefatigable industry, till we can't find a soul that's destitute of Christ in all the world."[39]

In another letter back home Carey mentioned "afflictions here [which] led us to the Lord."[40] He may have had in mind the terrible loss of his little daughter Lucy, a child of promise born in Leicester but buried there before her second birthday. Infant mortality was staggering in those days. Andrew and Sarah Fuller had 11 children, 8 of whom died before reaching the age of discretion. First Ann, and now Lucy—two little sisters who never knew each other. Carey mentioned her death in every letter he wrote, his sister recalled, for "he had been touched at a very tender point."[41] So too must Dorothy have been, though her suffering here, as in so many other ways, is veiled to us in silence.

The Missionary Trumpet Call

By the spring of 1791 matters at Harvey Lane had settled down and plans were made for Carey's formal installation as pastor. Fuller, Ryland, and Sutcliff were there again. The sermon of the evening, though, was preached by a new member of the inner circle, Samuel Pearce. His text was the motto of his life, as well as that of Carey himself: "God forbid that I should glory, save in the cross of our Lord Jesus Christ, by whom the world is crucified unto me, and I unto the world." (Gal. 6:14).

Pearce was a man of gentle disposition and deep spirituality. John Ryland referred to him as "the seraphic." As a young ministerial student at Bristol Baptist Academy, he penned this supplication, "May my affections to the crucified Savior be continually on a flame!"[42] The son of a silversmith from Plymouth, he was five years younger than Carey, whom he met for the first time the night of the installation at Harvey Lane. Pearce had accepted the call to Cannon Street Church in Birmingham the same month that Carey moved from Moulton to Leicester. Pearce and Carey were probably the two most promising young pastors among English Baptists at the time. Had either pursued the path of careerism, their lives might well have turned out quite differently. Instead, they were consumed with a desire to serve God rather than their own self-interest.

Pearce instantly became one of Carey's closest friends and one of his most ardent correspondents once the pastor of Harvey Lane was on the missions field. Pearce burned with the desire to join his friend in India, though he was never able to fulfill this holy ambition. But in his diary for October 10, 1794, we find this entry: "All prospects of pecuniary independence and growing reputation, with which in unworthier moments I had amused myself, were chased from my mind; and the desire of living wholly to Christ swallowed up every other thought."[43]

In the evening fellowship following the public consecration of Carey, Pearce requested that he read aloud to his fellow ministers from the *Enquiry*. Just one month earlier, on April 27, during the Easter meeting of the Northamptonshire Association at Clipstone, Carey had pleaded for the formation of a society to propagate the gospel in unevangelized lands. Fuller was the preacher that day. His topic was "The Danger of Delay" from

Haggai 1:2, "Thus speaketh the Lord of hosts, saying, This people say, The time is not come, the time that the Lord's house should be built."

Carey's influence resonated through every word of Fuller's message that day. If Luther had followed a strategy of overly prudent caution, he averred, the Reformation would never have happened. Why have the efforts to spread the gospel around the world been so feeble and few? Is Christianity less true now than it once was? Are there no opportunities to convey the gospel to the heathen? The truth is, he said, "We wait for we know not what. . . . We *pray* for the conversion and salvation of the world, and yet *neglect the ordinary means* by which these ends have been used to be accomplished. It pleased God, heretofore, by the foolishness of preaching, to save them that believed. . . . And how shall they preach except they be sent? Ought we not, then, at least try, by some means, to convey more of the good news of salvation to the world around us, than has hitherto been conveyed?"[44]

Despite Fuller's warning about the danger of procrastination, the ministers at Clipstone were not ready to heed Carey's summons to action. The fear of setting forth on an unbeaten path held them back. It seemed to them "too much like grasping at an object utterly beyond their reach."[45]

Yet Carey would not let his dream be quashed. The ministers had encouraged him to publish his *Enquiry*. He continued to revise his "piece" until it was ready to see the light of day. In early 1792 it was printed in pamphlet form by a female publisher in Leicester, a woman named Ann Ireland. It was sold for one shilling and six pence per copy. Booksellers in London and Sheffield as well as Leicester ordered copies. Soon Carey's case was before the churches. What George Smith has called "the first and still greatest missionary treatise in the English language" could not be ignored.[46]

Some 12 months passed from the evening Carey read portions of the prepublication version of the *Enquiry* to Fuller, Ryland, Sutcliff, and Pearce until the next spring meeting of the association. On this occasion ministers and messengers from the 24 associated churches gathered in Nottingham at the Baptist chapel in Friar Lane. It was the last day of May 1792. Letters from the churches were read reporting seasons of prayer and signs of revival. The next morning, a Wednesday, they gathered at 6:00 for an extended time of prayer. By 10:00 they were assembled for the first service of preaching that day. The appointed preacher was William Carey; his text, from Isaiah the prophet.

> Enlarge the place of thy tent, and let them stretch forth the curtains of thine habitations. Spare not, lengthen thy cords, and strengthen thy stakes; for thou shalt break forth on the right hand and on the left; and thy seed shall inherit the Gentiles, and make the desolate cities to be inhabited. Fear not. (Isa. 54:2-3)

Carey poured his soul into that sermon. How regrettable that it was never published! Since his early pastoral efforts in Moulton, the closing chapters of Isaiah had been a haven of comfort and encouragement in his own ministry. His chosen text follows Isaiah's great depiction of the Suffering Servant in chapter 53 and precedes God's open invitation to abundant life in chapter 55.

The whole passage is surrounded by imperative commands from the Lord: "Listen to me" (51:1,4); "Awake, awake" (51:9; 52:1); "Stand up" (51:17); "Rise up" (52:2); "Hear this" (51:21); "Shake yourself from the dust" (52:2); "See" (52:13); "Sing" (54:1); "Come" (55:1); "Do not fear, do not be discouraged" (54:4). The missionary call is sounded here in language which echoes through the New Testament: mountains made beautiful by the feet of messengers who bring good news and announce salvation, heralds of the King who proclaim, "Thy God reigneth" (52:7).

Carey took the prophet's words addressed to ancient Israel in a time of distress and applied it to the Church in his day. Indeed, there was much in his own experience of the Church to confirm the sullen image Isaiah paints: a barren widow, bereft of her husband, with no offspring to give hope or cheer. Yet the prophet calls for rejoicing, not lamentation; for celebration, not sorrow. The promise is this: God is about to restore the Church and His work will be extraordinary and wonderful. For this reason the command is given to lengthen the tent ropes and fortify the stakes of the tabernacle. There is to be an enlargement of God's people, a bringing-in of others on the right and the left, a winning of the Gentiles who are yet to be included in the covenant of grace.

The burden of the sermon came to a crescendo in a summarizing couplet, eight syllables, six words, "two plain, practical, pungent, quotable watchwords," as John Clifford once described them.

> Expect great things. Attempt great things.

Later tradition added two words to each of Carey's admonitions. Thus he is often quoted as having said, "Expect great things *from God;* attempt great things *for God.*" However, the earliest reports of the sermon do not contain these references to the Deity, which first surfaced in Ryland's summarizing account of Carey's message published in his posthumous account of Fuller's life in 1815, nearly 25 years after the event.[47]

Later biographers may have inserted the embellished motto into their accounts of Carey's life for polemical purposes, as has been argued recently, but there is an overriding reason why Carey himself would have felt no compulsion to include them in his original challenge anyway.[48] From first to last he was keenly aware of God's sovereignty in awakening the Church from its slumber and sending it forth to accomplish His eternal purpose in bringing the lost to a saving knowledge of the Redeemer. In this sense, both the "expecting" and the "attempting" were "*from* God." It was His mission, His Spirit, His call.

Other writers have reversed the order of Carey's watchword, placing the "attempt" before the expectation. But this too misses the spirit of his original intention.

> Carey's order reversed the vowels of his own name, and was the true sequence and reverence—Christian enterprise the fruit of Christian faith! Anything else . . . would be the cart before the horse.[49]

The effect of Carey's "deathless sermon," as it came to be called, was electric. Ryland, who also preached to the association later on the same day, recalled the impact made by the young friend he had baptized in the river Nene some 9 years before.

> Had all the people lifted up their voice and wept, as the children of Israel did at Bochim, I should not have wondered, so clearly did he prove the criminality of our supineness in the cause of God.[50]

By all accounts Carey's discourse was animated and eloquent. The ferment of his prolonged study and passion for spreading the gospel among the heathen overseas was poured into that one concentrated address. Writing to a minister in Yorkshire over one year after the event, Fuller could say, "I feel the use of his sermon to this day. Let us pray much, hope much, expect much, labor much; an eternal weight of glory awaits us!"[51]

On the morning following the sermon, a time was set aside for handling the business of the association. While many expressed appreciation for Carey's stirring message, the old feelings of doubt and hesitation were also present. As the time approached for the dismissal, it seemed that no specific action was going to be taken by the group. The inertia of the noncommitted was about to prevail.

Suddenly Carey seized Fuller by the arm. In "an agony of distress," as J. C. Marshman put it, he cried out loud, "Is there nothing again going to be done, sir?"[52] This was a catalytic moment in the history of the Church. How could those earnest Christians, however timorous, say no to what their ears had heard, their eyes had seen, and their hearts had felt?

Perhaps it was just to get the meeting over without further ado. Some of the messengers had a horseback ride of 60 miles and more before they could rest that evening. No doubt some of them saw it as a way of placating their overly zealous Brother Carey. After all, what could one small body of backwater Baptists *really* do to evangelize the *world*? Whatever their thinking, the Northamptonshire Baptist Association adopted a resolution before the benediction was pronounced that day. It was proposed by Fuller, at Carey's urging.

> Resolved, that a plan be prepared against the next ministers' meeting at Kettering, for forming a Baptist Society for propagating the gospel among the heathen.

One historian has expressed the meaning of that event like this: "Nothing less than a grand, God-glorifying, mission-oriented 'theology of hope' was entrusted to the church that day."[53]

EVERLASTING God! How much ground there is in the world where the seed of the gospel has never yet been sown, or where there is a greater crop of tares than of wheat! . . . Travellers bring home from distant lands gold and gems; but it is worthier to carry hence the wisdom of Christ, more precious than gold, and the pearl of the gospel, which would put to shame all earthly riches. . . . Must we not then pray God to thrust forth laborers into such vast tracts?

Desiderius Erasmus
The Art of Preaching, 1536

3

The Forerunners

CAREY'S sermon and Fuller's resolution set in motion a chain of events which led to the founding of the first society deliberately aimed at the evangelization of the non-Christian world. However, before we can tell that story, which is linked so directly with Carey's historic mission to India, it is necessary to see how this daring step by an obscure company of Midland Baptist ministers was related to other examples and precedents in the expansion of Christianity from a small Mediterranean sect into a worldwide religion of universal scope.

Missions and History

Carey himself was a keen student of the history of missions. The second section of his *Enquiry* reviews former undertakings for the conversion of the heathen beginning with the book of Acts and continuing through the early, medieval, and Reformation periods of church history. Carey believed the missionary mandate was integral to the Christian faith itself. It was the Church's obedient response to Jesus' command to proclaim the gospel to all segments of human society and to disciple believers from among *panta ta ethne,* "all peoples" (Matt. 28:19).

When, in the early fourth century, Eusebius of Caesarea set out to chronicle the course of Christian history from the days of the apostles up to his own time, he described the activity of those heralds of the faith through whom the spread of the gospel was first carried out.

Leaving their homes, they set out to fulfill the work of an evangelist, making it their ambition to preach the word of the faith to those who as yet had heard nothing of it, and to commit to them the books of the divine gospels. They were content simply to lay the foundations of the faith among these foreign peoples: they then appointed other pastors, and committed to them the responsibility for building up those whom they had merely brought to the faith. Then they passed on to other countries and nations with the grace and help of God.[1]

In this portrayal of early missionary activity, we find a three-fold strategy which recurs throughout the history of the Church: proclamation to the unsaved, indoctrination of new believers (i.e., their grounding in the Holy Scriptures), and the planting of local congregations led by a committed ministry. It was this very pattern which Carey called for in the *Enquiry* and which he implemented throughout his 40-year ministry in India.[2]

Carey also referred to a statement made by Justin Martyr, a Christian apologist writing around the middle of the second century. He declared that

there is not one single race of men, whether barbarians, or Greeks, or whatever they may be called, nomads, or vagrants, or herdsmen living in tents, among whom prayers and giving of thanks are not offered through the name of the crucified Jesus.[3]

Justin made this (no doubt exaggerated) claim in his debate with a Jewish scholar to prove that Malachi's prophecy of the universal worship of God (Mal. 1:11) had already been fulfilled in the Christian movement. Carey cited it to show that from the beginning of the Church's history, there was an urgent desire among believers to carry the good news of Jesus Christ into new territories, so that the Christian faith could become a universal force in the life of humanity.

A major shift in Christian consciousness occurred in the fourth century when the emperor Constantine embraced Christianity and endorsed it as the legal, official religion of the Roman Empire. This was the beginning of what is called the *corpus Christianum*, the fusing of church and society, religion and civil government, which has persisted in one form or another into the modern world.

Doubtless the church benefited in many ways from this altered situation. Christians were no longer persecuted. Believers in Jesus who formerly had to worship in catacombs and house churches were now free to build beautiful basilicas and cathedrals. But this reversal also carried great dangers. As Stephen Neill has put it, "With a new freedom, the church was able to go out into the world; at the same time, in a new and dangerous fashion, the world entered into the church."[4]

Carey deplored the "flood of corruption" which swept over the church in the wake of the Constantinian revolution. During the Middle Ages the missionary imperative was carried forward mostly by monks. The missions of Augustine to England, Patrick to Ireland, Columba to Scotland, Boniface to Europe, Cyril and Methodius to the Slavs are now fabled chapters in the history of world evangelization. Carey saw these efforts as a part of the extension of Christ's kingdom during difficult times.

All too often, however, the kind of Christianity which emerged from the so-called conversion of the barbarians was conditioned more by the pagan values of the surrounding culture than by the biblical and evangelical norms of the apostolic faith. Sadly, the missionary efforts of the Jesuits and other Roman Catholic orders did little to reverse the pattern of compulsion and superstition which had prevailed prior to the Reformation. Indeed, as Carey bluntly put it, "The professors of Christianity needed conversion as much as the heathen world."[5]

By the sixteenth century a reformation of the church "in head and members" was long overdue. The Protestant Reformation, however, was far more than a mere protest against the corruption and abuses in the Church. Essentially it was a rediscovery of the fundamental Christian doctrine of salvation. The last thing in the world the Reformers wanted to do was to start a new church. Their effort was to reform the one, holy, Catholic, and apostolic church by returning to the sources (*ad fontes!*) of its true life, namely the Holy Scriptures and the doctrine of the free grace of God in Jesus Christ. Thus the Reformers laid the foundation for the Great Awakenings of the eighteenth century and the modern missionary movement of the nineteenth century.

When Cyril and Methodius preached the gospel to the Slavs in the ninth century, they translated the Bible into their native Slavic tongue. By contrast, the medieval Roman church insisted that both the Bible and the Liturgy (the Mass) be available only in the official ecclesiastical language of Latin. Here and there were dissenting groups such as the Lollards in England who violated this sanction and passed around bits and pieces of the Bible which had been translated into the vernacular. The Reformers, however, building on the work of Christian scholars like Erasmus, broke down this barrier completely. Luther's Bible in German, Calvin's in French, and Tyndale's in English made the Word of God available, as Luther put it, to the "farm boy at his plough and the milk maid at her pail," as well as to learned clerics and theologians.

The newly invented printing press gave a great impetus to the dissemination of the Bible among the common people. Evangelical preachers and colporteurs carried with them Bibles, gospels, New Testaments, as well as catechisms and tracts and treatises by the Reformers, as they went from place to place planting churches, founding schools, and organizing the work of the new church.

The expository preaching of the Bible was a major homiletic innovation which the Reformers introduced. On January 1, 1519, Huldrych Zwingli entered the pulpit of the Great Minster of Zurich and began preaching, chapter by chapter, through the Gospel of Matthew. He followed this by similar series on nearly every book of the Bible. Calvin too adopted this pattern of preaching. In fact, when he returned to Geneva after a forced exile of three years, he walked to the pulpit of Saint Pierre, opened his Bible to the text he had been preaching on before his departure, and calmly continued the sermon! "The preaching of the Word of God is the Word of God," declared Heinrich Bullinger.[6] The Reformers knew that God alone could effect the conversion of sinners and that He had chosen "the foolishness of preaching to save those who believe."

Reformation preaching centered on the doctrine of justification by faith alone, "the article by which the church either stands or falls," as Luther put it.[7] The emphasis on the unmerited grace of God was a conscious protest against the sacramentalism and work righteousness of medieval Catholicism. Indeed, it called into question the basic presuppositions of humanism, mysticism, popular piety, and every other religious system which led human beings to believe they could in any measure save themselves.

Justification is by faith alone; but faith is not a human possibility, much less an achievement or good work. Luther insisted, especially in his commentary on Galatians, that faith is always, and only, a radical gift, dispensed freely in accordance with the good pleasure of God. Zwingli and Calvin agreed entirely with Luther on this point, although they stressed more strongly than he the concomitant responsibilities of the Christian life.[8]

Far from making this theology an excuse for inaction and unconcern, the Reformers confronted individuals with the claims of Christ and called on them to repent and believe the gospel. For example, Calvin's church in Geneva became a base for an aggressive evangelistic mission to France. Between 1555 and 1562 the Company of Pastors in that city commissioned 88 men who were sent forth as bearers of the gospel into nearly every corner of Calvin's native country. Also, in 1556 Calvin and his colleagues sponsored an ill-fated attempt to plant an evangelical church in Brazil, this some 50 years before the English established their first colony in the New World.[9]

This mission strategy was in keeping with Calvin's interpretation of the Great Commission. In commenting on the word *go* in Matthew 28:19, he wrote

> This is the point of the word *go* (*exeundi*): the boundaries of Judea were prescribed to the prophets under the law, but now the wall is pulled down and the Lord orders the ministers of the gospel to go far out to scatter the teaching of salvation throughout all the regions of the earth.[10]

In Carey's day Calvin's interpretation of Jesus' command had been almost completely forgotten. The missionary mandate was understood as restricted to the original apostles only! Since the world had already heard the gospel in the apostolic age, what need was there to offer it again? So pervasive was this thinking that it was reflected in an antimissionary hymn which made the rounds in the eighteenth century.

> Go into all the world,
>   the Lord of old did say,
> But now where He has planted thee,
>   there thou shouldst stay.

Carey and Fuller rejected this thinking as a perversion of the theology of the Reformers whose legacy they claimed as their own. For them the Great Commission had no statute of limitations. "Go ye" means you—and now!

The Pietist Advance

Despite the missionary impulse inherent in the work of the Protestant Reformers, their followers did not seize the initiative for world evangelization in the years after the Reformation. Indeed, at the end of the sixteenth century the Roman Catholic scholar Robert Bellarmine wrote a book blasting the Protestants for their lack of missionary activity. He could point to "many thousands of heathens" who had been converted by Catholic missionaries in the New World, while Lutherans and Calvinists could hardly boast "even so much as a handful."[11]

Why this failure? One scholar has suggested that the churches of the Reformation were so preoccupied consolidating their hard-won victories against medieval Catholicism that they had no energy for anything else. "A victim escaping from the folds of a boa-constrictor is presumably not in the condition of a vigorous athlete."[12] Other factors were the Wars of Religion, which left both church and society depleted; internecine quarrels among the various Protestant denominations; and a lack of vision stemming from the antimissionary theology referred to already.

The first real breakthrough toward a world missions effort among the Protestants began in Germany among the Pietists. Philipp Jacob Spener, a Lutheran pastor, had provided an impetus for this renewal movement in his book *Pia Desideria* (1675). His aim, like Luther's, was to call the Church back to basics. The preaching of God's word needed to sound forth with clarity again. Were Saint Paul himself to come back from the dead, not even he could understand some of the slippery geniuses who occupy our pulpits today, he said. The Scriptures must be read reverently and regularly, both in public worship and private devotions. We must reach out in Jesus' name to the poor and needy. Orthodoxy must be accompanied by orthopraxy: pure doctrine without holy living is mere hypocrisy.

Armed with these concerns earnest Christians all across Europe began to gather in small groups for Bible studies and prayer meetings. At Halle, August Hermann Francke, one of Spener's disciples, developed a major center of Pietist activities. There was an orphanage, a publishing house, a pharmacy to dispense medicine to the poor, as well as a school. From here the first two Protestant missionaries to India were sent out in 1705.

Bartholomew Zeigenbalg and Henry Plutschau were sponsored by the king of Denmark. At Tranquebar in south India they established a mission which was later directed by another Pietist from Halle, Christian Frederick Schwartz. He was a great missionary who served for 48 uninterrupted years.

Their mission was based on five foundational principles, each of which Carey and his associates would adopt and apply to their own labors in northern India.[13] First, church and school go together. The ability to read God's Word is basic to Christian nurture and growth. Second, the Scriptures must be made available in the common language of the people. Ziegenbalg translated all of the New Testament and much of the Old into the Tamil language before his death in 1719. Third, communicating the gospel requires an accurate knowledge of the customs and religion of the people. Fourth, the missionary must confront the lost with the claims of Christ and pray for the definite and personal conversion of every person encountered. And, fifth, an indigenous church with its own indigenous ministry must come into being as soon as possible.

More zealous than any of the Pietist groups in missions endeavors were the Moravians. Led by Count Nicolaus Ludwig von Zinzendorf, these earnest Christians dared to carry the gospel into some of the most remote and inhospitable regions on the face of the earth. From the icy slopes of Greenland to the sweltering tropics of the West Indies, members of the *Unitas Fratrum*, the Union of Brothers, as the Moravians were called, fanned out two by two "to win for the Lamb that was slain the reward of His sufferings."[14]

John Wesley was deeply impressed by the Moravians he met on board a ship returning to England from America. Their prayers and hymns and quiet calm amidst a storm at sea caused him to realize that he who had gone to America to convert others was as yet unconverted himself. It was at a Moravian prayer meeting at Aldersgate in London that Wesley felt his heart "strangely warmed" as he placed all his hopes for salvation in Christ alone.

Carey too was profoundly moved by the example of the Moravians. In the *Enquiry* he asks, "Have not the missionaries of the *Unitas Fratrum* encountered the scorching heat of Abyssinia and the frozen climes of Greenland and Labrador, their difficult languages and savage manners?"[15] Even in faraway Serampore, long before Carey had heard of the place, the Moravians had planted a small struggling mission, a precursor to a greater flowering of gospel work in that Danish settlement.

The Moravians were great singers. They carried their hymns wherever they went teaching them to Eskimos, Hottentots, Greenlanders, and African slaves. We can still catch something of the joy and confidence of their faith in the words of one of their first missionary hymns.

> Awake, Thou Spirit, Who of old
> Didst fire the watchmen of the Church's youth,
> Who faced the foe, unshrinking, bold
> Who witnessed day and night the eternal truth;
> Whose voices through the world are ringing still,
> And bringing hosts to know and do Thy will![16]

Eliot and Brainerd

Carey mentions two other forerunners in the *Enquiry,* men whose lives and labors were to inspire an entire generation of newly awakened evangels: John Eliot and David Brainerd, both pioneer missionaries among the native Indians of North America.

When the Pilgrim fathers set sail on the *Mayflower,* they believed they were heading for "those vast unpeopled countries of America," as William Bradford put it.[17] However, they soon discovered a land "peopled" with a race of human beings they had never encountered before. Almost from the beginning the conversion of the Indians was a stated goal of many believers.

They had come to New England not just for political or economic benefits, but to establish there "Mt. Zion in the wilderness."[18] Thus, when John Robinson, pastor of the Pilgrims, received a report that certain Indians had been killed in a skirmish with the Plymouth colonists, he replied in a letter to his faraway flock: "Oh, how happy a thing had it been if you had converted some before you had killed any!"[19]

John Eliot was the first person to take seriously the sentiment expressed on one of the earliest seals of Harvard College: an American Indian repeating the call of the messenger from Macedonia, "Come over and help us!" He had come to New England in 1631 on the same ship that brought over John Winthrop, governor of the colony. As a minister in Roxbury, near Boston, he developed a lifelong passion for preaching the gospel to the Indians, so much so that he was soon dubbed the Apostle to the Indians. Over the course of his ministry, some 4,000 Indians professed faith in Christ. A number of them were ordained as Christian pastors and served the 30-odd Indian congregations established by Eliot and his fellow workers.

The secret of Eliot's success was doubtless his habitual life of prayer. Cotton Mather, who was well acquainted with Eliot in later life, says that "he was perpetually jogging the wheel of prayer." Indeed, "his whole breath seemed in a sort made up of ejaculatory prayers, many scores of which winged messengers he dispatched away to Heaven upon pious errands, every Day. By them he bespoke blessings upon almost every person or Affair that he was concerned with; and he carried everything to God with some pertinent *Hosannah's* or *Hallelujah's* over it."[20] The habit of prayer he passed on to his converts whom he gathered into "praying Indian villages" all over New England.

Eliot was concerned with both the eternal destiny and the temporal well-being of the Indians. He taught them the system of agriculture he had learned as the son of a yeoman farmer in England. Like Carey later, he was an inveterate opponent of slavery. When certain New England Indians were captured by slave traders, he loudly protested this practice.

> The terror of selling away such Indians . . . for perpetual slaves . . . is worse than death. The design of Christ in these last days is not to extirpate nations, but to gospelize them. . . . To sell souls for money seemeth to me a dangerous merchandise.[21]

Eliot took extraordinary pains to learn the Algonquin language. He rejected outright the logic of those who argued that the Indians should be required to learn English before they were instructed in the Christian faith. Instead, he translated first a catechism, then the Psalms, New Testament, and eventually the whole Bible into the Algonquin dialect. Soon other books of piety and learning were added to "the Indian library": Richard Baxter's *Call to the Unconverted,* Lewis Bayly's *Practice of Piety,* Thomas Shepard's *The Sincere Convert,* and his own *The Christian Commonwealth* (1659) and *Communion of Churches* (1665). Remarkable scholarly work, this, for a busy pastor, ardent evangelist, and tireless church planter. At age 76 he began a complete revision of the Indian Bible. Well might his biographer ask, "Did ever a man more faithfully fulfil his ordination vow to teach and study the things pertaining to the Kingdom of God?"[22]

Eliot's life motto was appended to the grammar of the Algonquin language which he produced: "Prayer and pains, through faith in Jesus Christ, will do anything."[23]

If in so many facets of his career Eliot was a model for Carey—preacher, translator, agricultural reformer, organizer of churches, humanitarian—then Brainerd was his inspiration, a soul mate whose diary Carey devoured until, as Ryland later put it, it became "almost a second Bible to him."[24] When Carey and the other missionaries at Serampore drew up a covenant to serve as the basis for their life together in that settlement, it contained the following exhortation.

> Let us often look at Brainerd in the woods of America, pouring out his very soul before God for the people. Prayer, secret, fervent, expectant, lies at the root of all personal godliness. A competent knowledge of the languages current where a missionary lives, a mild and winning temper, and a heart given up to God—these are the attainments, which, more than all other gifts, will fit us to become God's instruments in the great work of human redemption.[25]

David Brainerd was born at Haddam, Connecticut, in 1718. According to his own testimony, he was "somewhat sober and inclined to melancholy" from his youth up. He was converted in 1739 during the Great Awakening and soon thereafter entered Yale College to prepare for the ministry. When the rector of the school, a man named Thomas Clap, forbade Yale students to attend the revival services led by George Whitfield, Brainerd remarked that he had "no more grace than a chair." This intemperate comment, for which he later apologized, got him expelled from the school.

Nonetheless, he was ordained by the revivalistic Presbyterians and commissioned to preach to the Indians under the auspices of the Society in Scotland for Propagating Christian Knowledge. For four years he carried on a remarkable missionary work among the Indians of New York, New Jersey, and Pennsylvania. Having contracted tuberculosis in his student days, he died in 1747 at the home of Jonathan Edwards at Northampton, Massachusetts. He was 32.[26]

Edwards's daughter Jerusha was engaged to be married to

Brainerd. Both she and her father were deeply impressed by the young missionary. Brainerd left his personal papers with Edwards with instructions for him to dispose of them as would "be most for God's glory and the interest of religion."[27] In 1749 he came out with *An Account of the Life of the Late Reverend David Brainerd.* It has been called the first full missionary biography ever published.

Carey carried this book with him to India and drew sustenance from it almost daily. Henry Martyn too, his younger contemporary who left the allurements of academic life in Cambridge to wear himself out on the missions fields of India and Persia, modeled his entire life on Brainerd. Martyn's own journal reflects his indebtedness to the saint of the "hideous and howling wilderness."

> Read David Brainerd today and yesterday, and find as usual my spirit greatly benefitted by it. I long to be like him; let me forget the world and be swallowed up in a desire to glorify God.
>
> Read Brainerd. I feel my heart knit to this dear man, and really rejoice to think of meeting him in heaven.[28]

Carey, Martyn, Judson, David Livingstone, Hudson Taylor, so many others read Brainerd and were never the same again. Indeed, as one historian has written, "David Brainerd dead was a more potent influence for . . . the missionary cause . . . than was David Brainerd alive."[29] What influenced Carey most was Brainerd's radical single-mindedness, his passion for souls, his desire to do God's will whatever the cost. How many times must Carey have read and reread these words from his hero's diary? How must he have thought Brainerd's ideas after him until they became his own.

> I cared not where or how I lived, or what hardships I went through, so that I could but gain souls for Christ. While I was asleep I dreamed of these things, and when I awoke the first thing I thought of was this great work. All my desire was for the conversion of the heathen, and all my hope was in God.[30]

Arm of the Lord, awake! awake!
Put on Thy strength, the nations shake;
And let the world, adoring, see
Triumphs of mercy wrought by Thee!

Say to the heathen, from Thy throne,
"I am Jehovah, God alone!"
Thy voice their idols shall confound,
And cast their altars to the ground.

Let Zion's time of favour come;
O bring the tribes of Israel home;
And let our wondering eyes behold
Gentiles and Jews in Jesus' fold!

Almighty God, Thy grace proclaim
In every clime, of every name,
Till adverse powers before Thee fall,
And crown the Saviour Lord of all!

William Shrubsole, 1795

4

The Church Awakes

THERE is a mystery in the timing of God which cannot be fathomed by rational explanation or historical accountings of cause and effect. Many of the forerunners did not live to see the full fruit of their labors. Brainerd's entire missionary career lasted only four years. Nor can his success be measured solely by the number of converts he won to Christ. Still, his life and witness inspired others to risk all for the sake of the gospel. In retrospect, he shines brightly indeed in "the great galaxy of missionary stars."[1]

The remarkable events which brought into being the Particular Baptist Society for the Propagation of the Gospel Amongst the Heathen, as it was first called, belong to a pattern of providential preparation by which the Church of Jesus Christ was aroused from a long slumber and revived to fulfill its true mission and purpose in the world. We have seen how Carey was called from the most humble and unlikely of origins to play a major role in this awakening. We must now examine three major factors which came together in just the right way and at just the right time to launch this historic missionary beginning: first, a revival of prayer among the churches and people of God; second, a theology of missions which gave a solid doctrinal foundation to the new outreach; and, third, a specific plan of action to set in motion the enterprise for world evangelization, an undertaking so fraught with the possibilities of failure, yet so pregnant with the promises of God.

The Call to Prayer

The year was 1784. The place, the Baptist Chapel in Friar's Lane, Nottingham. The occasion, a regular meeting of the

Northamptonshire Baptist Association. Carey was not present for he had just recently been baptized and still awaited his first call as pastor of a local congregation. Seven years were to pass before the "deathless sermon" would be preached before the same group and in this very place. In 1784 the sermons were delivered by others—John Gill, nephew and namesake of the greatest Baptist theologian of the century; John Sutcliff of Olney; and Andrew Fuller, newly come as pastor in Kettering.

On the second day of the meeting Sutcliff arose to address the ministers and messengers. He called on them to begin a concert of prayer in their local churches, meeting on the first Monday of every month to beseech God for revival and the spread of the gospel. His words were later printed in the circular letter of the association.

> The grand object in prayer is to be that the Holy Spirit may be poured down on our ministers and churches, that sinners may be converted, the saints edified, the interest of religion revived, and the name of God glorified. At the same time remember, we trust you will not confine your requests to your own societies; or to your own immediate connection; let the whole interest of the Redeemer be affectionately remembered, and the spread of the Gospel to the most distant parts of the habitable globe be the object of your most fervent requests.[2]

During the course of the next year churches throughout the association began to pray with an earnestness hitherto unknown. We can trace the impact of the prayer call by examining Fuller's diary in the following months.

> July 9. Read to our friends, this evening, a part of Mr. Edwards' *Attempt to Promote Prayer for the Revival of Religion,* to excite them to the like practice. Felt my heart profited and much solemnized by what I read.

> July 13. Spent this day in fasting and prayer, in conjunction with several of my brethren in the ministry, for the revival of our churches and the spread of the gospel: found some tenderness and earnestness in prayer several times in the day.

> July 19. Read some more of Edwards on prayer, as I did also last Monday night, with sweet satisfaction.

> December 6. An affecting meeting of prayer this evening for the revival of real religion.

March 7, 1785. Enjoyed divine assistance at the monthly prayer meeting, in speaking on continuing in prayer, and in going to prayer, though I felt wretchedly cold before I began.[3]

The prayer movement found a response not only in Northamptonshire but also among Baptists in Yorkshire and Congregationalists in Warwickshire as well. The monthly Monday evening prayer meetings were *really* meetings for prayer not social occasions for singing, eating, announcements, and business concerns. The night was set apart for deliberate intercession. They prayed for the state of public affairs in the nation, for revival among the churches, for the lost in their midst, and for the extension of Christ's kingdom throughout the earth.

Carey regularly participated in the prayer meetings, both in his own church and in other settings as well. At Harvey Lane in Leicester he arranged a special prayer service for his country members who came to town on market day, as well as the Monday evening one for the city dwellers. When the *Enquiry* was published in 1792, he did not fail to mention the role of prayer in preparing his own heart and those of others for the great task they were undertaking: "One of the first and most important of those duties which are incumbent upon us is fervent and united prayer. . . . I trust our monthly prayer meetings for the success of the gospel have not been in vain. It is true a want of importunity generally attends our prayers; yet unimportunate and feeble as they have been, it is to be believed that God has heard, and in a measure answered them."[4]

In many respects the writings of Jonathan Edwards were the single most important theological influence on Fuller, Carey, and the English Baptists who launched the modern missionary movement. We have noted already the great impact his edition of David Brainerd's life had on Carey and others. We shall soon observe how Edwards's ability to balance the sovereignty of God and human responsibility made possible a fresh interpretation of Calvinist theology, with historic implications for missions. We are now concerned with another of "Mr. Edwards's" books, the one Fuller could hardly put down during the summer of 1784.

Book titles in those days tended to be lengthy. The full title of Edwards's book set forth its theme.

An Humble Attempt to promote an explicit agreement and visible union of God's people through the world, in extraordinary prayer, for the revival of religion, and the advancement of Christ's Kingdom on earth, pursuant to scripture-promises and prophecies concerning the last time

This book was first published in New England, at Boston, in 1748, but its origin went back even earlier to an evangelical awakening in the Church of Scotland.

Edwards maintained a lively correspondence with a number of the Scottish evangelicals, notably John Erskine, who in 1744 organized a concert of prayer throughout the chief cities of Scotland as well as in many country congregations there. Edwards wrote his *Humble Attempt* to justify and encourage others to support the Concert for United Prayer drawn up by the Scottish ministers.

One historian has claimed that "no such tract on the hidden source of all true evangelistic success, namely, prayer for the Spirit of God, has ever been so widely used as this one."[5] Thirty-six years after its initial publication in Boston in April 1784, John Erskine included a copy of it in a parcel of books he sent to John Sutcliff. The reading of Edwards's treatise ignited a fire in Sutcliff's heart. He read prophecy after prophecy from Isaiah, Zechariah, and Jeremiah, promises of whole nations awakened to the truth, of the advancement of Christ's Church in the latter ages of the world. He meditated on the passage in Psalm 102 about the Lord appearing in His glory to build up Zion; words reserved, says the psalmist, for some future generation of God's people.

Sutcliff must have fastened on Edwards's commentary on this text: "Who knows but that the generation here spoken of, may be this *present* generation?"[6] Do not the Scriptures say that the time for Zion's deliverance will come when God's servants are brought by their prayerfulness to beseech the Lord for her restoration? Could this hour be now?

With words such as these ringing in his ears, Sutcliff called on his fellow Baptists to heed Edwards's challenge, to follow the lead of their Scottish brothers of the previous generation, to unite their voices, and to pour out their hearts before the Lord Who is "standing ready to be gracious, . . . waiting . . . to bestow this mercy, when He shall hear the cries of His people for it, that He may bestow it in answer to their prayers."[7]

Five years after the call to prayer at Nottingham in 1784, and two years before Carey's famous sermon in the same pulpit, Sutcliff brought out the first edition of Edwards's treatise published in England. In the preface to this edition, dated at Olney on May 4, 1789, he registered two points, each of which had a bearing on the developing missionary effort.

First he disclaimed an overly speculative interest in the details of the end time. There was a great interest in Bible prophecy in the late eighteenth century. World events fueled discussions of the end of the world. The year 1789 witnessed the storming of the Bastille. The rise of Napoleon, the American Revolution, renewed interest in the conversion of the Jews, all these gave rise to many date-setting schemes and prophetic timetables.

Edwards himself had written earlier works, outlining a progressive unfolding of the plan of redemption which he believed would culminate in the millennial reign of Christ on earth. He interpreted the Great Awakening as a sign that Satan's forces were on the run; Brainerd's ministry among the Indians was further evidence of the same. For Edwards these were encouraging portents, but they did not indicate that the golden age foretold by the prophets would be "brought to pass as it were at one stroke."[8] Quite to the contrary, Satan's complete downfall would likely require many, many years.

In a fascinating scenario, he projects a 250-year gradual advance of the gospel which, if carried out with "amazing and unparalleled progress," could conceivably usher in the millennium by the year A.D. 2000! According to this projection, the purity of the church would be restored among the Protestants in the half century from 1750 to 1800; the Roman Catholics would come to the full light of evangelical truth from 1800 to 1850; the Muslim world and the Jewish people would be converted from 1850 to 1900; and during the twentieth century the whole heathen world would be enlightened and accept the Christian faith "throughout all parts of Africa, Asia, America, and *Terra Australis.*" Then all things would be so adjusted and settled that "the world thenceforward should enjoy a holy rest, or sabbatism."[9]

In reprinting Edwards's treatise, Sutcliff did not endorse every detail of the great theologian's eschatology. "An author and an editor are very distinct characters," he reminds his readers.[10] Still, the Baptist missionary advocates shared with Edwards a sense that they were indeed living on the very edge of time. (Carey, for example, preached a series of weekly sermons on the book of Revelation during his pastorate in Leicester.) Their plan to carry the gospel into all the world was a vital part of God's providential ordering of history. The valley of dry bones was coming to life. Daniel's stone was ready to roll. The New Jerusalem was about to descend. Their unity in prayer was a God-given preparation for those awesome events. If, as Edwards surmised, the final fulfillment of these great works would still be several hundreds of years away, it did not follow that there would be no genuine revivals before then. For just such an outpouring of God's Spirit, they were to pour out earnest, diligent, and constant prayer.[11]

In the 1789 preface to the *Humble Attempt,* Sutcliff also referred to the unity of purpose and spirit which the "praying societies" had promoted among Christians from different denominational traditions and points of view. While the Baptists were to lead the way in organizing the first missionary society, they were soon joined in prayer and support by godly Presbyterians, Methodists, Congregationalists, Anglicans, and others. On the missions field the question of cooperation among Bible-believing Christians from varying denominations would become even more urgent.

Yet for the Church of Jesus Christ—"one holy society, one city, one family, one body," as Edwards called it—united in prayer for one sacred, transcendent cause, this was part of the founding vision from the beginning.[12]

> In the present imperfect state, we may reasonably expect a diversity of sentiments upon religious matters. Each ought to think for himself; and every one has a right, on proper occasions, to shew his opinions. Yet all should remember, that there are but two parties in the world, each engaged in opposite causes; the cause of God and of Satan; of holiness and sin; of heaven and hell. The advancement of the one, and the downfall of the other, must appear exceedingly desirable to every real friend of God and man. If such in some respects entertain different sentiments, and practice distinguishing modes of worship, surely they may unite in the above business. O for thousands upon thousands, divided into small bands in their respective cities, towns, villages and neighborhood, all met at the same time, and in pursuit of the same end, offering up their united prayers, like so many ascending clouds of incense before the Most High.[13]

The prayer movement itself was an example of the Spirit of God working across the boundaries of nation and denomination, class and social status, to accomplish His sovereign purpose among His people. A treatise written by a New England Congregationalist in support of Scottish Presbyterians reprinted by English Baptists who were inspired by it to launch a world missionary movement—the wind bloweth where it listeth!

Theology of Missions

One of the most famous incidents in Carey's early ministry occurred when he was still a young pastor at Moulton, trying to feel his way into Baptist circles. At a meeting of ministers at Northampton John Ryland, Sr., called upon his colleagues to propose a topic for discussion. After a few moments of awkward silence, Carey rose and proposed for consideration, "The duty of Christians to attempt the spread of the gospel among heathen nations." Ryland, Sr., was genuinely astonished and, with a rebuking frown, thundered back, "Young man, sit down. When God pleases to convert the heathen, He will do it without your aid or mine!" Some other topic was taken up, and Carey's question "tabled" for the time being. A later tradition says that the elder minister referred to Carey as a "miserable enthusiast" for even raising the issue.[14]

Ryland, Sr.'s, remark reflects a hardened attitude in Baptist thinking which had gained widespread support in Carey's day. Since the early seventeenth century, Baptists in England had been divided into two distinct branches: Particular, or Calvinistic, Baptists; and General, or Arminian, Baptists. The latter stressed the universal scope of Christ's atoning work and rejected the Calvinistic doctrines of Original Sin and Predestined Election. Early on the General Baptists were aggressively evangelistic in winning many to faith in Christ and planting churches throughout England. However, by the mid-eighteenth century they had ceased to be a vital force within evangelical Christianity. Swept along by the rising currents of rationalist theology, many General Baptists came to deny both the deity of Christ and the doctrine of the Trinity.

Still others, who remained formally orthodox for the time being, refused to subscribe to a Trinitarian confession of faith for fear that their Christian liberty would be abridged by this act. Historian Raymond Brown has aptly described the upshot of this posture: "Resistance to subscription became the prelude to heterodoxy. People who refused to sign the articles came eventually to deny them and those General Baptists who were theologically uncertain ultimately became committed Unitarians."[15]

Particular Baptists, on the other hand, resisted such liberalizing tendencies and affirmed strongly the orthodox Calvinist theology set forth in their First (1644) and Second London Confessions (1677, 1689). Carey; Fuller; Ryland, Jr.; Sutcliff; Pearce all belonged to this tradition. They were happy to call themselves Calvinists. They affirmed without reservation what Fuller called "the discriminating doctrines of grace" which can be summarized in five assertions: (1) the decree of election is absolute and unconditional; (2) the Atonement applies to the elect in a unique, particular way, although the death of Christ is sufficient to expiate the sins of the whole world; (3) because of the Fall, human beings are totally incapable of any saving good apart from the regenerating work of the Holy Spirit; (4) God's call to salvation is effectual, and, hence, His grace cannot be ultimately thwarted by human resistance; (5) those whom God calls and regenerates He also keeps, so that they do not totally nor finally fall away from faith and grace.[16]

Early Particular Baptists such as John Bunyan and Benjamin Keach embraced all of these doctrines without ever suspecting that they should be seen as a hindrance to evangelism and missions. However, in 1707 a Congregationalist minister named Joseph Hussey published a book entitled *God's Operations of Grace But No Offers of His Grace*. Hussey declared that anyone who claimed to believe in God's election and yet offered Christ to all was only a "half-hearted Calvinist."[17]

Hussey's writings formed the backdrop for the controversy over the Modern Question, so called from the title of a pamphlet published in 1737 by another Congregationalist minister, Matthias Maurice. In "A Modern Question Modestly Answer'd," Maurice raised the question of whether it was "the duty of poor unconverted sinners, who hear the gospel preached and published, to believe in Jesus Christ."[18] Those who answered this question in the negative saw little need for the promiscuous preaching of the gospel, since it was obviously useless to exhort unconverted sinners to do what they neither *could* do, nor indeed had any obligation to do!

There is no doubt that such views, which Fuller called "false Calvinism" as opposed to the "Strict Calvinism" which he embraced, gained currency among Particular Baptists in the late eighteenth century. Consequently, as Spurgeon was to put it in the next century, many churches were "chilled to the very soul." They omitted "the free invitations of the gospel" and denied "that it was the duty of sinners to believe in Jesus."[19] The "Modern Question" had first surfaced in Northamptonshire. It continued to shape the theology among many churches there for years to come. Clearly, this is the background of the "Young man, sit down" rebuke which Carey received from Ryland, Sr.

Andrew Fuller grew up in a church where the "noninvitation, nonapplication" scheme held sway. His pastor, a certain John Eve, seldom, if ever, addressed himself to the unconverted. Fuller cited three major influences on his own movement away from these views toward a more evangelical Calvinist position. First, his close study of the Bible with its many admonitions to the lost to repent and be converted; second, his reading of the lives of Eliot and Brainerd who were uninhibited in their addresses "to those poor benighted heathens"; and finally, his discovery of Jonathan Edwards's *Inquiry into the Freedom of the Will.*

What did Fuller learn from Edwards which was so crucial for his theological reorientation? Simply put, that evangelism and Calvinism could be reconciled. There was no contradiction between the universal obligation of all who hear the gospel to believe in Christ and the sovereign decision of God to save those whom He has chosen. The failure to believe stemmed not from any physical or "natural inability," but rather from a "moral inability" which was the result of a perverted human will. Edwards's distinction between natural and moral ability was the key which unlocked the mystery of divine sovereignty and human responsibility for Fuller.

By 1781 Fuller had committed some of his thoughts along this line to writing, although he was reluctant to have them published for fear of the controversy he was sure they would stir. The entries in his diary from 1784 reveal this apprehension.

August 23. The weight of publishing still lies upon me. I expect a great share of unhappiness through it. I had certainly much rather go through the world in peace, did I not consider this step as my duty.

October 21. Feel some pain in the thought of being about to publish *On the Obligations of Men to Believe in Christ*, as supposing I shall thereby expose myself to much abuse, which is disagreeable to the flesh.

November 22. Walked to Northampton. Some prayer that God would bless that about which I am going, namely, the printing of a manuscript on faith in Christ being the duty of unregenerate sinners.[20]

In the following year his defense of the indiscriminate preaching of the gospel rolled off the presses of Northampton. It soon became known by the leading phrase in its lengthy title, *The Gospel Worthy of All Acceptation*. Fuller was not disappointed in his expectation of controversy. As has been said of another tract for the times, this little book fell like a bombshell on the playground of the theologians. Fuller was pilloried by Arminians and Hyper-Calvinists alike. Yet others, including Carey, read his treatise with great profit. Eventually, the majority of Particular Baptists accepted Fuller's arguments as consonant both with the Scriptures and their own Calvinist heritage. The victory of Fullerism, as it came to be called, gave a solid doctrinal foundation for the launching of the modern missionary campaign.

The heart of *The Gospel Worthy of All Acceptation* was Fuller's argument for "duty faith" which he unfolded in six propositions.

1. Unconverted sinners are commanded, exhorted, and invited to believe in Christ for salvation.
2. Everyone is bound to receive what God reveals.
3. The gospel, though a message of pure grace, requires the obedient response of faith.
4. The lack of faith is a heinous sin which is ascribed in the Scriptures to human depravity.
5. God has threatened and inflicted the most awful punishments on sinners for their not believing on the Lord Jesus Christ.
6. The Bible requires of all persons certain spiritual exercises which are represented as their duty. These include repentance and faith no less than the requirement to love God, fear God, and glorify God. That no one can accomplish these things apart from the bestowal of the Holy Spirit is clear. Nonetheless the obligation

remains. In this respect "man's duty and God's gift" are the same thing, seen from different perspectives.[21]

Carey was to develop his missionary theology out of these basic insights. If sinners were *obliged* to repent and believe in Christ, was there not another "obligation" to be considered? Were not Christians, themselves delivered from darkness into light, most urgently *obliged* to present the claims of Christ to those who have never heard? Fuller was the theologian, Carey the visionary and activist of the missionary awakening.

Both Carey and Fuller were indebted to another senior member of the Northamptonshire Baptist Ministers' Fraternal, the elder Robert Hall of Arnesby. It was he who first put Fuller onto Edwards's *Inquiry into the Freedom of the Will* in the first place. It was also Hall's 1779 association sermon, published two years later under the title *Help to Zion's Travellers*, which made such an impact on young Carey. "The way to Jesus," said Hall, "is graciously open for everyone who chooses to come to him."[22] Many years later Carey said of Hall's book, "I do not remember ever to have read any book with such raptures as I did that. If it was poison, as some then said, it was so sweet to me that I drank it greedily to the bottom of the cup; and I rejoice to say, that those doctrines are the choice of my heart to this day."[23]

Such ideas could not be reserved for the study of ministers' discussion groups. They soon made their way into Carey's preaching. When Ryland, Jr., asked him to preach in the summer of 1788 at College Lane in Northampton, some who heard him there "called him an Arminian, and discovered a strange spirit." Ryland was dismayed at such "foolish cavils." "Lord, pity us," he wrote.[24] An Arminian Carey was not, nor ever became. Like Bunyan before him and Spurgeon after him, he was an evangelical Calvinist who could not but echo the warning of Evangelist in *The Pilgrim's Progress:* "Why standest thou still? Fly from the wrath to come. Do you see yonder shining light? Keep that light in your eye, and go up directly thereto."[25]

Carey's Plan

First the call to prayer, then theological renewal—what was needed next was a plan of action. This Carey provided with *An*

Enquiry into the Obligations of Christians to Use Means for the Conversion of the Heathens. It is a treatise noted for its remarkable restraint and preeminent common sense. No wild-eyed enthusiasm or fanatical rantings here; only the deliberate, logical, forceful presentation of a case based on careful research and argued from deep conviction.

The *Enquiry* consists of an introduction and five chapters dealing, respectively, with the Great Commission, historical precedents, a world survey, obstacles to missions, and the Christian's duty to promote the cause of missions. The last five words in the first paragraph of the introduction set the entire missions enterprise in the context of its ultimate, transcendent source— "the character of God himself."[26]

Unless one grasps this point from the beginning, it is easy to misunderstand the motivation for missions which Carey unfolds in the following pages. While his plan was a call for action based on genuine compassion for the lost, it was grounded in something deeper still; namely, the character of God Himself—eternal, holy, righteous, loving, giving. In the briefest terms Carey outlines the plan of salvation from the Fall to its effects in universal idolatry to the coming of the Messiah to overthrow Satan and open the gates of salvation. His life, death, Resurrection, Ascension are the only way of salvation for all peoples everywhere. His Commission to the Church, and "what might be done if the whole body of Christians" took it seriously, this is the theme of Carey's book.

In appealing to the imperative of Jesus in the Great Commission, it was necessary for Carey to counter the popular claim that these words applied only to the apostles and had been fulfilled already in the early history of the Church. If this line of reasoning prevailed, argued Carey, then not only the command to go into all the world has been abrogated, but so have the other parts of the Commission as well. Should we then stop baptizing or teaching? Is the promise of Christ's presence limited to the apostles too? Yet He expressly promised the contrary—to be with us to the end of the world.

In this section Carey also answered three commonly held objections to new missionary endeavors. First, there are the advocates of a do-nothing strategy who justify their inaction by appealing to Providence. We must not force our way in, we must wait for openings, they say. To which Carey replies that we ought not neglect those providential openings which are daily presented to us. Second, others claim that the time is not right for such initiatives since various biblical prophecies, such as the slaying of the witnesses in Revelation 11, await fulfillment. Carey denies such interpretations (appealing to Edwards's *Humble Attempt*) and points to outpourings of the Spirit which have occurred already before the final consummation. No prophecy must be fulfilled before the gospel is carried unto the ends of the earth. Third, to those who say that "we have work enough at home," Carey does not deny the great need for spiritual awakening in his native land.[27] But he does question whether this is a legitimate excuse for not sharing the good news of Christ with those who have no Bibles, no preachers, nor many other common advantages which are taken for granted at home.

Carey was an avid student of church history. In the second part of the *Enquiry* he reviews numerous missionary efforts from the days of the apostles until his own times. He begins with a complete overview of the book of Acts, the very first missionary manual ever written. He interprets the Pentecostal miracle of tongues as the supernatural gift of "speaking in all foreign languages" bestowed upon the apostles by the Holy Spirit. The result was a great ingathering of new believers from many different ethnic and linguistic people groups.

As Carey expounds chapter after chapter in Acts, we see the gospel breaking through the barriers of resistance—Jewish, Samaritan, Gentile, Roman—until finally the Apostle Paul is preaching Christ in the capital city of the empire itself. To be sure, Carey picks up on the other theme which resounds through Acts as well. Wherever a new work of God is established, there is a countermovement of opposition, persecution, demonic onslaught. Sometimes the opposition arises within the church (heresy, schism), sometimes from without (martyrdom).The theme of Acts, as Carey understands it, is the certain triumph of the gospel in the face of numerous obstacles and hindrances. Those who were persecuted went everywhere preaching the word (Acts 8:4). Despite imprisonments and false accusations, the churches planted by Paul on his missionary journeys "for ages after shone as lights in the world."[28]

Carey's review of the history of missions is a smorgasbord of names and places where the gospel of Christ had been carried across the ages. Four times he mentions India, though as yet he had no idea that his own destiny was to be linked to that distant land. Among the apostles, John and Thomas are said to have preached in India; later the monk Frumentius and also Francis Xavier, a Jesuit missionary of the sixteenth century, labored there.

Carey gives us here the first missionary roll call in the history of the church. James of Nisbia, Patrick, Finian, Columba, Augustine, Boniface, Modestus, Wycliffe, Hus, Eliot, Brainerd, the Moravians, the Methodists, all are here, among others, to form a great cloud of witnesses. These faithful messengers of grace were "the seed of the church" in many places. They being dead still speak through the example of the lives and their legacy of courage and service.

In reciting the precedent of such worthy forebears, Carey was not laying claim to an unbroken succession of true gospel churches. He was, however, identifying himself with the body of Christ extended throughout time as well as space. Carey was no Lone-Ranger Christian starting all over from scratch. He was building upon the labors of others and he knew it. From his study of history he knew no work of God is ever insignificant. Even a "few pious people" living obscurely in the valleys of Piedmont and Savoy were used by God to prepare the way for the greater lights of Luther, Calvin, Melanchthon, Bucer, and others.[29] Only such a perspective, again rooted in the character of God and His transcendent purpose in redemption, could sustain Carey during the incredible struggles and hardships upon which he was about to enter.

The centerpiece of the *Enquiry* was Carey's survey "of the present state of the world," divided by continent, country, and religion. Here he brought together in comprehensive overview the results of his reading and study over the past ten years. He had collected raw data for this survey from numerous sources— the world geographies he read, the newspapers he combed, the missions reports of the Moravians and others he devoured, the great libraries of his Leicester friends he was free to peruse. What Fuller had seen represented on his homemade map of the world in his workshop in Moulton was here spelled out in minute statistical detail.

Carey's survey was as complete and accurate as the best information available to him would allow. In this work he laid the foundation for the modern science of missiology. His survey was a forerunner of the *World Christian Encyclopedia* and other indispensable resources for missions research.

Carey had a special interest in islands recalling, no doubt, Isaiah's prophecy of "the isles" who wait upon the Lord (Isa. 51:5; 60:9). Captain Cook had opened his mind to the islands of the South Seas, and they are listed here: Oonalashaka Island, the Pelew Islands, the New Hebrides, the Sandwich Islands, the Friendly Isles, and many more. Even the tiniest dot on the map was not too small for his notice. For example, the minuscule island of Arroe, only eight miles long and two miles wide, finds a place next to Iceland, Madagascar, and New Zealand.

What mattered most to Carey were the inhabitants of these distant lands. He estimated a world population of 731 million people, more than half of whom were pagans. More than a fifth were followers of Muhammad. Still others were claimed by "the papists," for whom the clear light of the gospel was often obscured by their "ignorance of divine things."

In setting forth in such stark detail the religious conditions of the world's peoples, Carey was not pushing forward in a braggadocio sort of way his own denominational brand of the Christian faith. Indeed, he was quite critical not only of Catholics, but also of Anglicans, Lutherans, and Dissenters of all denominations (this takes in the Baptists) among whom, he lamented, were to be found "many errors and much looseness of conduct." All the while lost men and women were perishing for want of a clear witness to God's love and grace, poor heathens who are as "capable of knowledge as we are."

Carey's statistics were more than mere numbers on a chart. They represented persons, persons made in the image of God and infinitely precious to Him. How could any believer, much less any true minister of the gospel, look with studied indifference upon those vast millions destitute of the knowledge of Christ? No, such facts were "loud calls" to Christians to "exert themselves to the utmost" in fulfilling the Great Commission.

Carey knew his plan would be attacked by many as foolish and impracticable. In section 4 he anticipated five likely objections and then answered them one by one. The objections had to do with distance, the barbarism of the uncivilized peoples, dangers to the missionary, the difficulties of making a living, and learning a new language so far away from home.

As to the long distances involved in missionary travel, Carey pointed to the invention of the mariner's compass which had opened up the great oceans for discovery and exploration. "Men can now sail with as much certainty through the Great South Sea as they can through the Mediterranean or any lesser sea." Was not the development of trading companies and international business concerns a providential incentive for Christians to open a traffic in the merchandise of eternity? Should not believers have at least as much concern for the souls of their fellow sinners as traders have "for the profits arising from a few otter-skins"?

Carey was well aware that the alliance, if it can be called that, between missionary endeavor and economic expansion was a mixed blessing. Wherever Europeans had gone they had transplanted more of their vices than their virtues. Frequently the religious condition of the natives they met had been made worse rather than better from the exploitation they suffered at the hands of greedy entrepreneurs. Carey would soon face all these problems directly in his dealings with the East India Company. Still, he could not but believe that the Christian church stood before a great door of opportunity. The prophecy of Isaiah was coming true. The "ships of Tarshish," along with their cargos of silver and gold, could also deliver the good news of salvation to the far corners of the world. And, thus, "commerce shall subserve the spread of the gospel."[30]

The second objection focused on the uncivilized and barbarous way of life among the heathen. This was a flimsy excuse. What if the apostles and early missionaries to Britain and Germany had stayed at home because of the uncouth customs which prevailed in those countries then? Fortunately, "they did not wait for the ancient inhabitants of these countries to be civilized before they could be christianized, but went simply with the doctrine of the cross."[31] To turn the argument around, what more civilizing influence could be found than the spread of the gospel? What better way could be devised to turn "barbarians" into useful members of society? From the outset of his career, Carey was sure that while the *primary* goal of missionary work was the saving of souls for eternity—a priority he never lost sight of—the transformation of social structures and the cultivation of Christian virtues were also part of a faithful gospel witness.

The third and fourth objections, concerning the danger and difficulty of the missionary calling, were answered by an appeal to the example of the apostles who indeed "hazarded" their lives for the gospel's sake. Clearly, no one should enter this lifework "as a kind of sideline" or with motives of self-aggrandizement. Jesus calls us to bid farewell to friends, comfort, pleasures, to "venture all" for Him. No halfheartedness. No timidity. No turning back.

Carey combined this idealism of absolute commitment with the most practical realism possible. The missionary is not simply to "trust the Lord"; he is also to know how to "cultivate a little spot of ground." He should understand husbandry, fishing, fowling, and the like. He will need, of course, the necessary implements for such activities—fishing tackle, powder and shot, a few knives—together with essential clothing and the like. Preferably, married couples should be sent together to form a community of mutual support and care. In this way a self-supporting mission station could become the nucleus for the evangelization of an entire region or country. Carey never lost this common sense, no-nonsense approach to missionary life. It would serve him and his associates well for over 40 years in India.

Finally, the language barrier would be no more difficult for heralds of the gospel than for traders and agents of commercial interests. Interpreters could be employed until the native language was sufficiently mastered. As we have seen already, Carey thought this latter task could be done quite easily "in the space of a year, or two at most." Above all, though, the missionaries must be persons "of great piety, prudence, courage, and forbearance; of undoubted orthodoxy in their sentiments," men and women of God who will "enter with all their hearts into the spirit of their mission."[32]

The closing section of the *Enquiry* is like the crescendo near the end of a great musical movement. All of his previous argument, his pleading, the pouring out of his soul, is here brought together in a concentrated appeal for action. "Is nothing again to be done?" he had asked at Nottingham. What could be done?

First, *pray.* Here is something all Christians can do, and ought to do. "Fervent and united prayer" is the divinely appointed prerequisite for revival. So the prophecies of Zechariah say. The work of God in the heathen world will not be accomplished "by might nor by power," but only by the outpouring of the Holy Spirit (Zech. 4:6).

Second, *plan*. A "company of serious Christians" is needed to spearhead the effort. Missionaries must be recruited and screened and commissioned. A strategy for the mission must be devised. Information from the field must be gathered and assimilated. "In the present divided state of Christendom," Carey says, this work can best be accomplished by working within the established denominational structures. He proposes the formation of such a society within his own denomination, the Calvinistic Baptists of England. Still, "there is room enough for us all." All evangelical Christians should respond to the call from Macedonia. They should pray for one another, encourage one another, and countenance no "unfriendly interference" among one another in their common commitment to the cause of missions.[33]

Third, *give*. The missionary venture requires pray-ers, planners, givers, no less than those who go to the field far away. Those believers with whom God has entrusted great wealth have a special responsibility to give liberally. But *every* Christian has something to offer. Let there be special collections, even if it is only one penny per week, and sacrificial giving by all. If all Christians would tithe their income, Carey says, there would be an abundance of resources to support the ministry of the gospel at home as well as to sponsor the cause of Christ abroad. The ultimate reward for such stewardship will be realized fully only in the life to come. What a glorious sight in heaven to see the myriads of the lost who have come to know Christ through the labors and witness of God's faithful people.

> Surely a "crown of rejoicing" (1 Thess. 2:19) like this is worth aspiring to. Surely it is worth while to lay ourselves out with all our might in promoting the cause and kingdom of Christ.[34]

WHEN Christ was on board, the vessel could not sink, and those who doubted were reproved. . . . Surely, the Master hath been our pilot! Perhaps the greatest storms are yet to come! Be it so! Our eyes shall be up unto Him.

Andrew Fuller, 1793

5

To Venture All

FROM June 1792, when Carey returned home to Leicester after preaching his triumphant sermon to the association at Nottingham until the following June, when he finally bade farewell to his native land, he came to know the meaning of Paul's words about presenting oneself to Christ as a living sacrifice (Rom. 12:1-2). These 12 months were at once the most exhilarating and the most exasperating period of his entire life. Never before had he sought so desperately to know the will of God. Never again would he need such spiritual discernment in making sense of God's providential direction in the opening, closing, and reopening of doors of opportunity. It was a year he would never forget.

The Society Is Born

The summer of 1792 brought great sorrow to the Fuller household at Kettering. Andrew Fuller's wife, Sarah, had been afflicted with great depression since the death of their little daughter Sally in 1786. Now, expecting again, she became subject to hallucinations and for extended periods of time could not even recognize her husband. She died on Thursday, August 23, after giving birth to another little girl whom they named Bathoni after the last-born of Rachel in the Bible.[1]

Still grieving the loss of his dear companion, Fuller prepared to host the ministers' meeting called for at the close of the association in Nottingham. They gathered on the evening of October 2 in the home of Mrs. Beeby Wallis, whose deacon-husband had just died the previous April. He had been a man of "solid wisdom, strict integrity, and unaffected piety," frequently opening his home and hearth to visiting preachers, so that his house became known as the Gospel Inn.[2] Wallis's great-grandfather had been the founding pastor of the Kettering Baptist Church nearly a century before, and Beeby Wallis himself had served as deacon there for 24 years. On this occasion 14 men—12 pastors, 1 layman, and 1 ministerial student—crowded into the back parlor of Widow Wallis's stately Georgian home to pray and ponder what should be done.

Is it surprising that again there was wavering and hesitation? Fuller later said about his group, "There was little or no respectability amongst us, not so much as a squire to take the chair."[3] Apart from Fuller himself, who was only beginning to gain a wider reputation, and Ryland, Jr., who still lived in the shadow of his famous father, these men were all virtual unknowns. The churches they served were in tiny hamlets—Roade, Oakham, Foxton, Braybrook—far from the centers of influence and power. They were also young, too young some would say, to be launching such an ambitious project. Sutcliff, their eldest, was only 40; Fuller just 38; Carey himself 31; and Pearce barely 26. Their personal poverty was another drawback. Only one member of the group, Reynold Hogg of Thrapstone, was a man of any means. No doubt they anticipated the sneer which would later be thrown up by their detractors: "Are these the men and means with which the conversion of the world was to be attempted?"[4]

Just when it seemed delay would again win the day, Carey pulled from his pocket a copy of the latest issue of the *Periodical Account of the Moravian Missions*. He recounted the exploits of these gospel pioneers: how they were winning to Christ Negro slaves in the West Indies, building on Brainerd's work among the Indians of North America, and sending out new recruits to Africa and the Far East. Can the Baptists not at least make an attempt to carry the gospel somewhere into the heathen world?

It was Nottingham all over again. Here, as there, Carey carried his reluctant comrades to the point of resolution.

> Humbly desirous of making an effort for the propagation of the gospel amongst the heathen, according to the recommendations of Carey's Enquiry, we unanimously resolve to act in Society together for this purpose; and, as in the divided state of Christendom each denomination, by exerting itself separately, seems likeliest to accomplish the great end, we name this the Particular Baptist Society for the Propagation of the Gospel Amongst the Heathen.[5]

Out of their number a committee of five was appointed to

oversee the work: Fuller, as secretary; Hogg, the treasurer; with Ryland, Sutcliff, and Carey completing the inner circle. At the next meeting Pearce, who brought a sizable gift of 70 pounds from his church at Birmingham, was added to their number. Before they parted in prayer that October evening, the 14 pledged the first contributions to their infant society. Fuller passed around his circular snuffbox with the conversion of Saint Paul finely embossed on the lid. One by one the slips were collected and then added. Thirteen pounds, 2 shillings, and sixpence they had pledged. It was a paltry sum, considered in itself, yet the firstfruits of a great harvest yet to come.

One of the slips read "Anon," but pledged 10 shillings and sixpence, the smallest amount promised that evening. It was turned in by William Staughton, the theological student from Bristol. Baptized by Pearce at Cannon Street Church in Birmingham, this young man was destined to become one of the leading pastors among Baptists in America. He never forgot that evening, nor lost his zeal for missions. What Fuller was in England, Staughton became in America, an indefatigable advocate and fund-raiser for the cause of missions.

Years later, when serving as the corresponding secretary of the American Baptist Missionary Convention, Staughton recalled that small, but solemn, gathering in the back parlor of Widow Wallis's godly home. That gift he offered, his widow's mite, he saw as one of the best achievements of his life, he said. "I rejoice more over that ten-and-sixpence than over all I have given in my life besides."[6]

John Thomas

Carey missed the next two meetings of the society, although he followed closely their deliberations and plans. Rumors were beginning to circulate of his own appointment as a missionary. On November 27, 1792, he wrote to his father.

> Polly tells me that you are afraid lest I should go as a missionary. I have only to say to that, that I am at the Lord's disposal, but I have very little expectation of going myself, though I have had a very considerable offer, if I should go to Sierre Leone in Africa. I however don't think I shall go.[7]

Carey had referred to the settlement at Sierra Leone in the

Enquiry, calling for an evangelical mission there. This colony on the west coast of Africa had been established as a haven for freed slaves. Partly in response to Carey's appeal, an Anglican chaplain named Melville Horne did attempt a mission among the nationals there, although it proved an abortive effort.[8] In 1795 the Baptists sent their first two missionaries to Africa to this same place.[9]

In the fall of 1792 Carey was clearly torn between what must have been an inward compulsion to respond to the missionary call he himself had sounded with such persuasion and force and the major obstacles to such a commitment, these obstacles being the two primary support groups in his life, his church and his family. The former troubles in the fellowship at Leicester had vanished. Attendance was growing, new converts were being won and baptized, the building had just been expanded to accommodate the crowds. How could he up and leave this vital work just when God had answered their many prayers for revival?

Assuming Carey could persuade his congregation to release him from his pastoral work, there remained even stronger objections from his family. Dorothy Carey had never traveled beyond the limits of the county in which she was born. Illiterate when married to her cobbler-husband, she had barely learned to read and write her native tongue, perhaps from overhearing the lessons he gave to the village children. Already two precious daughters had been taken prematurely. The three sons who survived were full of life. Scampering about the cottage in Leicester, they were a handful to their mother who was weighted down with other duties expected of a pastor's wife. Now, in this very fall, the discovery of yet another little one on the way! The thought of her and her children being transplanted to some distant land was more than Dorothy could bear. Much was in the balance. There were reasons for Edmund Carey to be "afraid" for the fate of his eldest son and his growing brood.

While Carey's own future as a missionary remained uncertain for the time being, he was not slack in exploring new possibilities for the society. Evidently he thought of Tahiti as the most promising field for a new missionary initiative. The lure of the South Seas tugged at him since first he read of Captain Cook. But now his vision shifted as a new character walked onto the stage.

"I have just received a letter from Mr. Thomas, the Bengal missionary," wrote Carey to his colleagues, whose third meeting was held at Northampton on November 13.[10] They had just been discussing urgent matters of practical concern: What qualifications should missionaries have? Where do we find suitable candidates? What rules should be adopted concerning their mission? Above all, where were the most promising openings for missions work?

Carey's letter seemed a providential answer to their queries. Thomas was trying to establish a fund for a mission to Bengal, the leading province of India. He was now in London seeking a missionary companion to join him on his return voyage to this land where the seeds of a fruitful work had been planted already. Could his plan and that of the society be united into one common effort? Was this the crack in that great and effectual door (1 Cor. 16:9) for which they had been praying?

By all accounts John Thomas was a remarkable man. A native son of Gloucestershire, he was four years older than Carey. Through hearing the sermons of the great Baptist preacher Samuel Stennett and reading the commentaries of the learned John Gill, he came to a personal saving faith in Christ. "Many days and nights," he said, "were spent in the enjoyment of believing that Christ had suffered for *me* in particular. ME, ME, so insignificant, so worthless! that such an one as *I* should be a partaker of his benefits!"[11]

Commissioned as a ship's surgeon on the *Earl of Oxford*, he first saw Calcutta in 1783. Returning to London, where he set up a practice of medicine, he was baptized in the Soho Chapel and soon began "to exhort in private societies and to preach in different places in town and country."[12] Always inept in business matters, his surgical practice came to naught and he returned to India in 1785. Here he came into the good graces of Charles Grant, an evangelical Christian of high standing in the East India Company.

Grant, along with an Anglican chaplain named David Brown, was much concerned with the religious life of the Indian people. They went so far as to draw up a proposal for a Christian mission to Bengal. Send us, they asked, "fit men, of free minds, disinterested, zealous, and patient of labor, who would . . . aspire to the arduous office of a missionary. . . . Men who are ready to endure hardships and to suffer the loss of all things."[13] Good

Anglicans both, Grant and Brown directed their request to the king and his archbishop of Canterbury. As might have been expected, George III dismissed such ideas out of hand. The French Revolution was brewing still. Who knew but that a scheme like this could lead to the subversion of the established order of things?

Grant, however, was not one to give up so easily. What he could not do with the king's blessing, he might do on his own, under the table as it were. Thomas, albeit a Baptist, was a devout and gifted man with a burden for the conversion of the people of India. He had returned to Calcutta with the words of Isaiah burning in his heart, the same prophecies which a world away were just then stirring the Baptists of Northamptonshire, and not least Carey, to pray and plan and expect.

From Thomas's journal, under the date of July 6, 1786, we read these musings.

> Hath God revealed the spread of the gospel, for nothing? Do not all things revealed belong to us? But how much more especially *these* things—to us, in particular, upon whom the ends of the world are come? For the time is nigh at hand: "It shall come, that I will gather all nations and tongues; and they shall come, and see my glory, saith the Lord" (Isa. 66:18). If we live to see the dawn of this day only; surely it becomes us to leave a mark behind us of our eager expectation, from the trust we have of the faithfulness of God.[14]

Six months later his missionary zeal was no less ardent, for on January 16 he confessed, "I feel as though I could do anything for Christ: go or stay, live or die. . . . But if He should tear my heart from these heathens, there would be a bleeding, for my soul is set upon them."[15]

Under Grant's patronage, Thomas did begin to minister among the nationals of India, living first at Malda, then at Harla Gachi. During these years he learned Bengali and translated the Gospel of Matthew into that tongue. He also preached to many Hindus and made the acquaintance of several Brahmins, one of whom, Ram Ram Basu, would later become Carey's assistant.

Despite these worthy efforts, Thomas's missionary career soon suffered a relapse when he fell out of favor with Grant who cut off his financial support. Thomas, already heavily in debt, began to sink further toward financial ruin. Some of the blame for this broken relationship has to be laid at Thomas's feet. He was crude and censorious in his criticism of colleagues, blasting one for his Arminian leanings, others for their practice of infant baptism. At times he was presumptuous and tactless, forgetting that the virtue of love exceeds even those of faith and hope. Still, it is doubtful whether he deserved the epithets his former friends hurled at him: a bigot intolerable; a selfish, obstinate, overbearing, insolent, stubborn sectarian! He resolved at last to return to England with hopes of garnering more solid support for the work he had begun in Bengal.[16]

Holding the Ropes

Both Fuller and Carey were men of eminent good judgment; neither was one to suffer fools gladly. Upon hearing of Thomas, they investigated his "character, principles, abilities, and success," and found him worthy of trust in all respects, despite his worrisome debts and checkered past.[17]

On more than one occasion future events would prompt second thoughts about Thomas. But none of this was in view when the society gathered at Kettering for their first meeting of the new year on Wednesday, January 9, 1793. The morning session was given to prayer. In the afternoon Carey preached from the closing words of the book of Revelation, "Behold, I come quickly; and my reward is with me, to give to every man according as his work shall be" (Rev. 22:12).

Thomas had injured his foot and was not expected to be present. Fuller reported on his earlier meeting with him and passed around letters he had sent from India to leading Baptist pastors in London. From all of this it appeared to the society that "a door was open in India for preaching the gospel to the heathen."

They agreed Thomas would be their missionary and, if possible, a suitable associate would be sent with him to India that spring. Carey was then asked whether he would go with Thomas, to which the minutes attest matter-of-factly, "He readily answered in the affirmative."[18] It was his moment of surrender. From that hour on, his face was set, like flint, toward his Jerusalem.

While deliberations were still proceeding, to everyone's surprise it was announced that Thomas had arrived. Webster Morris of Clipstone, who witnessed so many turning points in Carey's career from his rebuke by Ryland, Sr., to the "Expect great things" sermon, was here as well. As Thomas limped into the room, he said, "Mr. Carey, impatient to embrace his future colleague, sprang from his seat, and they fell on each other's neck and wept."[19]

Later Fuller added his remembrance of that evening.

> From Mr. Thomas's accounts, we saw there was a gold mine in India, but it seemed almost as deep as the center of the earth. Who will venture to explore it? "I will go down," said Mr. Carey to his brethren, "but remember that you must hold the ropes." We solemnly engaged to do so; nor while we live, shall we desert him.[20]

Neither Ryland nor Sutcliff had been present at this meeting. To these stalwart friends Fuller wrote an account of the day's proceedings. "I am much concerned with the weight that lies upon us," he said. "It is a great undertaking; yet, surely, it is right. We have all felt much in prayer. We must have one solemn day of fasting and prayer, on parting with our Paul and Barnabas."[21]

How Carey broke the news to his wife we do not know. The date for departure was set on April 3, barely one month before her anticipated delivery! She could not be persuaded to go, but she did finally consent for Carey to take their eldest son Felix. He would return for the others in two or three years once a home base had been established in India. The church at Harvey Lane too was filled with sorrow when they learned of their pastor's plans.

To his father Carey wrote, seeking sympathy but fearing rebuff: "I am appointed to go to Bengal in the East Indies, a missionary to the Hindus. . . . I hope, dear father, you may be enabled to surrender me up to the Lord for the most arduous, honourable and important work that ever any of the sons of men were called to engage in. I have many sacrifices to make, I must part with a beloved family and a number of most affectionate friends. . . . But I have set my hand to the plough."[22]

The next several months were spent in a furious campaign of travel, preaching, and soliciting funds for the projected enterprise. On a trip to Yorkshire Carey bade farewell to his younger brother Thomas. They would never meet again, although the latter's two sons, then barely toddlers, would later follow their uncle to India.

All across England hearts were opened to the missionary

appeal. In Bradford, "good old Mr. Crabtree," some 70 years of age, canvassed the neighborhood, even calling on the vicar and curate, until he had collected more than 40 pounds. At Bath, where the church had an aversion to special collections, Thomas thought he would come away empty-handed, until a lady in the congregation offered 1 penny. Thomas thanked them and said he would enter into his ledger—*Bath, 1 penny!* Whereupon they passed the plate around and collected a sum of 22 pounds, 6 shillings.[23]

No one did more to encourage support for the mission than Samuel Pearce. By stagecoach and horse, on foot, and by boat, he darted hither and yon seeking help wherever he could find it. One ill-tempered fellow said to him, "I should feel more pleasure in giving the Methodists 10 guineas than you Baptists 1." To which Pearce kindly replied, "If you give them 20 guineas, sir, we shall rejoice in their success; and if you give us 1, I hope it will not be misapplied."[24] His own church, Cannon Street in Birmingham, gave twice as much to work abroad as they spent on their own needs at home. Sometimes, of course, they received "only beggars' fare," as Pearce put it. Even Fuller, not one easily discouraged, would sometimes retire from the public streets into the back lanes, so that he "would not be seen to weep for his so little success."[25]

Indeed, there was much to discourage the would-be mission strategists in the early months of 1793. Then, as now, London was the nerve center of British life, not excluding the Baptist denomination. The great names of Baptist influence—Stennett, Booth, Rippon—were clustered in the large metropolitan churches there. While as yet there was no official Baptist union, London was nonetheless the "headquarters" for Baptist goings-on. When the London leaders began to get wind of the missionary stirrings in the Midlands, doubtless some of them must have thought, Can any good thing come out of Kettering (forgetting that John Gill who was pastor of a London church for nearly 53 years was from that place)?

At Fuller's urging a group of 8 London ministers and 23 laymen did meet at Devonshire Square Church to consider their involvement with the mission. Some voiced lukewarm support, others were openly hostile to the idea. "Dr. Stennett predicts," wrote Fuller to Carey, "that the mission will come to nothing. People may contribute for once in a fit of zeal, but how is it to be continually supported?" The group decided that individuals might contribute (though Stennett himself gave nothing), but that no auxiliary society should be formed in London lest they seem to commit the whole denomination. Carey was not surprised at this turn of events. "I expected the London people would do just as they have done," he said. He remained unswerving in his determination to fulfill the "glorious errand" which he was sure God had called him to do. Not even the difficulty of booking passage by sea would stand in his way. If necessary, he declared, he would walk by foot all the way from Holland to India before abandoning their design.[26] No romantic wanderlust here. He knew the sacrifices he must make, the comforts he must forsake.

The Hoped-for, Dreaded Day

The church at Harvey Lane was at last reconciled to the loss of their beloved pastor. His final Sunday there was a triumphant day of worship and praise. It was a cold, blustery March in the Midlands. A Baptist wool trader from Yorkshire, Thomas Stutterd had arrived in Leicester drenched from the rains. He made his way to Harvey Lane for worship where he heard Carey's farewell sermon, from Matthew 28 on the Great Commission, and witnessed the baptism of 8 new believers.

When the tearful good-byes had been said, Stutterd stayed to talk with the pastor. He knew what Carey was leaving behind, having met him before in Yorkshire where he was inspired to subscribe to the campaign. In a letter to his wife he described his encounter that evening.

> I asked him if he felt his mind comfortable in his proceedings. He answered, "Yes, I do." He squeezed my hand to his breast, and said, "Yes, I do. My family and friends are dear to me. I feel much on account of leaving them. But I am clear that I am called to go. I am perfectly sure that it is the will of heaven that I must go. Therefore, I am happy in obeying that call!"[27]

The Sunday meeting was only a preliminary farewell compared to the send-off the society had planned for Carey and Thomas which took place, again at Harvey Lane, on March 20, a Wednesday. This was the "affecting, hoped-for, dreaded day" Pearce had written to Fuller about a month before. "Oh, how the anticipation of it at once rejoices and afflicts me!" he said. "Our hearts need steeling to part with our much-loved brethren, who are to venture their all for the Name of the Lord Jesus. I feel my soul melting within me, when I read the 20th of Acts, and especially verses 36-38."[28]

They came from all over the Midlands to this service: the faithful four, of course, Fuller, Ryland, Sutcliff, and Pearce, renewing their covenant to hold the ropes for their sent-forth friend; Staughton, who had gathered in Widow Wallis's parlor less than six months before; Dorothy and her little ones surrounded by sympathy and tears; dozens of new Christians recently won to Christ through the witness of their pastor.

The morning was for prayer, not routine or perfunctory, but wrenched from their souls, earnest entreaty for the health and safety of their Paul and Barnabas. In the afternoon Thomas himself addressed the crowded chapel. Thomas was a rousing speaker. On this occasion, as before, his "tongue was ready oiled to run smoothly" over the tales of life in India—the crying needs of humanity there, the idolatries of the natives, the learned Hindus he had nearly led to faith in Christ, the translation of the Scriptures already begun.[29] Following his message, the society drafted a letter to be carried by Thomas and Carey to their Hindu enquirers. "From Asia sounded out the word of the Lord into Europe," they observed. "Glad shall we be to have that joyful sound reverberate to Asia again, and extend to every other part of the earth!"[30]

In the evening service Reynold Hogg, treasurer of the society, preached first. It was a sermon of comfort and commitment from Acts 21:13-14, "What mean ye to weep and break my heart? . . . The will of the Lord be done." Then Fuller, overcome with emotion, delivered the charge to the missionaries-elect. He spoke with great fervor on four themes: the objects they were to keep in view, the directions they were to follow, the difficulties they would surely encounter, and the reward they might expect. Fuller concluded his address by exhorting the men, "Go, then, my dear brethren, stimulated by these prospects. We shall meet again. Each, I trust, will be addressed by our Great Redeemer, 'Come ye blessed of my Father—enter ye into the joy of your Lord.'" It was a farewell not unlike that given "at the edge of a grave in the prospect of an eventual resurrection." In days to come Fuller's words echoed in their minds and lifted their spirits in circumstances more trying than anyone imagined in Leicester that day.

The next two days were spent in settling Dorothy and the children with her family at Piddington. She, only weeks now from delivery, could not be persuaded to go, nor he to stay. On Tuesday morning they said farewell. Thomas and Carey (with little Felix at his side) made for London, accompanied by Pearce representing the society.

One final service was planned at Olney. Olney held happy memories for Carey. Here he first heard Fuller preach. Here too he had been duly appointed to the gospel ministry. The local schoolmaster, Samuel Teedon, was present that evening and left this record in his diary.

> I went to Mr. Sutcliff's Mtg. and heard Mr. Carey preach, the missionary to go to the Hindus with his son about 10 years of age [Felix was actually only eight]. A collection was made. I gave 6d. It amounted to 10 pounds. The Lord prosper the work.[31]

Carey's text for this message was the very one he had written to his father when he first revealed his decision to go to India, Romans 12:1-2. He would be the "living sacrifice" called for by Paul, the first Christian missionary.

Then the rafters at Olney rang with the closing hymn. Its question and response had become the litany of Carey's life.

> And must I part with all I have,
>   Jesus, my Lord, for Thee?
> This is my joy, since Thou hast done
>   Much more than this for me.
> *Yes, let it go:* one look from Thee
>   Will more than make amends
> For all the losses I sustain,
>   Of credit, riches, friends.[32]

Those last four words of the second verse he pronounced with added emphasis. His dear ones at Piddington, his ministry in Leicester, his native land, his dearest friends: "Yes, let it go."

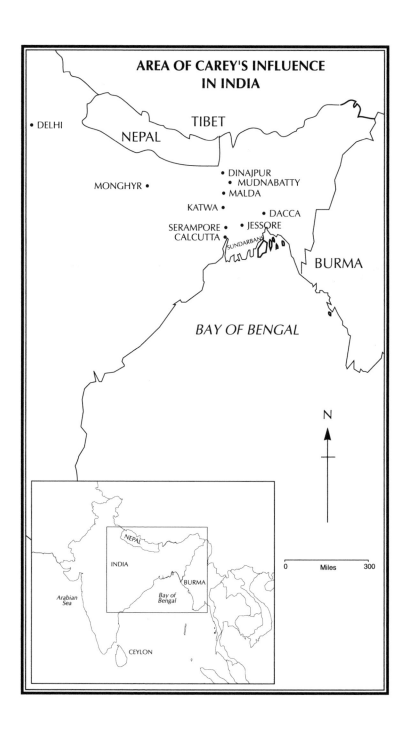

AREA OF CAREY'S INFLUENCE
IN INDIA

- DELHI

TIBET

NEPAL

- MONGHYR

- DINAJPUR
- MUDNABATTY
- MALDA

KATWA •

- DACCA

SERAMPORE •
CALCUTTA •
SUNDARBANS

- JESSORE

BURMA

BAY OF BENGAL

N

0   Miles   300

INDIA

NEPAL

BURMA

Arabian
Sea

Bay of
Bengal

CEYLON

H E is no fool who gives what he cannot keep to gain that which he can never lose.

Jim Elliot

6

No Turning Back

THE following Sunday found the missionary party in London. Carey was a curiosity even to those Londoners who remained skeptical about the missions enterprise. Some like the venerable Benjamin Beddome thought it was a waste to send such a "great and good man" to such a faraway land when there were so many destitute churches at home, "where charity ought to begin."[1] Carey had heard this "they have heathen at home" argument before, and had answered it in the *Enquiry*. It could not deter him now.

On Sunday morning Carey preached at John Rippon's church in Carter Lane, where Gill had served for so long and Spurgeon was yet to shine. In the congregation was a young man of 23, a printer named William Ward. Carey had met him once before on a preaching mission to Hull. Following the service the two men walked together beside the Thames as Carey presented his dream of translating the Bible into the languages of the Indian people. "You must come over and print it for us," Carey said, placing his hand on his shoulder. It was the summons to his lifework. Seven years later he would join Carey at Serampore, fulfilling the mandate he received that Sunday afternoon.[2]

These were days of frustration and worry as the missionaries sought official approval for their voyage to India. By Act of Parliament, any British subject going to India without a license from the East India Company was guilty of a high crime and misdemeanor. Stiff fines or even imprisonment could be meted out for breach of this law. At the very least illegal immigrants would be forced to return with all their belongings confiscated by the company.

Such thoughts were running through Carey's mind when he sought an interview with the saintly John Newton. Since 1780 Newton had been rector of Saint Mary Woolnoth's on Lombard Street. He was a friend of Wilberforce and a leading light among the evangelicals in the Church of England. As a young man Carey had felt Newton's lingering influence at Olney where he had written "Amazing Grace" and other hymns to stir the church. Now Carey sought his counsel and blessing.

"What if the company should send us home on our arrival in Bengal?" asked Carey. "Then conclude," replied Newton, "that your Lord has nothing there for you to accomplish." Then he added, "But if He have, then no power on earth can hinder you." Later Newton was to say of his Dissenter friend, "Such a man as Carey is more to me than bishop or archbishop: he is an apostle."[3] Thus was he encouraged to persevere in his purpose, despite all opposition.

Two Embarkations

At Carey's urging Newton tried to intervene with the East India Company, but to no avail. Charles Grant, who had returned to London from India, wished Carey well; but was dismayed to learn of his alliance with Thomas, of whose character and abilities he harbored only unpleasant memories. In any event, the policy of the company against the licensing of religious agents of any tradition was getting stiffer. That very fall Wilberforce would fail in his efforts to get Parliament to amend the charter of the company to include "religious improvement" among its duties of the people of India.

Just at this juncture Thomas proved most resourceful. He was able to persuade Captain White of the *Earl of Oxford*, on which he had twice served as a ship's surgeon, to take the party on board without a license. There were seven who boarded the *Oxford* in the Thames that April 4: Carey and Felix, Dr. and Mrs. Thomas and their daughter, along with two cousins of Thomas's from Smithfield. Only Pearce and one or two friends stood by the wharf to wave good-bye.

Southward they sailed to the Isle of Wight where they anchored in the harbor awaiting their convoy. Just two months earlier on February 11, France had declared war against Great Britain. No vessel dared plow the waters of the open sea alone. For six weeks they waited, taking lodging on shore in the city of

Ryde, since Portsmouth on the coast was too expensive.

The frustrating wait was broken by news from home, a letter from Dorothy which lifted Carey's spirits and prompted him to write in return.

My dear Dorothy,
I have just received yours, giving me an account of your safe delivery. This is pleasant news indeed to me; surely goodness and mercy follow me all my days. My stay here was very painful and unpleasant, but now I see the goodness of God in it. It was that I might hear the most pleasing accounts that I possibly could hear respecting earthly things. You wish to know in what state my mind is. I answer, it is much as when I left you. If I had all the world, I would freely give it all to have you and my dear children with me, but the sense of duty is so strong as to overpower all other considerations; I could not turn back without guilt on my soul. I find a longing to enjoy more of God; but, now I am among the people of the world I think I see more beauties in godliness than ever, and, I hope, enjoy God more in retirement than I have done for some time past.

Yesterday I preached twice at Newport, and once in the country. This place much favours retirement and meditation; the fine woods and hills and sea all conspire to solemnize the mind, and to lift the soul to admire the Creator of all. To-day I dined with Mrs. Clark (a former member of Harvey Lane) at Newport, and Felix found Teddy Clark, one of his old playfellows, which pleased him much. He is a good boy, and gives me much pleasure. He has almost finished his letter, and I intend to add a little to it. He has been a long time about it, and I question whether you can read it, when it comes.

You want to know what Mrs. Thomas thinks, and how she likes the voyage. She is very delicate, brought up very genteel, and cousin to Squire Thursby of Abingdon. But she is in good spirits, and the sea agrees with her very well. She sends her love to you, and is glad to hear the good news concerning your delivery. She would rather stay in England than go to India; but thinks it right to go with her husband. A young gentleman and his sister, cousins to Mr. Thomas, who have been brought up under the gospel, go with us.

I shall be glad to hear of you, and how you do, as often as possible. We do not know when we shall go, but expect it will be in a week at farthest. Tell my dear children I love them dearly, and pray for them constantly. Felix sends his love. I look upon this mercy as an answer to prayer indeed. Trust in God. Love to Kitty, brothers, sisters, etc. Be assured I love you most affectionately. Let me know my dear little child's name.

> I am, for ever,
> Your faithful and affectionate husband,
> William

To which he added this postscript.

> My health was never so well. I believe the sea makes Felix and
> me both as hungry as hunters. I can eat a monstrous meat supper,
> and drink a couple of glasses of wine after it, without hurting me at
> all. Farewell.[4]

In the meantime, Thomas's creditors were closing in on him.
One of them came calling at their lodging in Ryde, "with a writ
and bailiff," to arrest him for a sum of 100 pounds or less.
"They began to hunt; and I to flee as a partridge," he wrote
pathetically.[5]

Then, just as the consort ships pulled into sight, Captain
White received an anonymous letter from the India House in
London, stating that it was known that a person on board his
ship was sailing without the proper permit; and that if he were
allowed to continue, charges would be brought against the captain. Immediately the two missionaries and Felix were forced to
quit the ship, although Mrs. Thomas and the others were
allowed to continue the voyage.

Carey was in tears as the *Oxford* and her sister ships pulled
away and slipped out of sight. To Fuller he wrote, "I have just
time to inform you that all our plans are entirely frustrated for
the present. . . . I know not how to act. . . . All I can say in this
affair is, that however mysterious the leadings of Providence are,
I have no doubt but they are superintended by an infinitely wise
God."[6] Upon receipt of this despairing news, Fuller wrote to
Ryland, "Perhaps Carey has written to you. We are all undone. I
am grieved."[7]

In the next few days the "leadings of Providence" unfolded
in a way that no one could have anticipated. Having stashed
their baggage in Portsmouth, the two chagrined partners rushed
back to London to plot their next maneuver. Carey had in mind
to appeal in person to the director of the company or, if that
failed, to try the hazardous overland route from Europe to
India. Thomas, more streetwise about such matters, combed the
coffeehouses seeking information on the sailing of non-British
ships. After many inquiries one night, a waiter placed a card in
Thomas's hand, whereon were written, as he put it, "these life-
giving words."

A DANISH EAST INDIAMAN
No. 10, Cannon Street[8]

"No more tears that night!" They "fled" to the address, booked passage on the ship which they learned was hourly expected at Dover. Still nursing a hope that Dorothy might after all be persuaded to go, Carey, with Felix and Thomas in tow, caught the midnight coach to Northampton.

Dorothy was still fixed in her determination not to go. The new baby, Jabez, was only three weeks old. How could she pack their belongings and set out on such a dangerous journey with a newborn and three others under nine? Is William mad? she must have wondered, remembering the words of her father-in-law upon first hearing of the missionary venture. Neither Carey nor Thomas could induce her to change her mind. Needing to secure funds for their passage, the two men set out for Northampton. Carey was forlorn at the prospect of leaving his family. Thomas wanted to go back once more to plead with Dorothy.

"It's of no use," said Carey, "we are losing time." Undaunted, Thomas insisted, and this time prevailed. If she did not go with them, he said, her family would be dispersed and divided forever. And, *she would repent of it as long as she lived!* So urgent was Thomas's pleading that, as Dorothy later said, she was "afraid to stay at home." She would go on one condition, that her unmarried sister, Katherine Plackett, accompany her. She bravely agreed.

Carey and Thomas hurried away to Northampton to see Ryland. Nearly 700 pounds was needed now for the fares of their expanded party. Fuller had just received a note for 200 pounds from supporters of the society in Yorkshire, but there was no time now for a trip to Kettering. Ryland sat down and dashed off letters to Newton, Rippon, and Abraham Booth in London requesting an advance to cover the expenses of the voyage, with the promise that it would shortly be repaid.

With the loans secured Thomas completed the negotiations for the passage. He and Kitty, as Dorothy's sister was called, would go as "attendants" for a much reduced price, taking their meals in the servants' mess. Only the Careys would have a cabin with eating privileges at the captain's table. Such selfless concern always endeared Thomas to Carey, despite the former's exasperating foibles and flaws.

On Monday, May 27, Carey with his wife, children, and sister-in-law went by boat from London to Dover to await the arrival of their ship, the *Kron Princessa Maria*. Thomas took a coach to Portsmouth for the baggage. After some difficulty, he hired a fisherman who agreed to transport the packages by boat for 9 guineas. The next evening they landed safely at the Dover wharf, "having run through all the privateers in the dark," Thomas remarked.[9]

So much had happened so quickly. The missionaries' disappointment had turned to opportunity, their despair into joy. Two years to the day after Carey had admonished his brethren to "expect and attempt great things," Samuel Pearce wrote to his wife the following words summing up the whirlwind events of recent days.

> Prepare, my love, to rejoice and wonder and be grateful! On the evening of the day you left I received a letter from Ryland, and what do you think he wrote? Why, Carey *with all his family* are gone to India!! When? How? you are ready to ask, and I cheerfully satisfy you.
>
> By this time I suppose they have sailed. O what a wonder-working God is ours! Tell the whole now to others for the honour of our great Redeemer and the encouragement of His people. Three advantages are now secured: (1) The missionaries will go out more honourably, and the enemies of the Cause will not be able to reproach the Society with duplicity in transporting them under false pretences; (2) as the Danes are a neutral power, there is no fear of their being captured by the French on their way; and (3) Carey has the satisfaction of his whole family being with him, and the world has lost thereby one objection often raised against his going.[10]

Five Months at Sea

Two weeks more they waited at Dover as their ship, en route from Copenhagen, battled the heavy winds and black waters of the North Sea. Finally, at 3:00 in the morning on June 13, they were awakened by the sound of the guns signaling the ship's arrival in the wharf. Overcome with joy, Thomas jotted a note to his friends in London, "We are going with a fine fair wind. Farewell, my dear brothers and sisters. Farewell. May the God of Jacob be ours and yours, by sea and land, for time and eternity! Most affectionately adieu!"[11]

At last, all were safely aboard. On a receding tide, the *Kron Princessa Maria* continued on her journey to India accompanied as far as the Bay of Biscay by a British frigate, the *Triton,* for fear of attack by French vessels. As darkness fell the white-chalked cliffs of Dover blended into the mist and the verdant English countryside faded from sight. None of those in the missionary party, save Kitty, would ever look upon their native land again. Yet, more clearly now than ever before, Carey saw the hand of God in the stop-and-go circumstances of the past several months. Before retiring that first night at sea, he opened his journal with these words.

> This, I hope, was a day of joy to my soul. I was returned to take all my family with me, and to enjoy all the blessings which I had surrendered up to God. This is an Ebeneezer which I raise to God, and I hope to be strengthened whenever I reflect upon it.[12]

He spent his days being tutored in Bengali by Thomas and helping the latter attempt a translation of Genesis. With his innate flair for languages, he admitted "some delight" in these exercises, but only insofar as they related to his "great work"; that is, the conveyance of the Scriptures in the languages of those who had never read them before. He was wise enough to know that this task could not be accomplished in one lifetime or by one person alone. He envisioned his sons as apprentices with him in his ministry. "I am very desirous that my children may pursue the same work; and now intend to bring up one in the study of Sanskrit, and another of Persian. O, may God give them grace to fit them for the work!"[13]

One of the men on board ship was a Frenchman named Barnard. He was a Deist who denigrated the authority of the Bible and all the truths of revealed religion. Carey refers to him as a "daring, presumptuous wretch" and claims that he never "found a man so hardened and determined to turn Scripture into ridicule as he." He and Carey carried on a running dialogue throughout the voyage, with neither convincing the other of the errors of his way. In later years Carey would confront other representatives of "enlightened" religion in India whose subtle perversions of the gospel would recall his ocean debates with "the old Deist."[14]

The long sea voyage was also a time for soul searching and deepening the disciplines of the spiritual life. On July 5 Carey records this confession: "I have need to read the Word of God more; and, above all, I want a heart to feed upon it." On August 2: "I have in general reason to mourn that I have no more of the spiritual warfare maintained in my soul, and no more communion with God." By November 9 this: "I think that I have had more liberty in prayer, and more converse with God, than for some time before." His prayers, as always, centered on the conversion of the heathen and the blessing of God on the society which had encouraged and supported him so generously.

Dorothy left no journal for us to trace her impressions of the long five months at sea. For much of the trip she and Kitty both were nauseated from the squalling winds and swellings of the waves. Doubtless she was filled with fears and doubts and many second thoughts. "So that," as Thomas wrote, "she was like Lot's wife, until we passed the Cape; but, ever since, it seems so far to look back to Piddington, that she turns her hopes and wishes to our safe arrival in Bengal."[15]

Some 20 years later another missionary wife, with a sense of calling as strong as that of her husband, would confide to her journal something of what Dorothy Carey must have felt during those long days and nights. On the eve of leaving Salem, Massachusetts, for India, Ann Hasseltine Judson wrote

> Still my heart bleeds. O America, my native land, must I leave thee? Must I leave thee, Bradford, my dear native town, where I spent the pleasant years of childhood; where I learned to lisp the name of my mother; . . . where I learnt the endearments of friendship, and tasted all the happiness this world can afford; where I learnt also to value a Saviour's blood, and to count all things but loss, in comparison with the knowledge of him? . . . Farewell, happy, happy scenes, but never no, never to be forgotten.[16]

Dorothy's anxiety was eased a little by the kindness of Captain Christmas, the owner and pilot of the ship. Carey said he was "one of the most polite, accomplished gentlemen that ever bore the name of sea captain." He had assigned the Careys the most spacious cabin on board, a room with papered walls and sash windows. He also provided for Kitty and Thomas as though they were full-paying passengers. And, when seasickness kept the women from dining at the table, he sent soup and other niceties to their rooms. He also offered to recommend the missionaries to the governor of the Danish settlement at Serampore, just 16 miles from Calcutta, once they were in India. Little did any of them know that this very spot would become the permanent base for their mission, though not till 7 years after their arrival.

Though not a deeply religious man himself, Captain Christmas permitted Carey and Thomas to conduct public preaching services every Sunday. Few people came, at most six besides the Carey party, though they were a veritable "common market" of a congregation—a German, Norwegian, Dane, a Frenchman (most likely not the Deist), and a Fleming. In addition, family worship was held twice daily, each morning and evening.

Soon after the ship had rounded the southernmost tip of Africa, near Cape Agulhas, it was seized by a terrible storm. Just after midnight on August 26 everyone was aroused by a violent rolling of the ship. Chairs, stools, glasses, anything not tied down went flying through the air. Carey instructed his wife and children to stay in bed while he went on deck to help repair the damaged masts and rigging. The ship was plunging into waves which seemed to Carey 50 or 60 yards high!

> I saw her going, and with others concluded she could not recover it. I had but a moment to reflect: I felt resigned to the will of God; and to prevent being tossed overboard by the motion, caught hold of what was nearest to me. The plunge was dreadful. . . . At last, we cleared the wreck and set our main-sail, which kept the ship a little steady.[17]

It took 11 days to repair the damage to the ship. Carey gave thanks for their deliverance, perhaps calling to mind a favorite text from his beloved Isaiah (43:2), "When thou passeth through the waters, I will be with thee; and through the rivers, they shall not overflow thee." He was greatly strengthened by the knowledge that hundreds, yea thousands, of believers in England were lifting his name to God in prayer. He carefully calculated the difference in time, 6 hours from England to the Bay of Bengal, and paused each Sunday at the times of public worship back home to unite his prayers with those of his friends and fellow believers there.

Throughout the voyage he was comforted again and again by two promises from the Bible: the blessing of Moses on the children of Israel, "As thy days, so shall thy strength be," and the assurance of the Risen Christ to all His commissioned disciples,

"Lo, I am with you alway, even to the end of the world" (Deut. 33:25; Matt. 28:20).

Carey had hoped their ship would stop in southern Africa, so he could visit with the Dutch Christians there and also post back to England a packet of letters. The storm delay and condition of the winds prompted the captain to plow straight on for the Bay of Bengal. Thus, on October 17, with their destination only weeks away, Carey sat down to write his first letter to the society back home. He reviews the details of their voyage, reporting how little Jabez had grown so "stout," how all the children had been "complete sailors," and the women too (he would later confide to his sisters) doing "much better than I ever expected." He asks that they send him certain publications: a Polyglot Bible, the gospels in Malay, Curtis's *Botanical Magazine,* and Sowerby's *English Botany.* Wherever he had lived he had kept a garden. India would be no exception.

Then, in words which were later quoted and reprinted by the friends of missions both in England and America, he sets forth again his vision for the spread of the gospel throughout the world.

> I hope the society will go on and increase, and that the multitudes of heathen in the world may hear the glorious words of truth. Africa is but a little way from England; Madagascar but a little way further; South America; and all the numerous and large islands in the Indian and Chinese seas, I hope will not be passed over. A large field opens on every side, and millions of perishing heathens, tormented in this life by idolatry, superstition, and ignorance, and exposed to eternal miseries in the world to come, are pleading; yea, all their miseries plead as soon as they are known, with every heart that loves God, and with all the churches of the living God. Oh, that many laborers may be thrust out into the vineyard of our Lord Jesus Christ, and that the Gentiles may come to the knowledge of the truth as it is in Him!

India was only the beginning.

India at Last!

While still at sea Carey threw overboard the ill-fitting wig he had worn ever since a fever had deprived him of hair years ago. Since medieval times canon law had prescribed the shaving of the head, called tonsure, for the initiation of monks into their order. Carey, with the world for his cloister, entered his apostolic labors in India nearly bald, except for a clump of hair around the base of his skull.

After so many months at sea, everyone on board was anxious for landfall. Yet no one in the missionary party had a permit to enter the country. Before disembarking the commander of every vessel was required to submit an affidavit stating that he carried no contraband or unlicensed passengers. To avoid this danger, the missionaries, with the connivance of Captain Christmas, transferred to a small fishing boat, called a *pansi,* which carried them from the mouth of the estuary up the Hooghly River towards Calcutta. On November 14 the *Calcutta Gazette* announced the arrival of the *Kron Princessa Maria,* her only cargo, "Sundries." Three days before the missionaries had slipped into the vast city unnoticed and unmolested by the company officials.

Traveling this same route, Ann Judson described the scene Carey first saw that November morning in 1793.

> On each side of the Hoogli, where we are now sailing, are the Hindu cottages, as thick together as the houses in our seaports. They are very small, and in the form of hay-stacks, without either chimney or windows. . . . The grass and fields of rice are perfectly green, and herds of cattle are everywhere feeding on the banks of the river, and the natives are scattered about, differently employed. Some are fishing, some driving the team, and many are sitting indolently on the banks of the river. The pagodas we have passed are much larger than the houses.[18]

Even before reaching Calcutta the two missionaries "began our labors," as Carey has it. At a market town along the river, the party stopped and Thomas preached. Throngs of natives gathered round and listened "for 3 hours" to the discourse. Afterwards, the Careys enjoyed their first Indian supper, kindly provided by one of the natives: rice and curry served on plantain leaves and eaten with fingers rather than forks.[19] What hospitality shown to Christian evangelists! They concluded the visit amidst warm invitations to come again.

From the outset Carey was drawn to the people, "remarkably talkative and curious," he described them. The fields were indeed white unto harvest. Ten thousand missionaries would not suffice to publish the gospel to so many. "Yet they are very willing to hear, and you are sure of a congregation, go where you will."[20] How long before he too could join Thomas in declaring God's good news of Redemption through Jesus Christ? "To see people so interested, inquisitive, and kind, yet so ignorant, is enough to stir up any with the love of Christ in their heart."[21]

When Carey landed at Calcutta in 1793 he entered a city 200 years old. For the past 20 years it had served as the capital of the Indian Empire. It was a city teeming with people: 200,000 Asians, Carey estimated; in addition to the British, the Armenians, and the "Portuguese," as the Eurasian descendants of earlier settlers were called. It was a city of culture and refinement for those of the ruling British class who had succeeded well in the mercantile world. One lady of the upper crust described the social routine of the day: "We dine at one or two o'clock, . . . take a siesta afterwards, and then dress and take the air at sunset in carriages."[22]

Over the years such self-indulgence had led to decadence. Carey criticized the "pomp and grandeur of Europeans here" for he knew that it mitigated against an effective Christian witness among the people. As an Indian remarked to one of the chaplains he met, "Christian religion! Devil religion! Christians much drink, much do wrong, much beat, much abuse others."[23]

As Carey walked for the first time through the busy streets of Calcutta; as he looked upon the grand houses, the beautiful gardens, the impressive white buildings lining the river; as he saw too the squalid poverty, the pitiful outcasts, the many evidences of a false religious system leading multitudes towards destruction ("Go where you will, you are sure to see something of an idolatrous kind: flowers, trees, or little temples by the wayside"), he resonated with another missionary on his first visit to another City of Palaces long ago.

> I feel something of what Paul felt when he beheld Athens, and "his spirit was stirred within him." I see one of the finest countries in the world, full of industrious inhabitants; yet three-fifths of it are as uncultivated jungle, abandoned to wild beasts and serpents. If the gospel flourishes here, "the wilderness will in every respect become a fruitful field."[24]

What could he do, this lone, little man, against the principalities and powers of darkness? Here is his resume: education, minimal; degrees, none; savings, depleted; political influence, nil; references, a band of country preachers half a world away. What are his resources? A weapon: love; a desire: to bring the light of God into the darkness; a strategy: to proclaim by life, lips, and letters the unsearchable riches of Christ.

Cowper of Olney had said it: "God moves in a mysterious way His wonders to perform."

L IKE most of the master minds of all ages, Carey was educated in the school of adversity.

Francis Wayland

7

Through Many Dangers, Toils, and Snares

JOHN Robinson, the pastor of the Pilgrim fathers, once described the dismal circumstances and unsettled condition of his hounded flock in this way: "That we have been here and there, up and down, without sure footing is our portion in this present evil world."[1] Such too was the experience of Carey and his family during the first years of their new life in India. Hardly in the annals of missionary history is there a story more moving or more pathetic.

The writings of Jonathan Edwards were the mainstay of Carey's spiritual reading during those early days, next to the Bible, of course, and Brainerd's diary, which Edwards had edited. Among the precious, slender volumes of sermons he had brought over from England there were no commentaries. Still, having preached through Revelation before leaving Leicester, Carey may well have hidden in his heart these words from the great Puritan divine's "Notes on the Apocalypse": "God tries the graces of his people by persecutions, that the truth and power of his grace in them may appear to his own glory, both before men, angels, and devils."[2]

From his boyhood days in England, Carey's life had been one extended readying for the work he was now about to do. His love for plants and gardens, his gift for languages, his global vision of humanity, his cobbler's common sense, his genius for friendship, his pastoral labors and pulpit work, all these were but preparatory promptings for his larger part in the drama of the ages. Still he was not ready yet. There were other waters to cross and flames to pass through ere the refining work was done.

The Slough of Despond

Newcomers to Calcutta were expected to be armed with letters of introduction attesting their character and social status and admitting them into the amenities of polite society in the Anglo-Indian world. Our missionary-outlaws, of course, had no such testimonials to present. In certain quarters the very knowledge of their arrival would have jeopardized their stay.

Somehow Mrs. Thomas got word to her husband about where she was staying. The *Earl of Oxford* arrived safely on October 4. Since then Mrs. Thomas, nearly as reluctant to leave England as Dorothy Carey, had anxiously awaited the arrival of the two men and little boy she had last waved good-bye to off the Isle of Wight.

How surprised she must have been when the whole party of eight showed up on her doorstep! During his earlier sojourn, Thomas had become acquainted with George Udney, a Christian in the employ of the East India Company, who was yet to play a decisive role in the missionaries' labors. Through the kindness of Mrs. Udney, Mrs. Thomas had found temporary lodging in Calcutta. Here on November 11 the entire clan set up housekeeping under a single roof.

Almost immediately they found themselves in dire financial straits. In the first place, Thomas grossly underestimated what it would cost them to live in India. The society had raked and scraped to put together the fare for their passage, so there was no cash left. The "venture" they had sent ahead with Mrs. Thomas, cases of silverware and other merchandise they had hoped to sell for a profit in Calcutta, brought much less than expected because of a glut of such items on the market. The expense of maintaining a large household in Calcutta was quickly draining their meager resources.

After three weeks they moved to Bendel, an old Portuguese settlement 30 miles up the Hooghly River. With mosquitoes buzzing around them in the summerlike air, it was an uncomfortable journey made in a long, oar-driven boat which passed between the low banks of the river lined with trees.[3] Here they rented a cheap house from a German innkeeper, but this too was a makeshift arrangement.

For a while they considered settling at Nuddea, the "Oxford" of India, where Sanskrit scholars and learned Brahmin dispensed the wisdom of the Hindu religion. Carey and Thomas visited this ancient center of learning and received a warm welcome from its leaders. What a beachhead for the gospel a mission in Nuddea could be!

In his first letter to Sutcliff back in England, Carey wrote that if this "bulwark of heathenism" could be carried for Christ, then "all the rest of the country must be laid open to us."[4] From the outset Carey knew that, at bottom, Christianity was about truth. Ultimately, the claims of Jesus Christ would have to be pressed against competing ideologies and worldviews on this basis.

Before any of this could pan out, however, personal circumstances forced another shift of direction. To his dismay, Thomas discovered one of his creditors in London had issued a writ for his arrest in India. His only hope, he felt, was to move back to Calcutta, set up practice as a surgeon, and begin to repay his pursuers. Carey had grave misgivings about his friend's plan, knowing well by then "the fickleness of his mind."

He was furious when he discovered that Thomas had spent not only his own portion but also all of Carey's allotment of their meager savings in order to set himself up in a fine house with 12 servants and a coach to carry him about the city![5] To his diary Carey confided: "Now all my friends are but one; I rejoice, however, that He is all-sufficient, and can supply all my wants, spiritual and temporal."[6]

Now, bereft of all resources, forsaken by his colleague, no help from England, not even words of encouragement even possible yet for months to come, Carey was cast into the very abyss of despair. "I am in a strange land," he wrote, "alone, no Christian friend, a large family, and nothing to supply their wants."[7]

Disappointments multiplied. A job at the botanical gardens he had been recommended for was given to someone else. Desperately seeking help, he walked 5 miles under a sweltering sun to see David Brown, an Anglican chaplain he had heard about from John Newton in England. He received Carey with "cool politeness," but, upon hearing of his association with "that chap

Thomas," he sent him on his way empty-handed, not even offering a cool drink to relieve the burden of the heat.

His family was now living on the outskirts of Calcutta in a shack of a house made available to them out of pity by a native moneylender Carey had met. The constant shifting to and fro, unsanitary living conditions, and near-starvation diet had taken their toll. Dorothy and the two older boys, Felix and William, were suffering from dysentery. Felix was so sick Carey did not think he would survive.

Kitty, on whose shoulders the care of them all fell, joined her sister, Carey says, in "continually exclaiming against me." Was it fair for the Thomases to be living in Calcutta in affluence while they were forced to subsist on the charity of a native, without even the necessities of life? With no friends, unacquainted with local customs, unable to speak the language, they were indeed "lonely in the midst of a hundred thousand people." This was more than they had bargained for. "If my family were but hearty in the work," Carey wrote to Sutcliff, "I should find a great burden removed."[8]

The whole month of January Carey was preoccupied with trying to scrape together emergency funds for the family. "January 17. Went to Calcutta for money, but to no purpose. Was very much dejected all day." "January 20. This has been a day of seeking money." "January 28. This morning I was at Calcutta. Again disappointed about money. Was much dejected and grieved."[9]

Had God after all led him all the way to this strange land only now to abandon him? There were days when it seemed so. He complains of "spiritual barrenness," of "the strange stupidity" of his heart. When will the Lord take full possession of my mind and abide there forever? he asks. And yet, in the midst of such storms, he found an anchor.

One evening, depressed from the day's frustrations, he uncrumpled his copy of Fuller's farewell sermon at Harvey Lane. His spirit was charged again to read those endearing words of his soul mate far away. "Oh! I think again, I am not only ready to be offered, so as to suffer anything, but if I be offered, upon the service and sacrifice of the faith, I joy and rejoice in it."[10] Miserable accommodations in wretched wildernesses, hunger and thirst, nakedness, weariness, hard work, but little worldly encouragement—he had written of such things in the *Enquiry,* and now they were his lot.

Another evening, walking back home in the dark, he was impressed with the "all-sufficiency of God and the stability of His promises." He felt a quietening peace within that night and resolved to labor on, even if he should lose his life in the process. When he arrived at the house, things were calmer than usual, for which he thanked the Lord. Before going to bed, he prayed for faith and for the gift to wait patiently for Christ.[11]

Amidst such pressing cares, Carey never forgot his primary reason for being in India: to make Christ known. Every Sunday he and Thomas preached in the open-air markets and street bazaars of Calcutta. Remarkably, Carey was still willing to work alongside this man who had treated him and his family so shabbily. He never questioned Thomas's personal integrity or sincerity, only his poor judgment and instability. With Paul, Carey could say, "What does it matter? One way or another . . . Christ is set forth, and for that I rejoice" (Phil. 1:18 NEB).

In their joint missions Thomas did most of the preaching for Carey was still learning to express himself in the Bengali language. Even on his own, however, Carey took every opportunity to present the gospel. His diary records this encounter which occurred on February 1.

> February 1. Spent to-day in preparations for our departure on Monday to the intended place of our residence. Was very weary, having walked in the sun about fifteen or sixteen miles; yet had the satisfaction of discoursing with some money changers at Calcutta, who could speak English, about the importance and absolute necessity of faith in the Lord Jesus Christ. One of them was a very crafty man, and tried much to entangle me with hard questions; but at last, finding himself entangled, he desisted, and went to his old occupation of money-changing again. If once God would by his Spirit convince them of sin, a Savior would be a blessing indeed to them; but human nature is the same all the world over, and all conviction fails, except it is produced by the effectual working of the Holy Spirit.

Carey's long career in India was built on this fundamental truth: only God can open blinded eyes. Only God can convert lost sinners. Frenzied human efforts at evangelism, unless invigorated by the Holy Spirit, must come to naught. Yet, in His mercy, God has chosen to declare His plan of Redemption not with tongues of angels, but through the stammering lips of ordinary men and women. What greater motive, then, to tell this good news to all peoples everywhere? This was the driving motive of Carey's life—to witness faithfully, obediently, consistently to God's amazing, surprising, and always overcoming grace.

God an All-Sufficient Portion

Since first arriving in India, Carey intended to establish his mission on the basis of the two principles he had learned from the Moravians, and set forth in the *Enquiry*, namely: (1) missionaries must be on equal footing, companions, of the people among whom they minister; and (2) as soon as possible, they should become self-supporting.[12] Against his better judgment, he had acceded to Thomas's schemes. Now he would pursue the strategy he had conceived from the first.

Carey learned that a plot of land some 40 miles east of Calcutta was available rent-free for 3 years for homestead farming. Nearby was the town of Debhatta where the Salt Department owned a bungalow his family might occupy, if it were vacant. Dorothy, who had just suffered a relapse, and Kitty, envious of the "pomp and grandeur" of the Europeans in Calcutta, could hardly abide the thought of being transported into a "wilderness." This, after all, would be their fourth major move in less than three months!

Had the women known more about the dangerous territory in which their new home was situated, doubtless their fears and complaints would have been even greater. Debhatta was in the Sundarbans, a vast tract of swampy jungle land through which several tributaries of the Ganges drain southward into the Bay of Bengal. In 1832 missionary John Mack described this untamed region of India which, if possible, was even more primitive 40 years before when the Careys first ventured there.

> The Sundarbans are a land of monsters dire. The rivers swarm with hideous alligators, which we often see basking on the shores, or rather imbedded in the mud, of which the banks consist; tigers of the fiercest kind pass and repass every night over the ground where the people are at work in the day; and snakes of monstrous size and deadly poison abound.[13]

Carey himself calls it a jungle forest; uninhabited by humans;

swarming with tigers, leopards, rhinoceroses, deer, buffaloes, etc.[14] Thither with a sick wife, a forlorn sister-in-law, an infant son, and three others under 10, Carey sailed for 3 days along the rivers and salt lakes toward what he hoped would be his first permanent settlement since leaving Leicester. William Ward hit the mark when later he referred to this episode of Carey's life as that of a latter-day Abraham who "went out, not knowing whither he went" (Heb. 11:8).

The bungalow they had set their hopes on was taken already. It would be weeks before Carey could construct a bamboo hut for their abode. Again facing disaster, what Carey's nephew later called a favorable dispensation of Providence, now fell upon them.

Charles Short, an official of the company's salt works in the area, graciously invited the whole party to reside with him for 6 months, or even longer if need be, until they could be properly settled. Short was not a Christian and showed no sympathy for Carey's missionary ideas. Yet his kindness was met by a responsive chord. He and Kitty struck up a friendship that February which was to blossom into romance in the days ahead. On November 15, 1794, they were united in marriage.

There was a new person who took up residence with the Careys in the home of Charles Short. He was Ram Ram Basu. A High-caste Brahmin of great learning, he had worked with Thomas during his earlier stay in Bengal. He had also professed faith in Christ, but had never taken the decisive step of repudiating his caste and receiving baptism. In fact, when Thomas returned to England, Ram Ram Basu had relapsed into the idolatrous practices of his Hindu past, partly because he had been "forsaken" by the Christians he knew, and partly to placate his family while seeking their help in a time of distress. Still, he professed to "love Christianity the best," and linked up with the missionaries soon after their arrival in Calcutta.[15]

Carey engaged Ram Ram Basu as his pundit, or *munshi*, a learned scholar whose expertise in the languages and mores of his people proved invaluable to the novice missionary-translator. Carey promised room and board and a nominal salary for his assistance. Carey believed that he was "a truly converted man," and continued to encourage a more unequivocal response from him. Later, when he fell into adultery and other sins, Carey was deeply disappointed and, with much regret, dismissed him from his service. To Pearce he wrote that it appeared "as if all was sunk and gone."[16] Still in those early days, with Thomas so fickle, Ram Ram Basu was a wise helper and "trusty friend" to Carey. He also composed the first Christian hymn in the Bengali language, a verse sung for many years by believers in that area.

> O who besides can recover us,
> O who besides can recover us,
> From the everlasting darkness of sin,
> Except the Lord Jesus Christ?[17]

By day Carey worked to clear his plot of ground and plant the makings of a crop. Dangers were constantly lurking in the shadows. In the previous year some 20 men had been killed by tigers in the district of Debhatta. Thousands had fled the area in fear. How carefully must the women have watched the children at play! As word got out about Carey's project, however, the natives began to return. Soon there were several hundred gathered around the settlement, giving Carey hope of a Christian community taking root there. Things were more tolerable at home too. Dorothy and Felix recovered from the attacks of dysentery, helped along no doubt by the abundance of berries, mangos, fresh fish, and leafy vegetables to eat.

Of necessity, much of Carey's time was spent "managing my little farm with my own hands."[18] Yet he did not neglect his studies. Daily he increased his knowledge of Bengali finding it a "very copious" language, abounding "with beauties."[19] With the help of Ram Ram Basu, he continued to correct the translation of Genesis which Thomas had begun on board the *Kron Princessa Maria*. The translation and publication of the Bible in Bengali was a goal he intended, with God's help, to reach.

In the evening hours, when the day's work was done, Carey and Charles Short talked about the ultimate matters of life and death, of time and eternity. Short was a Deist of sorts and raised many of the same objections to the Christian faith that Carey had encountered in his discussions with the French skeptic at sea. Was the Bible really the Word of God? Was Carey not "illiberal and uncharitable" in claiming that faith in Christ was necessary for salvation? Was it not unfair to consign the heathen to eternal misery?

Carey replied he was no more "uncharitable" than the Bible,

and that God would be proven "gloriously just" in all His dealings with humankind. "I feel a pleasure in being valiant for the truth," wrote Carey, "and much wish that God would convert his soul. He is indeed a kind and hospitable man."[20] Following his marriage to Kitty, Short did become a Christian. Until his death in 1802, he remained close to Carey who had repaid his great act of compassion in the most benevolent way possible: by introducing him to the Saviour.

During his Debhatta days, Carey confided to his diary the ups and downs of his spiritual struggles. "In this wilderness, O how my soul wanders! I thirst, but find nothing to drink. O Lord, I beseech thee, deliver my soul!" "Feel very much degenerated in my soul; scarcely any heart for God." How could he teach others of God's grace when he himself was so destitute of it? His soul was like a pendulum swinging to and fro. Yet he knew that it could find rest only at its true center, God. "O when shall I serve God uninterruptedly, and pursue everything in a subserviency to his divine will, and in such a manner as to commune with Him in everything I do?"[21] How he desired for his soul to be like the well-watered garden he was cultivating— manicured, orderly, fruitful; how instead it resembled the jungle which threatened to devour him— turbulent, unruly, dark.

While such smiting of the soul may sound strange to modern Christians brought up on a sunnier sort of spirituality, it is at the heart of the Puritan quest for a holy life which Carey had learned through the likes of Newton, Fuller, the elder Robert Hall; and the writings of Doddridge, Edwards, Law, Watts, Gill, Bunyan, and a host of others. Christ did not come to heal those who were full of health, but rather the broken, the hurting, the helpless. To sense one's unworthiness and to know one's desperate need for Christ is as much a prerequisite for spiritual renewal as a glass being empty is for its filling.[22]

The shadows did give way to sunshine for Carey. He took great comfort from reading Brainerd, always Brainerd, though there were no woods to retire to for fear of the tigers! Edwards's sermons were also a blessing, especially one entitled "The Most High, a Prayer-Hearing God." "What a spirit of genuine piety flows through all that great man's works!" he exclaimed. "I hope I have caught a little fresh fire today."[23]

On April 15 this cheering note: "Bless God, that His presence is not departed. This evening, during the approach of a violent storm of thunder, I walked alone, and had sweet converse with God in prayer. O! I longed to have all my fetters knocked off, that I might glorify God without any hindrance, either natural or moral."[24]

One of the things which grated hardest on Carey during these months was his isolation from other Christians. In the Sundarbans jungle, there was no fellowship with other believers, save his family with whom he regularly prayed and read the Scriptures. Even at sea there were five or six who came by his cabin for worship. Now he was alone. It was "now a year and 19 days" since he had left his "dear charge at Leicester." Perhaps he counted the hours as well.

Reading Ryland's circular letter on zeal reminded him of how sorely he felt the loss of those "public opportunities which I enjoyed in England."[25] Sundays were the most difficult days of all.

> March 16. Such another Sabbath I hope I shall never pass. What a hell it would be to be always with those who fear not God.

> May 12. A Sabbath not quite unprofitable but attended rather with perplexity than any enjoyment. . . . God grant that I may see much more the beauty of His ways!

> May 19. A Sabbath almost fruitless.[26]

Deprived of the blessing of public worship, he valued it now as never before. Removed from the sweet fellowship of his dear Christian friends, he was driven into the arms of his Sovereign Lord. "April 14. I feel that it is good to commit my soul, my body, and my all, into the hands of God. Then the world appears little, the promises great, and God an all-sufficient portion."[27]

The Move to Mudnabatty

With the kind reception from Charles Short, their bamboo house under construction, and the beginnings of a promising crop in the ground, Carey's announcement that they would soon be making yet *another* family move must have fallen with a thud on his dismayed household. Again it was Thomas who played such a pivotal role in this major direction.

Back in Calcutta Thomas, stricken with remorse for his relapse from the mission, wrote to Carey apologizing for his conduct. He admitted he had been "desperately drinking into the spirit of the world," and desired to make a new start. George Udney's brother and sister-in-law had recently drowned in a tragic accident on the Hooghly River. Thomas wrote a gracious letter of sympathy and treated the family, especially Udney's mother, with great pastoral sensitivity. This led to a reconciliation between these old friends and to an offer from Udney for both Thomas and Carey to supervise the manufacture of indigo dyes on two tracts of land he owned in the region of Malda in northern Bengal. Both planters were to be paid salaries of 250 pounds each per year. They were also promised a share in the proceeds of the business should it succeed. More important still, as indigo planters the two missionaries would have for the first time a legal standing in British India, preventing their preemptory expulsion by the East India Company. Too, he would be near Thomas again. Together they could resume their public ministry and preaching to the natives.

Considering all these advantages, Carey accepted the offer gladly. "For a long time," he wrote in his journal, "my mouth has been shut, and my days have been beclouded with heaviness. But now I begin to be something like a traveller who has been almost beaten out in a violent storm, and who, with all his clothes about him dripping wet, sees the sky begin to clear."[28]

It took three weeks to make the long 250-mile journey from Debhatta to Mudnabatty, a village 32 miles north of Malda on the Tangan River. Here the Careys moved into a two-story house newly built for the director of the indigo works. It was their first permanent abode since Leicester and would be their home for the next 5 years. Thomas's plantation was at Mahipaldighi, some 16 miles away, close enough no doubt for families who had once lived uncomfortably under the same roof!

There was much work to be done. Some 90 natives were assigned to Carey's operation, from whom he hoped the nucleus of a Christian congregation could soon be formed. Bricklayers and carpenters constructed the vats where supplies of the harvested indigo plant would be beaten by the native workers, standing waist-deep in water. Once the water had turned a deep blue color from this action, it was drained into still lower vats and allowed to solidify into hardened cakes. These, in turn, were gathered and shipped to Calcutta for sale and export. Carey's love for plants and his knowledge of the agricultural process made him an ideal director of such a project.

Requiring his full-time supervision only 3 or 4 months a year, the indigo works also gave much opportunity for Carey to pursue his missionary interests, as a bivocational minister, so to speak. This he did with Udney's full blessing and support. The business operation was never an end in itself. Rather it was the God-provided means to accomplish a larger, worthier ideal. As Carey reminded himself, "If, after God has so wonderfully made way for us, I should neglect the very work for which I came thither, the blackest brand of guilt and infamy must lie upon my soul."[29]

Communication between Carey and his supporters back home was slow and uncertain due to the continuing hostilities between England and France. Carey's first letter to the society, written on board ship before he reached India, was not received until a year later when he was already settled at Mudnabatty.

He himself was keenly disappointed when the ship *Nancy* docked at Calcutta without a single communication from his friends who had pledged to "hold the ropes" for their colleague on the field. "Surely you have not forgotten us," he wrote to the society on August 5, 1794.[30] By January 1795 Carey still had not heard a word. He did not doubt the firmness of their friendship, he wrote in his journal, but "hope deferred makes the heart sick."[31]

It was never Carey's plan to remain permanently dependent on the society for financial support. Quite the contrary. Missionaries, he believed, should support themselves by their own labors, freeing up money raised at home to be used in starting new missions endeavors. In the letter of August 1794 just referred to Carey informed the society he would no longer require their monetary assistance, thanks to the business arrangement he and Thomas now had with Udney.

Back home in Northamptonshire, Carey's letter was received with suspicion and alarm. They had not sent Carey to India to become an entrepreneur! Was he intending to make himself rich by this new scheme? Such questions arose primarily from newer members of the society, with less personal knowledge of Carey than the old stalwarts. At a meeting when Fuller was absent, they fired off a curt letter to Mudnabatty questioning the wisdom of the indigo plantation. They insinuated Carey was a money grubber for whom "the spirit of the missionary" had been swallowed up by "the pursuits of the merchant."[32]

Carey was deeply offended when this letter finally made its way into his hands in January 1796. He refused to grovel or justify his actions: "If my conduct will not vindicate itself, it is not worth vindicating." All the same, he responded with a stern blast of his own. He was putting upwards of one-third of his income from the indigo works back into the mission. He vigorously denied that the love of money had motivated his course of action. "I am indeed poor, and shall always be so, till the Bible is published in Bengali and Hindostani."[33] Besides, the society had contributed less than 200 pounds to his support the 3 years he had been in India. Hardly the basis for so censorious an attack! Fuller was able to smooth over the misunderstanding and restore friendly relations between the society and their premier missionary-pioneer. Still, this episode foreshadowed even greater difficulties in the future. Those problems too involved the financial integrity of the mission. Unfortunately, they would prove impossible to resolve once the mediating hands of Fuller had been removed by death.

Though several hundred miles to the north, the topography of the Malda region was much the same as the rest of Bengal: meandering rivers, clumps of trees and brush, and the seemingly unending fields of rice and jute, flat as a pancake. "There is not a single mountain or hill in the country," wrote William Ward.[34]

The weather was a study in contrasts. In what the natives called the "time of the dew," from early January till mid-March, it could be quite cold. Carey said he shivered even under his overcoat during this time. This is followed by the springtime and then the coming of the hot season from May through July. "During these months," Ward said, "the heat is often very oppressive; the body is in a state of continual perspiration; the sweat drops from the body as a person sits in the shade, and two or three changes of linen are necessary during the day."[35] The heat, in turn, is followed by the monsoon season from July through October when storms of wind and rain devastate the land, uprooting trees, overturning houses, flooding the fields of young green rice, leaving stagnant pools of malarious water standing everywhere. "In Bengal," said Ward, "nature always appears in an extravagant mood."[36] The rain comes down in sheets, the wind scorches you by its ferocity, the sun burns up everything.

The Careys moved to Mudnabatty in the summer of 1794 just as the oppressive heat was giving way to the torrid rains. Carey's diary records the effect of such weather: "very much fatigued," "very poorly today, from being exposed to yesterday's heat," "fevers are frequent in the rains . . . perhaps arising from the number of rice-fields which are full of water."[37]

Up to this point Carey had been spared serious illness since coming to India, although Dorothy and Felix had been afflicted for over eight months. Now Carey himself fell victim to a malarious fever which was attended "with a violent vomiting and dysentery." Then just as he was beginning to recover (Udney had brought him medicine), his 5-year-old son Peter contracted an even more virulent fever and died. "He was a fine engaging boy," Carey wrote, so full of life and promise. Already he could speak Bengali with a fluency which amazed his father. What hopes Carey must have set upon him! Now he was gone.

So rigid were the rules of caste that Carey could find no one willing to help with the burial of little Peter. No one to make the casket, or dig the grave, or bear the body to its place of rest. Contact with a corpse was strictly forbidden. Finally, when the grieving parents had resolved to carry their son's body to the grave themselves, an outcast was found to do this deed for them. The personal distress caused by these events only reinforced Carey's conviction that the claims of Christ and the system of caste were incompatible. Caste is "one of the strongest chains with which the Devil ever bound the children of men."[38] Only God, he said, can break it.

Dorothy never recovered from Peter's death. She could see none of the "wise ends" her husband claimed God must have in such circumstances. Only bitterness and hurt remained for her. She would bear another son at Mudnabatty, born in January 1796. They called him Jonathan, "gift from God." But he could never take the place of Peter. Separated now even from her sister Kitty, she became more distant and disturbed. Much of her anger focused on Carey who privately complained of "very sore trials in my own family, from a quarter which I forbear to mention," while he prayed for greater faith and patience. When the new baby was 3 months old, he confided in a letter to his sisters back home, "My poor wife must be considered as insane, and is the occasion of great sorrow."[39]

Carey continued to struggle in prayer and search the Scriptures for that enjoyment of God which he found so elusive yet so alluring. He bemoaned his lack of progress. "I think my peevishness, fretfulness, and impatience is astonishing. O that the grace of God might but be in me, and abound!"[40]

Six months after Peter's death, alienated from a wife who was daily losing her grip on reality, still awaiting his first letters from England, Carey confessed to his journal:

> This is indeed the valley of the shadow of death to me, except that my soul is much more insensible than John Bunyan's Pilgrim. O what would I give for a kind sympathetic friend, such as I had in England, to whom I might open my heart! But I rejoice that I am here, notwithstanding; and God is here, who not only can have compassion, but is able to save to the uttermost.[41]

Witness to the Truth

During the years at Mudnabatty Carey laid the foundations for his future ministry in India. He was especially anxious to preach again and rejoiced to have his "tongue loosed" at Malda, even though his congregation consisted only of the Udneys and a few of their European friends.[42]

Once he was settled at Mudnabatty, he began regular Sunday preaching trysts for the natives, drawing between 200 and 600 every week. Muslims and Hindus came in about equal number to his services. He admitted that their holy books, the Koran and the Hindu *Shastras,* contained many good observations and rules, but they provided no remedy for sin, no way of forgiveness.

> I told them that their books were like a loaf of bread, in which was a considerable quantity of good flour, but also a little very malignant poison, which made the whole so poisonous that whoever should eat of it would die.

He then presented "the suitableness and glory of the gospel," focusing on the "infinitely great sacrifice for infinite guilt" offered by Christ on the cross. Eternal life and the benefits of grace were to be found in Christ alone, a "free salvation for poor and perishing sinners."[43]

Such was the pattern of Carey's early preaching to the Indians. By March 1795 he had acquired enough fluency in Bengali to preach for a stretch of about 30 minutes, although he frequently had to stop and ask help in finding the proper word to express his ideas. Still, he found that he was "tolerably well understood."[44]

With such a limited vocabulary, his sermons varied little. He dwelt on the essential truths of the gospel: the universality of sin; the justice of God; the Incarnation and Atonement of Christ; the necessity of conversion, repentance, faith, and holiness in the Christian life. He found his audiences remarkably attentive and polite. Dozens of inquirers stayed to talk about the things of God. "I hope in time I may have to rejoice over some who are truly converted to God," Carey remarked.[45]

The Hindu gods whom their devotees sought to appease by offering sacrifices to their innumerable shrines and altars were vengeful deities, much like the autocratic ruler in this dialogue which Carey wrote to help schoolchildren learn the Bengali language.

> Bearer, pull off my boots.
> As you order, sir, I am pulling them off.
> Bearer, bring some hot water.
> Sir, I have put the water on the fire. When it is ready, I will immediately come and bring it.
> What? Is not the water hot yet? Did not I order it when I went out in the coach?
> Sir, it is almost ready.
> What do you say? I suppose you pay no attention to me. The work which I ordered at daybreak, it is not ready yet.
> Sir, there is a fault. Don't be angry any longer.
> What kind of fault is this? Suppose any other gentleman had come to breakfast. . . . If they had come what could have been done! I should have been greatly ashamed.
> Sir, your slaves have committed a fault, there be orders to forgive.
> Hirkarrah, pull the Bearer's ears. Let him remember not to do so again.[46]

Many Muslims in Bengal, although technically followers of the one God, Allah, also believed in multiple deities which they often identified with the spirits of departed relatives and friends.

Over against such eclectic systems of belief and worship, Carey presented the true claims of the Christian faith: the Almighty God, Who made everything out of nothing, cannot be appeased by the trifling acts of sinful humans who deserve His wrath and judgment, but in mercy and grace He has taken their sins on Himself in the person of His Son Jesus Christ and now provides true salvation to all who will turn from their idols and trust in Him.

Carey treated with respect and fairness those he was seeking to win to faith in Christ. When a certain bricklayer at the indigo works constructed an idol of the goddess Sorosuadi, with a shed for her covering and large dishes of rice and fruits placed around her image, Carey did not forbid outright this religious practice, for he thought such an imperious act would be persecution. Instead, he sought to convince the man of both the foolishness and sinfulness of his act and to persuade him to abandon his idol worship.[47] Carey remembered well the legal strictures imposed on Baptists and other Dissenters in England. He knew the gospel in India would make its way not by coercion and force but only as the Holy Spirit broke through the barriers of ignorance, superstition, and unbelief to bring the lost out of darkness into the light of truth.

Carey soon encountered the difficulty of communicating the gospel in a cross-cultural context. Hinduism was a syncretistic religion which could absorb without offense many elements from other faith systems. Vishnu, for example, was a god of love who went through many incarnations in order to help the human race. His greatest incarnation was Krishna who lived among the poor, performed deeds of charity, was killed by wicked men, and will come yet again. Was not the Christ of the missionaries just another version of Krishna? Only the Bible could show the uniqueness of Christ. This is why Carey yearned so much for it to be translated and disseminated among the people.

There were other misunderstandings as well. Hell, for example. Believing in the transmigration of souls, the Hindus saw life on earth as one stage in a long process of begetting and becoming through which the soul passes on its way to Nirvana, the ultimate release from desire and life when the individual self is absorbed into the great impersonal Force of the universe. Before reaching this stage, however, the soul might have to pass through as many as 7 heavens, 1 of them on earth, and 21 hells!

In one of his sermons Carey mentioned hell as the ultimate destiny of unbelievers. Several of his hearers stayed to talk with him about it. "I suppose, sir," said one of them, "we shall be used there as we should in Dinagepore jail." Carey answered, "No. In prison only the body can be afflicted, but in hell the soul. A person may escape from prison but not from hell. Death puts an end to imprisonment, but in hell they shall never die. There God's wrath will be poured upon them for ever, and they must dwell in endless fire."[48] Carey did not dwell in a morbid sense on the details of eternal damnation; his central theme and emphasis was the grace of God in the cross of Christ. At the same time, as a true herald, he did not shrink from proclaiming the whole counsel of God.

No person was too insignificant, no question too trivial, for Carey to take with the utmost seriousness. In 1807 when Felix, then a grown man, was preparing for a mission to Burma, Carey shared with him the strategy of personal witnessing that he had pursued since coming to India.

> Preach the never-failing word of the cross. Do not be above sitting down to the patient instruction even of one solitary native. . . . Cultivate the utmost friendship and cordiality [with the natives], as your equals, and never let European pride or superiority be felt by the natives in the mission house at Rangoon.[49]

Carey's business interests required that he travel extensively throughout the Malda region, making sure the indigo crop survived the storms and arranging for the shipment and sale of the finished product. He traveled from village to village along the lakes and flooded fields with two small boats. One was equipped with a table, chair, bed, and lamp—a floating hotel! The other boat was used for cooking and storage and for taking back the many specimens of Bengali flora and fauna Carey was collecting. On these tours, which he made mostly during the dry season from November to March, Carey tramped back into the inland villages, walking up to 20 miles a day sometimes, "preaching, or rather conversing, from place to place, about the things of the kingdom of God."[50]

Meanwhile, back in England, Fuller and other members of the society remained anxious about the progress of the mission, or lack thereof. They were also increasingly suspicious and mistrustful of Thomas, not without good reason to be sure. His debts continued to mount. Then, in 1797, he abandoned his position with Udney, and with his sickly wife and daughter traveled hither and yon attempting one venture after another. Shortly before Thomas's death in 1801, he renewed contact with Carey and proved useful in the conversion of the first Hindu Christian won through the witness of the mission.

Carey stood by his erratic friend to the end. Earlier he responded to Fuller's blast against him by saying that "if anyone wounds Mr. Thomas, he wounds me."[51] He knew his faults quite well, but he also admired the great heart and genuine compassion of this first medical missionary who could have made a fortune, Carey thought, had he stayed in Europe rather than blazing a trail for Christ in Asia.

Near the end, his life became completely unraveled. He wrote a pitiful letter describing himself as "a hunted flea, a broken vessel, . . . a sunken worm."[52] One of his last conversations was with a Brahmin to whom he spoke about Christ. Carey preached his funeral sermon from John 21:19, "This spake he, signifying by what death he should glorify God." Joshua Marshman summed up his legacy best of all. "To him it is owing, under God, that the Hindus now hear the word of life."[53]

Carey knew his friends in England were anxious to read glowing reports of his work among the natives. Samuel Pearce had begun to edit his letters, along with portions of his journal, and publish them in the *Periodical Accounts* of the society, a title and idea borrowed from the Moravians. After all, Carey had told them to "expect great things."

Yet Carey knew, as not all of his supporters did, that true greatness in the divine measuring was not always quantifiable in terms of size and numbers. To Pearce he wrote in October 1795, "I cannot send you any account of sinners flocking to Christ, or of anything encouraging in that respect." One thing he could say with assurance: the name of Jesus Christ is "no longer strange in this neighborhood."[54]

Visible results there were. Just one month after writing to Pearce, Carey conducted his first baptism in India. Samuel Powell, Thomas's young cousin who had sailed on to India with his wife and daughter aboard the *Earl of Oxford,* now openly professed faith in Christ. Carey was happy to report back to the society that "a Baptist church is formed in this distant quarter of the globe."[55] The charter members were only four—Carey, Thomas, Powell, and a certain Mr. Long whom Thomas had baptized during his earlier ministry. Still, it was a beginning. For the first time since Harvey Lane days, Carey presided at the administration of the Lord's Supper.

The seed of a second church was sown the following year when Ignatius Fernandez, a Portuguese merchant in the neighboring city of Dinajpur, became a Christian. He supported Carey financially and also erected on his own property a brick church, the first Protestant house of worship in Bengal outside Calcutta. Later Carey's son William responded to the missionary call and worked for a while with Fernandez. In 1808 Carey wrote to his son:

> You are in a post, my son, very dear to my remembrance, because my first Indian years were spent in its neighborhood. I, therefore, rejoice greatly in your exertions. The conversion of one soul is worth the labor of a life. . . . Hold on, therefore; be steady in your work, and leave the result with God.[56]

By 1796 Carey had been in India long enough to develop a strategy for having the greatest missionary impact on his adopted country which he never intended to leave. He knew there would need to be more missionaries. He wrote to Fuller suggesting that seven or eight families should be sent out together. They could live in a single community sharing resources and laboring together in the work of the mission. At least one person in the group should be a teacher, with responsibility for educating the children.

By modeling Christian life in such a community, they would be an encouraging example to others. "Our families should be considered nurseries for the Mission."[57]

With an eye to his own desperate home situation, he added that "it is absolutely necessary for the wives of missionaries to be as hearty in the work as their husbands." And not only missionary wives but also single female missionaries were needed, women of "piety and evangelical sentiments" who are "disposed to consecrate their talents for the literary and religious improvement of their own sex." Carey was a pioneer in recognizing that the evangelization and nurture of women converts required a special approach and wisdom "different from, and far beyond, what men can or will bestow."[58]

Carey's dream of missionary families living together in a disciplined community spearheading the gospel witness for India became a reality at Serampore. Central to his plan were education and publication. Unbeknownst to him at the time, God was preparing even then a schoolmaster and his wife and also a printer to launch this great work with Carey.

In the meantime, the society had already sent reinforcements in the person of a young man named John Fountain. He arrived in Calcutta in September 1796 and immediately made his way northwards to Mudnabatty. In his first letter back home he described his first impressions of Carey.

> After getting a boat at Calcutta, and other necessary things, I left it on the 24th of September, and arrived at Mudnabatty on the 10th of October. Brother Carey most kindly received me. When I entered, his Pundit stood by him, teaching him Sanskrit. He labors in the translation of the Scriptures, and has nearly finished the New Testament, being somewhere about the middle of Revelation. He keeps the grand end in view, which first induced him to leave his country, and those Christian friends he still dearly loves. He reads a chapter and expounds, every morning, to twelve or sixteen persons. On a Sabbath morning, he also expounds, and preaches twice in the day besides, to forty or fifty persons; after which, he often goes into some village in the evening. In the intervals of preaching to the natives, we have worship in English. He indeed appears to be the character he describes in his publication, where he says, "A Christian minister is a person who, in a peculiar sense, is not his own; he is the servant of God, and therefore ought to be wholly devoted to him."[59]

Fountain is an interesting footnote in missionary history. One of his contemporaries described him as "a man of small stature and of small mind."[60] He certainly had an outspoken mind, especially about political affairs. He detested the corrupt policies of John Company, as the East India Company was sneeringly called. For all their rich exports from the East, they had imported "nothing but vice and misery." King George himself was more of a Rehoboam than a Solomon![61] These were dangerous words from a young man who had no legal basis for being in India.

Fuller threatened to disown him if he did not tone down his rhetoric. Carey was prompted to caution Fuller to warn other missionaries sent under the auspices of the society "to say nothing about politics, especially upon their arrival in Calcutta." The mission was still a fragile enterprise. Despite the good graces shown to Carey and Thomas, the entire missionary venture could be placed in jeopardy by loose talk or careless remarks overheard by the wrong ears.

Despite this flap, Carey and Fountain got on very well. He learned the language quickly, and ably assisted in the preaching and translation work. From his houseboat on the Hooghly River, Carey wrote to the society about his young colleague. "He is a good man, and greatly desires the salvation of the heathen."[62] He taught in the fledgling school Carey had begun at Mudnabatty, which by 1799 could boast some 40 students. He also helped to install Carey's first printing press which Carey purchased with the help of a loan from Udney. Seized by a fever, Fountain died in the home of Ignatius Fernandez at Dinajpur on August 20, 1800. His kind host, impressed by his steadfast faith in his dying hours, placed over his grave an inscription which read: John Fountain, Missionary to the Heathen, Aged 33, a Sinner Saved by Grace.[63]

In 1799 a devastating monsoon season left the indigo works at Mudnabatty inoperable. Carey had to look for another home and base for his missionary labors. He decided on Kidderpore, some 12 miles away. Felix was 16 now. William and Jabez were getting bigger, and soon little Jonathan could help with the family business as well. At Kidderpore they could develop their own indigo plantation. Here too the missionary community he longed to see could take root and flourish.

Much later Carey looked back on his early years in India and recalled how he had had to labor and "get forward by inches" in the work of the mission.[64] They were years of struggle and doubt, of hurt and hope, the sorrow of a lost child mingled with the sounds of new life. Partly fearing, partly hoping, Carey kept his hand to the plow knowing God would one day give the increase. To his sisters back home he wrote:

> I feel as a farmer does about his crop: sometimes I think the seed is springing, and thus I hope; a little time blasts all, and my hopes are gone like a cloud. They were only weeds which appeared; or if a little corn sprung up, it quickly dies, being either choked with weeds, or parched up by the sun of persecution. Yet I still hope in God, and will go forth in His strength, and make mention of His righteousness, even of His only.[65]

Guide us, O, thou great Jehovah!
Pilgrims on the boisterous sea;
We are weak, but Thou art mighty,
Thou canst make each danger flee.
Bread of heaven, Bread of heaven,
Feed us till we want no more.

When we see the shores of India,
Bid our anxious fears subside;
Let each heart be friendly toward us,
Land us safe by Carey's side.
Songs of praises, songs of praises,
We shall ever give to Thee.

Composed by William Ward and sung by the
missionaries on board the *Criterion*

8

The City of Refuge

ON Tuesday, May 7, 1799, the Baptist church at Olney was filled to overflowing for the commissioning of the new missionaries. Accepting Carey's challenge, they had volunteered to go to India to live in community and work as his assistants. William Ward, printer and former editor of the *Hull Advertiser,* was the only single man in the group. He had never forgotten Carey's stirring words to him about publishing the Scriptures in India. There was also a single woman, Miss Tidd, who planned to marry John Fountain. Three married couples and their children rounded out the company: Mr. and Mrs. Daniel Brunsdon; Mr and Mrs. William Grant, parents of two; and Joshua and Hannah Marshman, keepers of a charity school in Bristol, who had three little ones.

Samuel Pearce, whose devotion to Carey and the mission was exceeded by none, was not able to come to Olney due to an illness which was soon to take his life. From his deathbed he wrote a letter of benediction for Fuller to read out loud.

> My most hearty love to each missionary! Happy men! Happy women! You are going to be fellow laborers with Christ Himself! I congratulate, I almost envy you; yet I love you, and can scarcely now forbear dropping a tear of love, as each of your names passes across my mind. Oh, what promises are yours; and what a reward!
> . . . Oh, be faithful, my dear brethren, my dear sisters, be faithful unto death, and all this is yours![1]

Ward had served for several months as Pearce's associate at the Cannon Street Church in Birmingham. As the missionaries prepared to depart from London, he wrote a final letter to his saintly friend. "Would that you could join us! Lord, strengthen our hearts, and give us the apostolic spirit. Thank God, my dear, dearest brother, you can say with Bunyan's Hopeful, 'I feel the bottom'; 'the bitterness of death is past.'"[2] He begged Pearce to send him a copy of his signature, a farewell memento he could "clasp to his heart" on the long voyage to India.

On May 13 Fuller and Sutcliff joined the missionaries in London. That evening they prayed together and celebrated the Lord's Supper; a few days later they had a tearful farewell with their families and friends. They prayed, and sang "Was it for crimes that I had done?" They exchanged gifts, tokens of tenderness: a pocketknife, a watch ribbon, a vest. Then the embarkation. As the ship slipped anchor, the whole party stood on deck blowing their last kisses and waving good-byes to the loved ones on shore. "We cheered them again and again on the water. Their hearts were overcharged. We again cheered and saw them no more."[3]

Ward says he felt a "tender melancholy" which was impossible to shake.

For who, to dumb forgetfulness a prey,
This highly favor'd country e'er resigned,
Left Fuller, Pearce, and Ryland in a day,
Nor cast one longing, ling'ring look behind?[4]

And yet, before retiring that evening, he had turned from looking back to looking toward the mission which beckoned him forward. "Blessed be God," he writes in his journal, "that I have seen this hour and that I am now on board a vessel which will, I trust, carry me to India, to print the New Testament."[5]

The Serampore Brotherhood

Anticipating the difficulties of entry into India, the missionaries had sailed aboard the *Criterion,* an American frigate, guided by Captain Wickes, a Scotch-Irish Presbyterian from Philadelphia. Wickes was a devout believer and proved an invaluable friend to the mission. Their plan was to disembark before reaching Calcutta and secure passage on local boats up the Hooghly to the Danish settlement at Serampore. Here they would seek asylum until they could join Carey at Kidderpore many miles to the north.

Things went according to plan until the *Calcutta Gazette* ran a story reporting the arrival of "papist missionaries" at Serampore. The authorities of the company were alarmed for England was still at war with France. Rumors abounded of Napoleon's plans to march into India and recapture the land from the British. Could these "missionaries" be French spies in disguise? Ward and Brunsdon were hailed before the police in Calcutta who soon discovered that their "papists" were really "Baptists"!

Still, this incident gave instant notoriety to the missionaries. The officials warned them to stay in Serampore or else face arrest and expulsion. Now what was to be done? Carey awaited their arrival in Kidderpore, but the company had forbidden their settlement there. In the meanwhile Governor Bie, the Danish governor of Serampore, had shown them great kindness and invited them to establish their mission in his territory.

Ward was chosen to bear these tidings to Carey and seek his counsel. He arrived on a Sunday, December 1, 1799.

> I felt very unusual sensations, as I drew near, after a voyage of fifteen thousand miles, and a tedious river passage! . . . At length I saw Carey! He is very little changed from what I recollected: has rather more flesh than when in England, and, blessed be God, he is a young man still.[6]

In fact, Carey was 38 at the time, toughened no doubt by his strenuous years as a missionary-planter.

Ward presented the dilemma. Carey weighed the pros and cons of his joining the others at Serampore. He had sunk his life savings, over 500 pounds, into the land and buildings at Kidderpore. Already a church had been formed and a gospel witness established in the area. He had many misgivings about moving so near to Calcutta, remembering perhaps his own earlier, desperate days there.

In prayer they sought God's will and divine guidance was given. The next day Ward recorded the decision. "Carey has made up his mind to leave all, and follow our Savior to Serampore."[7] In this circumstance, as in so many others before, God had closed one door only to open wide another one.

Carey and his family arrived at Serampore on January 10 of the new year. The city was situated on the west bank of the Hooghly, 16 miles, or 2 hours by rowboat, from Calcutta.

Carey called it a city of refuge for debtors and derelicts. Now it became a haven for other debtors, latter-day Pauls who felt an obligation to preach the gospel to "Greeks and barbarians" alike, to pagan peoples no less than to hardened, "civilized" Englishmen. Serampore, in fact, was a melting pot. Danes, Germans, French, English, Portuguese, Armenians, Greeks, Sikhs, Muslims, Hindus—all sinners needing a Saviour.

Governor Bie welcomed Carey warmly. With his help the missionaries soon purchased an attractive piece of land along the river. On it was a spacious house with a separate apartment for each family, but with a large commons which doubled as a refectory and chapel. Other buildings on the property were suitable for the printing operation and the boarding school which they planned to open soon.

Already grief had struck the little group. William Grant died of cholera and dysentery less than a month after their arrival, a casualty to the cause before the others had put their sandals on. Fountain and Brunsdon would soon be carried off by similar seizures. Amidst such calamities Carey proposed a pattern of communal living for the group.

Like their Moravian colleagues and the early Christians of the book of Acts, they agreed to have all things in common. All the proceeds from their labors would be funneled back into the common treasury, save for the bare essentials required by each family. All profits would be used for the furtherance of the missions work. In the course of Carey's life, it is estimated, some 90,000 pounds were thus contributed to the cause in this way.

Twice each day the whole community gathered for the reading of the Scriptures and prayer. Meals were taken at a common table. Such strong-willed people living together in such close quarters was bound to produce friction. Ward was especially anxious about this matter. "I tremble," he wrote, "almost before we begin to live together. . . . One man of the wrong temper could make our house a hell."[8]

It was never Carey's plan to rule over the brotherhood, as he called it, in an authoritarian way. They would rotate preaching and presiding responsibilities. Each Saturday evening there was a community meeting to regulate matters and air any differences which might have arisen during the past week. The rule was speak up or shut up! "Should any be hurt in their minds, and not mention it then, they would meet with little pity afterwards."[9] Honesty, Intimacy, Equality were the watchwords of the community.

For Carey and the others the brotherhood was not an end in itself, but rather a means toward the extension of their primary work, the sharing of Jesus Christ with the lost of India. This ideal was clearly set down in the covenant, or Form of Agreement, which they adopted in 1804. This document was to be read publicly three times a year. In this way they renewed their vows to God and their commitment to one another. The covenant contained 11 statements of purpose.

1. To set an infinite value on men's souls.
2. To acquaint ourselves with the snares which hold the minds of the people.
3. To abstain from whatever deepens India's prejudice against the gospel.
4. To watch for every chance of doing the people good.
5. To preach "Christ crucified" as the grand means of conversions.
6. To esteem and treat Indians always as our equals.
7. To guard and build up "the hosts that may be gathered."
8. To cultivate their spiritual gifts, ever pressing upon them their missionary obligation, since Indians only can win India for Christ.
9. To labour unceasingly in biblical translation.
10. To be instant in the nurture of personal religion.
11. To give ourselves without reserve to the Cause, "not counting even the clothes we wear our own."[10]

By May 1800 the community had settled into a regular routine. Everyone arose at 6:00 each morning. Carey spent the morning hours in his garden not only pruning the plants and cultivating the flowers but meditating, praying, preparing for the day's labors. Ward and Felix went to the printing office to get ready for the day's output. The Marshmans gathered materials for the school. Breakfast was at 8:00, followed by the morning's work. A light lunch was followed by rest, more work, and the main meal at 3:00 in the afternoon. The late afternoons and evenings were devoted to preaching expeditions, prayer meetings, and conversations with inquirers. Each Thursday evening the community held an "experience meeting" where members shared testimonies, prayer requests, and new insights gained from the Scriptures.[11]

Carey was delighted with his new helpers. "Ward is the very man we needed," he wrote. "I have much pleasure in him, and expect much from him. Marshman is a prodigy of diligence and prudence. Learning the language is mere play to him. He has acquired in four months as much as I did in eight."[12]

These three—Carey, Marshman, and Ward (the Serampore Trio)—formed a close-knit alliance of mutual support and admiration which was to make their labors together one of the most illustrious examples of missionary teamwork in the history of the church. Marshman was 7 years younger than Carey; Ward, 8. Both men respected the wisdom and piety of the senior colleague, while he, in turn, was loyal and enthusiastic about them. They stood by one another inseparably, in good times and bad, during years of severe trial, and through seasons of harvest and joy.

In 1811 a Burman missionary passing through Serampore referred to these three as Peter, James, and John. Concerning Carey he wrote, "He is a very superior man, and appears to know nothing about it."[13]

With Dorothy Carey completely incapacitated by her confining illness, Hannah Marshman took the reins as the true mother of the mission. Under her wings she sheltered Grant's widow and 2 children; the widow of John Fountain, who was pregnant when her husband died at Dinajpur; as well as a host of Indian women and girls who flocked to the mission. She also intervened when she noticed Carey's two older boys Felix and William growing obstinate and disrespectful because they had been, as she put it, "left in great measure without control." Doubtless it was her influence, together with Ward's, which saw these young men through their teenage rebellious years and helped to redirect them both into the path of missionary service. As John C. Marshman said of Felix, "From being a tiger, he was transformed into a lamb."[14]

Hannah Marshman assisted her husband in running the boarding school. As early as 1800, she had also opened a "school for young ladies." She took a special interest in the plight of the Hindu women. "The women are in general very dirty, and almost as unmoved as Stoics. Boiling their rice, and bathing their children is nearly all they do."[15] The school started by Hannah became a model for others. In 1826 Carey could report 14 such schools which had been established for "the mental instruction of the poor females of India."[16]

In addition to her other responsibilities, Hannah also supervised the domestic side of things within the community. When they began, there were 10 adults and 9 children to feed. Eventually that number would grow to around 60, including special guests and visitors who sometimes showed up unexpectedly. The dinner was prepared in a kitchen detached from the main building. Then it was brought over to the dining hall in a large wooden box with four handles, carried by 2 of the helpers. While supplies lasted, the fare was sumptuous and hearty.

> In every dinner we expend four very large dishes of boiled rice piled up on a heap; four dishes of curry, three or four joints of meat, sometimes eight or nine large fish, seven or eight dishes of vegetables from our own garden, three tureens of soup with bread. . . . Our victuals are always boiled in earthen pots, except when we have rump of beef. It is all in the English way, except the curry. We have often puddings and pies made by our own cook. . . . We have very good butter made twice a day; it will not keep good any longer. We have one plate of toast, six large plates of bread and butter, besides two very large dishes of the same.[17]

Though one historian has referred to Hannah as "Marshman's domineering wife," her son was more nearly correct when he described his mother as "a woman of feeling, piety, and good sense, of strong mind and great disinterestedness, fitted in every respect to be an associate in the great undertaking to which the life of her husband was devoted."[18] To which Carey agreed, praising her extraordinary patience, godliness, and zeal.

On April 24, 1800, the brotherhood celebrated a day of thanksgiving for the completion of their buildings. They formed themselves into a church, with Carey as pastor, Marshman and Ward the deacons. Looking back over the past months, they could see with clarity the hand of God in knitting their hearts and lives together. They were sure too that He had a special purpose in leading them to such a "populous, well-ordered, healthful, and beautiful town."

Preaching with Boldness

In 1792, the very year the Baptist Missionary Society was organized, the Moravian missionaries abandoned their post at Serampore after several years of fruitless labors. In the early days of their settlement there, the Baptists too must have wondered whether their ministry would suffer a similar fate. Despite the kind reception of Governor Bie, Carey declared that the local natives "appear to me to be some of the vilest of the vile."[19]

From the outset, however, Carey and the others, as soon as they could speak the language, took to the streets, *ghats* (river-bank stairways), and bazaars calling on their hearers to "turn from dumb idols to serve the living and true God." Next to Serampore itself was one of the Jagannath shrines where thousands of pilgrims came to witness the tortuous practice of "swinging." In this ritual two iron flesh hooks were pierced into the back of the devotee. Then suspended by ropes attached to the hooks, he would be drawn up some 40 feet in the air and twirled around for a considerable time. Sometimes the hooks gave way and the victim plummeted to his death.

At Puri there was a car devoted for the god Jagannath which was pulled by means of hooks fastened into the flesh of the disciples. Numerous individuals were crushed to death beneath the wheels of the Jagannath car. Such frenzied acts were committed in hopes of making a self-atonement, thereby securing release from the cycle of existence.

Carey felt such practices had to be condemned and the false ideas on which they were based challenged directly. Often he engaged the Brahmins in dialogue. On one occasion he came across a group of these revered members of the Hindu priestly caste sitting around the gateway of a temple. They had smeared their faces with white ashes taken from the Jagannath shrine nearby.

"What do you call that mark on your face?" Carey asked. "It is the *telak*," they answered. "But why do you put on such a mark?" he probed further. "It is a piece of holiness, and we are commanded to do this in the *Shastras*." "Where in the Shastras do you find this?" Carey continued. "And how do you know these books are divine?"

An older Brahmin, known for his learning, joined the conversation, he sitting on one mat, Carey on another. The crowd grew larger as the discussion became warmer. The Brahmin declared that the way to salvation was through deep meditation and good works. Carey replied that no one could perform acts truly pleasing to God until there was a change within. "You may as well expect to see mangoes produced on the Indian fig," said Carey, "or coconuts on the toddy tree, as to see fruits of holiness proceed from a sinful heart." He then moved on to present clearly the gospel solution to the human dilemma.

> Brahmin, said I, you and I, and all of us are sinners, and we are in a helpless state. But I have good tidings to tell you. God, in the riches of His mercy, became incarnate, in the form of man. He lived more than thirty years on the earth, without sin, and was employed in doing good. He gave sight to the blind, healed the sick, the lame, the deaf, and the dumb; and, after all, died in the stead of sinners. We deserved the wrath of God, but he endured it. We could make no sufficient atonement for our guilt, but he completely made an end to sin. Now he has sent us to tell you that the work is done, and to call you to faith in, and dependence on, the Lord Jesus Christ. Therefore, leave your vain customs, and false gods, and lay hold of eternal life through Him.[20]

As soon as the printing press was set up, Carey hit on the idea of publishing copies of the Gospel of Matthew and distributing them as tracts to the people. Soon the story of Jesus was being read in Bengali for the first time. Natives from all over the region began to show up at Serampore with crumpled copies of Matthew's Gospel in their hands desiring to know more about Jesus Christ.

Carey led the way in evangelizing the Indians, but soon the others were at it as well. By the end of their first year in Serampore, Carey could write, "Our brethren now begin to stand upon their own legs in preaching."[21] Marshman was especially effective. He was all eagerness for the work of God even if this sometimes led to an unfortunate lack of sensitivity. For example, in 1810 Carey described Marshman's witnessing style to John Ryland, who had recruited the former Bristol schoolmaster for the missions field. He would "eye a group of persons," Carey said, "exactly like a hawk, look on his prey, and go up to them with a resolution to try the utmost strength of gospel reasons on them."[22] In point of zeal, Carey said, he is a Luther, I am Erasmus!

Unlike the placid crowds who listened politely to Carey at Mudnabatty, the audiences around Calcutta and Serampore could be openly hostile. On more than one occasion, the missionaries had to run for cover from flying pebbles and sticks accompanied by insults, taunts, and threats. Marshman often came home with his face besmirched with blood from such encounters.[23] Carey reported to Fuller that they were frequently assaulted "with all the insulting language that malice could invent."[24]

Music too played its part in the itinerant preaching of the Serampore missionaries. Carey was a hearty singer and loved the great hymns of Cowper, Newton, Watts, and the Wesleys. According to one eyewitness, he "stamped his foot vigorously to set the time" during the regular worship services on Sunday.[25]

Hindu ballad singers were commonly seen on the streets and in the marketplaces of that day. On one occasion (March 30, 1800), Carey, Marshman, and Ward assumed this role for themselves. Standing at a busy intersection of four roads, they began to sing a "Christian ballad." People looked out of their houses, stopped their business activities, and gathered around in astonishment at the sight.[26]

Ward had printed up copies of the ballad they sang and gave them out to the curious onlookers. It was a hymn Carey had composed in Bengali depicting an Indian renouncing his idolatrous past and embracing Christ as his Lord.

> In serving vain idols, why thus spend my days,
> Since nought but destruction attends all my ways?
> The Lord of the world did descend from on high,
> And was born in our nature all sin to destroy.
>
> Seeb, Doorga, and Kallee, could give me no aid,
> No Debta nor Debbee, of off'rings were made,
> No Brammhan, no Yogee, no deed done by me,
> No, not all these united can set my soul free.
>
> My sin, and my holiness, now are my shame!
> My passions, my wishes, my honour, my name;
> I now lay all down at Christ Jesus' feet,
> And trust, though a sinner, I mercy shall get.
>
> Ho! All sinful people, this good news attend,
> Salvation and Righteousness, now apprehend;
> This, this is the order he gives unto you,
> And then after death you to glory shall go.[27]

They preached on faithfully week after week, month after month, with not a single native converted to Christ. True, they knew well that only God could give the increase. Like their friend Henry Martyn they could say, "I am willing to continue throwing the net at the Lord's command all the long night of life, though the end may be that I shall have caught nothing."[28]

But such thoughts were no pretext for a lack of compassion or unconcern about the lost. The missionaries yearned and prayed fervently for God to open the hearts of those to whom they had been sent. They were not complacent but distressed to see their hopes frustrated by the lack of response. What would their friends in England think? Would they continue to pray and give to missions with so little to show for all their exertions? To see so many of the lost refuse the only way of salvation and deliverance added an urgency to their prayers and labors. When would the day come when the gospel would take root among the people? When would the name of Christ be vindicated from the dishonor daily cast upon it?[29]

Discouraged they were but not defeated. Surely God's providence had not led them thus far in vain. To John Williams, a friend of missions in New York, Carey wrote, "I have no doubt but in the end the God of all grace will exert His almighty power and establish the glory of His own name in this country. Our labors may be only like those of pioneers to prepare the way, but truth will assuredly prevail and this among other kingdoms of the earth shall assuredly see the salvation of our God."[30]

A Day of Rejoicing!

In October 1800, shortly before his death, John Thomas came to Serampore to see Carey once again. The two men were so different. Carey was a plodder, deliberate, scientific, persevering, blessed with an abundance of common sense. Thomas was the opposite: impetuous, quixotic, short-fused, a meteor in the night.

Yet, despite his obvious shortcomings, Thomas had been the catalyst which sparked the mission to India in the first place. When it seemed that Carey might spend his days raising rice and peas in the jungle swamps of Debhatta, Thomas had negotiated their move to the north which led to the profitable ministry there. Now, again, at Serampore he played a crucial role in the opening of a new chapter in the witness of the mission.

Krishna Pal was a Hindu carpenter. Years before he had done

work for the Moravians at Serampore from whom he first heard about Jesus and His love for all people. In the meantime, he became a follower of a certain guru named Ram Charan Pal who taught him to repeat mantras and seek release from his sins by good works and ritual acts such as bathing in the holy waters of the Ganges.

One morning, it was November 26, 1800, as Krishna Pal was going down the steps to the river to perform this rite, he slipped and fell, dislocating his right shoulder. Having heard that a doctor was staying at the missionary compound nearby, he sent two of his children for help. Thomas left his breakfast and went immediately to care for Krishna. With Carey and Marshman holding the arm, Thomas jerked the damaged shoulder into the socket.

He then stayed to talk with Krishna about his sin and remedy provided through the death of Christ. Before leaving he gave him a tract, recently printed on the mission press. It contained the words of a *gayati*, a brief chorus chanted by Hindus as they went about their daily business. This chant, however, spoke of salvation, not through human effort or devotion to an ephemeral deity, but through Christ alone.

> Sin confessing, sin forsaking,
> Christ's righteousness embracing,
> The soul is free.

Krishna began to attend the Bible studies at the mission house. He brought along his wife and daughter. They listened intently as Carey, Ward, and the others explained the meaning of God's love in Christ, His death and Resurrection, and the new life they had received through faith in Him.

One day Thomas encountered Krishna on the street. "I am a great sinner," he said. "But I have confessed my sin and I am free!" Thomas replied, "Then I call you brother. Come and let us eat together in love."

For a Hindu to eat with a European meant the forswearing of his caste. Just as Jesus' contemporaries were shocked and offended by his public eating with all classes of people, so the Indians of Serampore were outraged that one of their own had broken caste by taking dinner with the missionaries. Carey, like Jesus, saw it as a sign of the in-breaking of God's kingdom.

Ward exclaimed, in words that breathe the spirit of the New Testament, "Thus the door of faith is open to the Gentiles. Who shall shut it? The chain of caste is broken; who shall mend it?"[31]

Krishna was called upon to suffer many things for his open commitment to Christ. Hundreds of his fellow Hindus mobbed him and shouted, "*Feringhi*," ("Traitor"). His teenaged daughter, who had been pledged to a Hindu neighbor as a child bride, was abducted and forced to live against her will with her unbelieving "husband." (Happily they both later embraced the gospel and joined Krishna and other Hindus who had broken caste in one of the first native-led churches in India.)

From the beginning Carey felt that the holding of caste was incompatible with faith in Christ. He refused to baptize anyone who continued to maintain caste distinctions. The renunciation of caste was also a means to test the sincerity of new converts. As much as the missionaries desired to win the lost to Christ, they steadfastly refused to lower the standard of Christian discipleship in order to puff up their numbers. Hypocrites in the church, of course, was as much a problem in England as ever it was on the missions field. Still, Fuller agreed with Carey's strategy. Writing to Ward in 1801, he said, "A willingness to lose caste may be as great a proof of sincerity with you as anything which our converts [in England] can offer can be with us."[32]

At last Carey was ready to baptize the first Hindu convert, along with his son Felix whose waywardness had given way to the stirrings of God's call in his life. It was December 28, 1800, the last Sunday of the year.

Ward describes the happy scene in words which were sent back to England and read with great rejoicing by many who thanked God for such a glorious breakthrough.

> Sunday, December 28, 1800. After our English Service, at which I preached on baptism, we went to the riverside, immediately opposite our gate when the Governor, a number of Europeans and Portuguese, and many Hindus and Mohammedans attended. We sang in Bengali, "Jesus, and shall it ever be?" Carey then spoke in Bengali, particularly declaring that we did not think the water sacred, but water only, and that the one from amongst them about to be baptized professed by this act to put off all sins and all debtahs, and to put on Christ. After prayer, he went down the bank into the water, taking Felix in his right hand, and baptized him. Then Krishna went down and was baptized, the words in Bengali. All was silence.

The Governor could not restrain his tears, and almost every one seemed struck with the solemnity of this new ordinance. I never saw in the most orderly congregation in England anything more impressive. "Ye gods of stone and clay, did ye not tremble, when in the Triune Name one soul shook you from his feet as dust?"[33]

That evening they celebrated the Lord's Supper for the first time in Bengali. Felix preached his first sermon to the gathered community. Carey rejoiced that God had permitted him to "desecrate the Ganges" by baptizing the first Hindu believer. Many others were to follow. By 1821 the missionaries had baptized over 1,400 new Christians, more than one-half of them Indians.

Krishna himself became a great witness among his own people. Two years after his baptism he wrote to the Serampore brotherhood, expressing joy in his new walk with Christ and committing himself to spread the good news to others.

The love of God, the gospel of Jesus Christ, was made known by holy Brother Thomas. On that day our minds were filled with joy. In this rejoicing, and in Christ's love believing, I obtained mercy. Now this word I will tell to the world. Going forth, I will proclaim the love of Christ with rejoicing. To sinners I will say this word: Here sinner, brother! Without Christ there is no help. Christ, the world to save, gave his own soul! Such compassion, where shall we get?[34]

THE tidings which I bring unto you are, that there is a REVOLUTION and a REFORMATION at the very door, which will be vastly more wonderful than any of the deliverances yet seen by the church of God from the beginning of the world.

Cotton Mather, 1702

9

A New Reformation

CAREY'S mission to India inaugurated a new era in the history of the Christian church. In the summer of 1794 John Ryland summoned David Bogue, a Congregationalist minister from Gosport, along with several other colleagues in Bristol, to listen to one of Carey's first mission letters back home. They were so inspired by what they heard that they soon gathered with other friends at Baker's Coffee House, Change Alley, London, to pray and plan for a new missions initiative. Out of this ferment the London Missionary Society was organized in 1795.

Speaking at one of the first meetings of this group George Burder of Coventry recalled how "the apostolic spirit revived in the glorious Reformers" following the "long and awful night" of medieval superstition and decline. Luther, Calvin, other great lights of the Reformation recovered the gospel in their day. "But oh! Where is the primitive zeal? Where are the heroes of the church—men who would willingly spend and be spent for Christ; who have the ambition not to tread in a line made ready for them, but to preach Christ, where, before, He was not named?" Chief among such pioneers, Burder asserted, was "Mr. Carey, of Leicester . . . now a preacher on the banks of the Ganges."[1]

By the following year the infant society, organized on an interdenominational basis, had purchased its own ship and recruited 30 missionaries to carry the gospel to Tahiti, Carey's long-envisioned destination. On August 10, 1796, at 6:00 A.M., their ship, the *Duff,* lifted anchor and began to glide down the Thames as those on board sang, "Jesus, at Thy command, we launch into the deep."[2]

Carey's work in Bengal also made a deep impression on

Charles Simeon, the leading Anglican evangelical pastor at Cambridge. He inspired a generation of young students to devote their lives to the cause of missions. Among these was Henry Martyn who sailed for India in 1805. Encouraged by Wilberforce, John Newton, Thomas Scott, and other luminaries, Simeon became the catalyst in the formation of the Church Missionary Society, which since 1799 has had a continuous and distinguished record as the primary mission-sending arm of the Church of England.[3]

In 1816 the British Methodists and their Arminian cousins, the General Baptists, launched their own missionary efforts. On the other side of the Atlantic, the American Board of Commissioners for Foreign Missions was founded by Congregationalists in New England in 1810. Four years later the General Convention of the Baptist Denomination in the United States of America for Foreign Missions (later known as the Triennial Convention) was organized at Philadelphia. By 1834 there were 14 societies in England, as well as several others in American and Europe, devoted to the missionary cause. All of them were inspired by the example of Carey and the Serampore missionaries. In the words of J. G. Greenhough, "The light, which Carey had kindled, spread from hill to hill like beacon-fires, till every Christian church in turn recognized the signal, and responded to the call."[4]

Carey was a keen student of history and saw the missionary awakening as the first wave of a new Reformation. Again and again he appealed to the example of Luther and the Reformers as a paradigm for his own evangelical labors. The publication of a treatise exposing the errors of the Hindu system with its exalted priestly caste of Brahmins was "something like those thundering addresses against the idle, corrupt, and ignorant clergy of the church of Rome at the commencement of the Reformation."[5] The Christian-Hindu debates about whether salvation was by grace or through human efforts echoed the earlier Protestant-Catholic disputes over works righteousness in the sixteenth century.[6] The protection given to the Serampore Mission by the Danish governor was comparable to the support Luther received from his territorial prince, Frederick the Wise of Saxony.

The very timing and circumstances of the mission were part of a providential pattern which recalled God's guidance in the lives of other Christians in ages past. Speaking at William Ward's funeral in 1823, Joshua Marshman asked, "What would Luther have done had he been born a century earlier, or in some remote part of the earth?"[7] Just as God had prepared Luther for his reformatory mission and then placed him in the precise sphere of usefulness suited to his talents and the need of the hour, so also He was working now to call forth those men and women who would be heralds of good news to the entire world.

Wycliffe of the East

One of those "thundering addresses" of the Reformation to which Carey likened his own publications was Luther's treatise *The Babylonian Captivity of the Church* written in 1520. In this writing Luther set forth the principle of Scripture alone (*sola Scriptura*) over against the Roman Catholic appeal to the authority of the church.

> It is the promises of God that make the church, and not the church that makes the promise of God. For the Word of God is incomparably superior to the church, and in this Word the church, being a creature, has nothing to decree, ordain, or make, but only to be decreed, ordained, and made.[8]

Carey held firmly to this same conviction. The Bible was the very Word of God, uniquely inspired by the Holy Spirit; a totally truthful revelation from God; an infallible authority for doctrine, ethics, and all matters pertaining to the Christian life.

From his earliest days as a young believer, Carey had evaluated the competing claims of various theological systems in the light of the Bible. He became a Baptist only after he was convinced that believer's baptism by immersion was the *scriptural* pattern of baptism. Likewise, he rejected the Hyper-Calvinistic ban on witnessing and evangelism because it lacked a clear biblical warrant and indeed contradicted the clear command of Jesus in the Great Commission.

Every morning Carey began his day by reading a chapter from the Bible in each of the languages he had mastered—Latin, Greek, Hebrew, Dutch, French, as well as his native tongue.[9] He was aware of the pioneering work of John Wycliffe, William Tyndale, Miles Coverdale, and other Reformers who had translated the Bible into English at great personal risk. He prayed that the pentecostal gift of tongues might be poured out in his own day, so that Christian scholars could translate God's Word into all the languages of the world. In the sixteenth century Erasmus had set forth his *Paraphrases of the New Testament* for, as he said, he desired to see the sacred Word in the hands of "women and cobblers, clowns, mechanics, and even the Turks."[10] Nearly 300 years later one of the cobblers himself took up the work Erasmus and Luther had begun. His goal was no less ambitious than theirs: to make the Word of God accessible to the masses of India.

As we have seen already, Carey began learning Bengali on board the *Kron Princessa Maria,* being tutored daily by Thomas. With the help of Ram Ram Basu, he soon mastered the language to the extent that he was able to correct Thomas's defective translation of Matthew's Gospel. During the difficult days at Debhatta and Mudnabatty, he worked tirelessly to improve his knowledge of the language. His children, especially the younger ones, were his best teachers, for they quickly became fluent in the local dialect.

Carey's philosophy of learning a new language is reflected in the advice he gave to Felix when the latter was preparing to embark on his mission to Burma in 1807.

> With respect to the Burman language, let this occupy your most precious time and your most anxious solicitude. Do not be content with acquiring the language superficially, but make it your own, root and branch. To become fluent in it, you must attentively listen, with prying curiosity, into the forms of speech, the construction and accents of the natives.[11]

Carey frequently struggled to find the precise verbal equivalents in Bengali for many key biblical words such as *love* and *repent*. Even *Devil* and *Son of God* required careful nuancing.

> If I say "Shaitan," that is the Devil, they do not understand who I mean unless I should add, he is a "Burra Hurram Taddi," which though used to signify a rascal, etc., yet in plain English is "a son of a whore." If I say the "Son of God," they can scarcely one in a hundred understand the word for "Son"; but if I say "God's Boy," this is exactly conformable to their idiom. This sometimes discourages me much, but blessed be God.[12]

By 1796 Carey had worked through such problems and

could report the completion of his first translation of the New Testament.

When Carey moved to Serampore, he took with him the wooden printing press he bought in Calcutta. With the help of William Ward, the first edition of the Bengali New Testament was finally completed on February 7, 1801. For 7½ years Carey had labored to see this day. He lovingly placed the first bound copy on the communion table at Serampore as the mission families and recently baptized converts gathered around to give thanks to God for this great breakthrough. To his friends back in Hull, Ward described the joy he had found in his new vocation. "To give to a man a New Testament who never saw it, who has been reading lies as the Word of God; to give him these everlasting lines which angels would be glad to read—this, this is my blessed work."[13]

The translation of the Bible into the language of the people was a powerful tool of evangelization. Marshman referred to the first 2,000 copies of the Bengali New Testament as 2,000 missionaries. One of the copies of this first edition made its way to the distant city of Dacca. When the missionaries finally established a work there some 17 years later, they discovered several villages of Hindu peasants who had abandoned the worship of idols. They were waiting for a teacher who would explain to them the faith they had learned from the frayed pages of a little book preserved in a wooden box in one of their villages. The book was Carey's Bengali New Testament.[14]

Carey knew his translation was imperfect and he worked constantly to improve it. A major revision of the New Testament appeared in 1806, a third in 1811, the fourth in 1816, and so on, until the eighth and final edition was published in 1832. After correcting the last sheet of this definitive edition, Carey exclaimed, "My work is done; I have nothing more to do but wait for the will of the Lord." The Bengali Old Testament proceeded at a slower pace, being published in segments from 1802 to 1809. It went through five revised editions before Carey's death.

Bengali was the language of the most heavily populated province in India. Carey's translation of the Bible into this language was his first love. His Bengali dictionary and grammar were also major contributions to the development of modern Bengali literature. To these must be added numerous translations of literary and scientific texts, as well as the first weekly Bengali-language newspaper, first published in 1818. The *Darpan,* as this paper was called, was intended to familiarize the native Bengalis with the printed version of their language and thus "render easy the future perusal of the Sacred Scriptures."[15] In sum, Carey's influence on the Bengali language is comparable to that of Dante on Italian, Luther on German, or Calvin on French, this despite the fact it was not his mother tongue.[16]

Even before he had completed his Bengali Bible, however, Carey was planning multiple translations of the Scriptures in the numerous languages and dialects of India and even countries far beyond. As one scholar has said, "Carey refused to allow his horizons to be limited by the flat swamps of the Ganges Delta in which he lived."[17] Thus in 1803 we find him writing to John Ryland back in Bristol.

> We have it in our power, if our means would be for it, in the space of about fifteen years to have the Word of God translated and printed in all the languages of the East. Our situation is such as to furnish us with the best assistance from natives of the different countries. We can have types of all the different characters cast here. . . . The languages are the Hindustani, Maharastia, Ooriya, Telinga, Bhotan, Burman, Chinese, Cochin-Chinese, Tongkinese, and Malay. On this great work we have fixed our eyes. Whether God will enable us to accomplish it, or any considerable part of it, is uncertain.[18]

Although Fuller and others thought this scheme too ambitious, Carey moved forward with it undaunted. [19] Fuller loyally raised the funds for this enormous undertaking, traveling literally thousands of miles to and fro across England and Scotland. From America too funds poured in. In 1806 and 1807 Carey acknowledged the receipt of nearly $6,000 from friends of missions in the United States.[20] The British and Foreign Bible Society, established in 1804 with Carey's encouragement, was another source of financial support, despite some early tensions between this Anglican-dominated group and the Baptists at Serampore. (One of the disputes centered on Carey's insistence that the Greek word *baptizo* be translated literally as "dip," or "immerse.")

By 1837, the year of Marshman's death, Carey and his associates had translated the Bible into some 40 languages and dialects. Carey himself was responsible for translating the entire

Bible into Bengali, Ooriya, Marathi, Hinki, Assamese, and San-skrit, as well as portions of it into 29 other tongues. By any standard this is a remarkable achievement, and places Carey in the front ranks of Bible translators in Christian history alongside Jerome, Wycliffe, Luther, Tyndale, and Erasmus.

How did he do it? He certainly had help, as he frequently acknowledged. Marshman was a better Greek and Hebrew scholar than he, and Carey often ran doubtful renderings by him. In addition, he gathered a team of Indian pundits with whom he worked closely in checking each translation for accuracy and readability. Still, Carey himself was either the primary translator or general editor of all the translations published at Serampore. Writing to Fuller in 1808, he explained his normal translation routine.

> I never . . . suffer a single word, or a single mode of construction to pass without examining it, and seeing through it: I read every proofsheet twice or thrice myself, and correct every letter with my own hand. Bro. Marshman and I compose with the Greek, or Hebrew, and Bro. Ward reads every sheet. Three of the translations viz the Bengalee, Hindoosthanee and Sangskrit I translate with my own hand. . . . I constantly avail myself of the help of the most learned natives, and should think it criminal not to do so, but I do not commit my judgment to any one.[21]

By translating the Bible into the vernacular, Carey was able to provide a potent weapon to new converts and missionary recruits in their efforts to win others to faith in Christ. Like Wycliffe's "poor priests," or Lollards as they were called, who fanned out across England in the fourteenth and fifteenth centuries carrying snippets of the Scriptures into every corner of the land, so Carey's evangels moved along the rice fields and market towns of northern India, witnessing to the gospel and leaving behind religious tracts and portions of God's Word.

Whenever Carey began translating the Bible into a new language, he first published separate editions of the Gospel of Matthew, Acts, and Romans. These three books he felt were sufficient to lay a foundation of Christian teaching for new believers. The first contained a complete account of Christ's life, death, and Resurrection; the second, the earliest record of the New Testament church; and the third, a summary of Christian doctrine and ethics. As soon as possible, though, the entire

Bible was made available for the building up of the faithful and preaching of the whole counsel of God.

While Carey could reach the masses with his vernacular translations, the learned Brahmins looked with disdain on holy books written in any language other than Sanskrit, the sacred language of ancient Hindu civilization. While still at Mudnabatty, Carey began to learn Sanskrit. In 1808 he brought out his first edition of the Sanskrit New Testament. Ten years later the Old Testament was published as well.

One of the primary purposes for the Sanskrit Bible was to give to the cultured elite of India the "true *Shastra*" in place of their false ones. Carey cultivated a great respect for this ancient language and felt that it was especially suited to convey the nuanced meanings of the Christian Scriptures.

> The language itself, with its copiousness and exquisite structure seems fitted to *receive* the divine oracles beyond almost any other, while its being a language in which the meaning, not only of the terminations but of every individual word has been fixed for ages, enables it to retain and preserve the precious treasure with as much firmness perhaps as the Greek itself.[22]

In place of the Hindu Vedas and Upanishads, with their myths of transmigration and pseudoincarnations, Carey set the Sanskrit Bible, the true story of God's love for His lost creation, the record of redemption through His Son Jesus Christ.

Carey also published a Sanskrit dictionary and grammar, thus laying the foundations for the modern critical study of this classical language. In addition, he undertook the translation of many of the great epics of the Hindu tradition such as the *Ramayana,* a poem comparable in scope to Homer's *Iliad* and *Odyssey.* When Fuller read Carey's translation of these Hindu writings, he wondered whether his dear friend were not wasting his time on such "obscene" literature.

In the face of such objections, Carey continued to work with texts from the corpus of sacred Hindu writings. He had three reasons for doing so. First, he felt that he could not adequately counter the arguments of the Brahmins unless he knew firsthand their own Scriptures. Second, by mastering these writings, he was better able to translate the Bible into Sanskrit, and so offer a positive witness to the gospel. Finally, there was an economic motive. Because there was a demand for such texts, their publication was a profitable venture for the Serampore Press. Carey saw humor in the fact that his unmasking of the "mysterious, sacred nothings" of ancient Hindu writings was providing revenue for the publication of the Christian Scriptures and the promulgation of the true gospel.

Professor Carey

Carey's *Enquiry* had spoken of the Christian's obligation to use *means* for the conversion of the heathen. Next to preaching and Bible translation, education was the most important means employed by the Serampore missionaries in their efforts to evangelize India. Carey frequently reminded his missionary sons of the strategic value of this work. When William was considering opening a new mission station in Dacca in 1811, he wrote: "One of the first things to be done there will be to open a charity school and to overlook it."[23]

Soon after Jabez had begun his work in Amboyna, Carey sent this advice: "Pay the utmost attention to the schools. I consider schools as one of the most effectual means of spreading the light of the gospel through the world."[24] When Jabez came back to India and moved to a hitherto unevangelized city, again his father recommended the same strategy: "Your ministry embraces two things. The establishment of schools and spread of the gospel. The first of these if it can be secured will I trust be an effectual introduction to the other."[25]

The Bible, translated in the vernaculars of India, was itself a great educational tool. Yet a basic literacy was required if the Bible was to be read and understood as Carey envisioned. Here again Carey's concern echoed that of Luther in the sixteenth century. "The Scripture cannot be understood without the language," Luther had argued, "and the languages can be learned only in school."[26]

Carey's first school for natives was established at Mudnabatty. In 1798 he wrote to Fuller that "our school now consists of 21 children who every day write and read to us some portions of the Scriptures, join us in the morning worship, sing hymns very pleasantly and improve considerably in writing and accounts."[27]

From this humble beginning a vast network of native schools (with the instruction in Bengali), boarding schools (English instruction offered for children of Europeans), girls' schools, and Sunday Schools was developed from the base at Serampore. Carey, Marshman, and Ward had all been teachers in England; but it was Marshman, together with his energetic wife, Hannah, who supervised what became in time a veritable education empire.

In 1816 Marshman published a manual for teachers in the Serampore school system: *Hints Relative to Native Schools with an Outline of an Institution for Their Extension and Management*. In this treatise he adapted the pattern of education advocated by the British pedagogical Reformer Joseph Lancaster to the schools in India. The curriculum included a strong emphasis on spelling, grammar, and arithmetic; along with courses in composition, history, geography, the natural sciences, as well as ethics and morality.

Carey's philosophy of education was to instill divine truth into the minds of the students "as fast as their understandings ripen." He desired to promote "curiosity and inquisitiveness" among the rising generation and so lead them to contemplate both the discernible facts of the natural world and the deeper theological truths on which they were based, and only in the light of which they made sense.[28]

Carey rejected the dichotomy between science and religion, which has characterized educational theory and practice since the Enlightenment. Indeed, he believed that only as Hindu students were instructed in the unity of truth which embraced all facets of reality could the pagan superstitions and mythology of their faulty worldview be exposed. The first five axioms in an elementary-level copybook on science demonstrate this holistic approach.

1. The Earth has been created nearly 6,000 years.
   God hath created all things out of nothing.
   The Earth is 21,875 miles in circumference.
2. The Earth in 24 hours turns round on its own axis like a wheel.
   This motion causes day and night.
   The length and shortness of the days are caused by the annual motion of the earth.
3. The eye of God is in every place beholding both the evil and the good.
   The clouds are never more than 3 miles above the Earth.
   The highest mountains are little more than 5 miles above the level of the sea.

4. God hath created of one blood all the nations of the Earth. India has been known to the European part of the world above 2,000 years.

It is said that Menu the first sovereign of India reigned about 3,000 years ago.

5. God has appointed all men once to die and after that to receive judgment.

The Earth and the other planets move round the sun.

From the exhalations of the Earth the clouds are formed from which proceeds rain.

The soul of a man is of more value than the Sun, the Moon, and all the stars.[29]

By 1817 the Baptist missionaries had opened 103 schools with an average attendance of 6,703 pupils.[30] Carey and his associates faced much opposition in the development of these schools. It was generally believed that a woman who had been educated would become a widow shortly after marriage. Thus little girls were forbidden by their parents to imitate their brothers' attempts to read and write. Other parents were reluctant to send their children to the mission schools for fear that they would be kidnapped and shipped away to England.[31] Despite such prejudice and superstition, the missionaries' efforts to promote literacy and education among the people of India had a lasting influence on the culture of the country and also served the primary purpose of their mission by training a generation of native leaders for the indigenous churches.[32]

Carey's personal prestige in literary and government circles was greatly enhanced by his appointment as a professor (or tutor, as he was first called because of his status as a Dissenter) at Fort William College in Calcutta. This school was founded by Lord Wellesley, the governor general, to provide advanced training for the sons of company officials stationed in India. Modeled on the colleges of Oxford and Cambridge, it catered to the cultured elite who would become the leading civil servants of the next generation.

Needing someone to fill the important chair of Bengali, David Brown and Claudius Buchanan, who served as provost and vice-provost of the college, respectively, recommended Carey. When first notified of this proposal, Carey conferred with his comrades Marshman and Ward. As Marshman described it, "We laid our heads together with the gravity of a conclave of

Cardinals."[33] Would this assignment divert him from his primary responsibility as a missionary? Could a person with no formal training or academic credentials be accepted in such a post? The Serampore Trio committed the matter to prayer and agreed to leave it to God "to fulfill or frustrate."

Persuaded by Brown and Buchanan that he was the best qualified person available to fill the chair, Carey consented "with fear and trembling."[34] Soon after beginning his work at the college, Carey wrote to Ryland, "My ignorance of the way of conducting collegiate exercises is a great weight on my mind."[35] Despite this shaky start, Carey soon mastered the art of college teaching and had responsibility not only for Bengali but also for Sanskrit and Marathi. From April 1801 until May 1830, four years before his death, Carey carried out his work at Fort William College with great distinction.

Far from distracting him from his missionary calling, Carey's professorship aided the evangelical causes at Serampore in at least four major ways. First, Carey's entire salary was funneled into the common treasury of the mission, with the exception of a minimal amount for his personal family budget and occasional gifts sent back to England to help his aging father and his sister Polly, by now an invalid. Along with income from the Marshmans' boarding school and proceeds from their publications, Carey's professorial salary (1,500 pounds a year after 1806) was the primary financial support for the Serampore ministries.

Second, Carey's scholarly labors at the college complemented his translation work. Not only did he produce grammars and dictionaries of several languages, he was also able to gather round him some of the most learned pundits in the land. In reality, Carey functioned as a senior research professor with a team of able scholars who assisted his many translation projects with their native knowledge of the Indian languages and dialects.

Third, Carey used his academic base in Calcutta to carry on continuous preaching and evangelistic activities in the city. He had accepted the teaching appointment with Lord Wellesley's full knowledge and consent to his role as a missionary. In 1802 he was meeting weekly for prayer and conversation in the home of a certain Mr. Rolt. The following year he wrote to Fuller, "We have opened a place of worship in Calcutta, where we have preaching twice on Lord's Day in English, on Wednesday evening in Bengali, and on Thursday in English."[36] By day Carey busied himself with teaching the Anglo-Indian aristocracy and with numerous translation projects; in the evening he preached the good news of salvation through Christ alone to the poor and outcast of Calcutta's slums.

Yet another benefit to the mission resulted from Carey's enhanced esteem in the eyes of the governing authorities. On May 8, 1801, the Serampore community awakened to find the British flag flying over their settlement. Their friend Governor Bie was under house arrest. Back in Europe, England was at war with Denmark, and the British soldiers across the river at Barrackpore had captured Serampore without firing a shot. The Danish protection which had given the missionaries a legal standing in the country was in jeopardy. Because of Carey's position at Fort William College and the favor of the governor general, the missionaries were permitted to carry on their work as before until Danish rule was restored 15 months later. When the community met to reflect on these happenings, it was clear there was a divine purpose behind it all. "Now we could unravel the providence in respect to Carey," said Marshman. "The tokens of divine care over us are almost as visible as over Israel in the wilderness."[37]

During his long tenure as professor at Fort William College, Carey's time was divided between Serampore and Calcutta. Each Tuesday through Thursday was spent in the city, the long weekends at Serampore. Every week he rowed the 16 miles there and then back again. Writing to Ryland in 1806, Carey describes his typical day.

> I rose this day at a quarter before six, read a chapter in the Hebrew Bible, and spent the time till seven in private addresses to God and then attended family prayer with the servants in Bengalee. While tea was pouring out, I read a little in Persian with a Moonshi who was waiting when I left my bedroom. Read also before breakfast a portion of the Scriptures in Hindoosthanee. The moment breakfast was over I sat down to the translation of the *Ramayana* from Sangskrit, with a pundit. . . . Continued this translation till ten o'clock, at which time I went to College, and attended the duties there till between one and two o'clock. When I returned home, I examined a proofsheet of the Bengalee translation of Jeremiah, which took till dinnertime. . . . After dinner translated with the assistant of the chief pundit of the college, greatest part of the eighth chapter of Matthew, into Sangskrit. This employed me till six

o'clock. After six sat down with a Telinga pundit . . . to learn that language. Mr. Thomas called in the evening; I began to collect a few previous thoughts into the form of a sermon, at seven o'clock, and preached in English at half past seven. . . . The congregation was gone by nine o'clock. I then sat down to write to you. After this I conclude the evening by reading a chapter in the Greek testament, and commending myself to God. I have never more time in a day than this, though the exercises vary.[38]

The crowning work of Carey's educational career was Serampore College, founded in 1818. The college began with 37 students, 19 of whom were Christian nationals, the others Hindus. An auspicious building with ionic columns was erected and occupied in 1821. On this occasion, Carey wrote, "I pray that the blessing of God may attend it, and that it may be the means of preparing many for an important situation in the Church of God."[39]

Carey knew that English missionaries alone would never be able to evangelize the whole of India. It was the purpose of Serampore College to provide theological education for Christian students of various denominations to carry forth this work. However, rather than following the model of a free-standing seminary, such as Carey would have known about at the Bristol Baptist Academy where Ryland was principal, Serampore College incorporated its divinity school into a wider liberal arts curriculum. The faculty was interdenominational, although all professors were required to embrace the essential evangelical doctrines such as the deity of Christ and His substitutionary Atonement. The original charter declared that "no caste, color, or country shall bar any man from admission into Serampore College."[40]

Carey served both as professor of divinity and as lecturer on botany and zoology at Serampore College. Around the grounds of the school he developed one of the most magnificent gardens in all of India. His boyhood love for the outdoors, for plants and all living things, came to fruition in his cherished garden. In his old age he once remarked that he was afraid that when he was gone, Marshman would permit cows to run loose in his garden!

Compassion and Reform

In his *Enquiry* Carey admonished would-be missionaries that they should "take every opportunity of doing . . . good" to the people among whom they intended to serve. As we have seen, Carey never forgot that his *primary* mission was to proclaim God's redemptive message of salvation to lost sinners. This did not mean, however, that he lived out his ministry in a "gospel ghetto" sequestered from the real hurts of humanity or the structural evils of Indian society. Quite to the contrary. Carey and the Serampore missionaries threw themselves into social reform activities precisely because their commitment to Jesus Christ compelled them to do so.

Even before he left England, Carey's conscience had been awakened to the evils of the slave trade. He joined with other Christians in boycotting West Indian sugar which was produced by slave labor. In 1803, having heard that the Jamaican House of Assembly had forbidden the education of slaves and their religious meetings, Carey wrote to John Williams in New York: "We must wrestle in prayer for their deliverance. Certainly God's hand will fall heavily on those Isles (i.e., the British) whose trade is maintained by robbery and cruelty. . . . Yet may their oppressors be converted rather than destroyed!"[41] Near the end of his life word reached him of the emancipation of the West Indian slaves. He was overcome with rejoicing and tearfully thanked God for this deliverance. At his request the Baptist churches at Serampore and Calcutta set aside one month to offer special thanksgiving for this remarkable answer to their many, many prayers.

From his very first hours in Calcutta in 1793, Carey's spirit was deeply troubled by what he saw—not only the open idolatry but also the degradation of human life which frequently accompanied it. In 1799 Carey and Thomas, while riding near Malda, came across a basket suspended from a tree. Inside was the remains of an infant which had been exposed; only the skull was left, the rest having been devoured by white ants.[42]

Carey soon realized that this horrible discovery was not an isolated incident. Infanticide was a way of life in India. If babies were sickly or deformed or refused the mother's milk, they would be exposed since they were believed to be possessed by evil spirits. When Carey moved to Serampore, he became aware of the ritual infanticides at the island of Saugor where the Hooghly branch of the Ganges opens into the Bay of Bengal. After he had taken up his post at Fort William College, he was asked by the governor general to investigate this practice. William Ward discovered that upwards of 100 children per year were thrown into the river where they were eaten by alligators. Mothers who took this drastic action had vowed to the river Ganges that, if blessed with two children, one would be offered back to the sacred river. As a direct result of Carey's research and his agitation against this custom, the authorities in Calcutta outlawed ritual infanticide and sought to curtail its practice.[43]

While infanticide was much more common than abortion in the India of Carey's day, he also deplored the wanton destruction of unborn human life. When his first pundit, Ram Ram Basu, committed adultery and then procured an abortion to eliminate the unwanted child which had been conceived, Carey released him from his employ and tried to show him the horrible wrong which had been done. Even in this decision, Carey was not vindictive and later at Fort William was reconciled to his repentant assistant.[44]

Just as the lives of the unborn and the newborn were deemed dispensable by many in Indian society, so too the indigent and aging were often disposed of in the most inhumane manner. Ward described the custom of exposing the sick and dying on the banks of the Ganges, a practice the missionaries referred to as "*ghat* murders" (*ghats* were the steps leading down to the river).

> When a person is on the point of death, his relations carry him on his bed, or on a litter, to the Ganges. . . . Some persons are carried many miles to the river; and this practice is often attended with very cruel circumstances: a person, in his last agonies, is dragged from his bed and friends, and carried, in the coldest or hottest weather, from whatever distance, to the riverside, where he lies, if a poor man, in the open air, day and night, till he expires.[45]

Frequently Carey and other members of the Serampore community rescued those who had been left along the river near the mission compound. They loudly protested such cruelties and called upon the governing authorities to take legal action to prevent them.

Many of these barbaric practices were perpetrated under the

cloak of religion as requirements of the Hindu system of purgation and self-annihilation leading eventually to the ideal state of Nirvana. This was especially true of *sati,* a ritual in which Hindu widows cast themselves upon the funeral pyres of their dead husbands in hopes that this act would bring blessings on her family and contribute to her own eternal salvation.

In 1799 Carey himself witnessed the immolation of a Hindu widow. He never forgot the gruesome scene which he vividly recounted in a letter to Ryland.

> We were near the village of Noya Serai. . . . Being evening, we got out of the boat to walk, when we saw a number of people assembled on the riverside. I asked them what they were met for, and they told me to burn the body of a dead man. I inquired if his wife would be burned with him; they answered yes, and pointed to the woman. She was standing by the pile, which was made of large billets of wood, about 2½ feet high, 4 feet long, and 2 wide, and on the top of which lay the dead body of her husband. Her nearest relation stood by her, and near her was a small basket of sweetmeats. . . . I asked them if this was the woman's choice, or if she were brought to it by an improper influence. They answered that it was perfectly voluntary. I talked till reasoning was of no use, and then began to exclaim with all my might against what they were doing, telling them that it was a shocking murder. They told me it was a great act of holiness, and added in a very surly manner, that if I did not like to see it I might go farther off. . . . I told them that I would not go, that I was determined to stay and see the murder, and that I should certainly bear witness of it at the tribunal of God. I exhorted the woman not to throw away her life; to fear nothing, for no evil would follow her refusal to burn. . . . No sooner was the fire kindled than all the people set up a great shout—"Hurree-Bol, Hurree-Bol." . . . It was impossible to have heard the woman had she groaned or even cried aloud, on account of the mad noise of the people, and it was impossible for her to stir or struggle on account of the bamboos which were held down on her like the levers of a press. We made much objection to their using these bamboos, and insisted that it was using force to prevent the woman from getting up when the fire burned her. But they declared that it was only done to keep the pile from falling down. We could not bear to see more, but left them, exclaiming loudly against the murder, and full of horror at what we had seen.[46]

Just as Carey had collected evidence of infanticides which led to their restriction, he also investigated the incidents of *sati* and publicized the details of its practice throughout both England and India. His studies of the Hindu sacred books also revealed that this cruel custom was by no means required by these writings, contrary to the common view. The government was reluctant to forbid a practice so long sanctioned by tradition and religion. Still, Carey continued to campaign against the *sati*. Eventually, in 1829, his appeals were heard by those in authority and the burning to death of thousands of widows was legally proscribed.[47]

The Baptist missionaries were not the only ones to protest these horrifying cruelties. They were joined by their missionary colleagues of other denominations, as well as Indian Reformers and political leaders such as Wilberforce in England. Nonetheless, even Indian historians admit that the persistence of Carey and his friends "allowed fresh air to enter the enlightened Indian minds to blow away the abominable practices harmful to human dignity and depressing to human conscience."[48]

Carey never permitted his involvement in movements for social reform to substitute for, or take precedence over, the clear proclamation of salvation through faith in Jesus Christ alone. He knew that the amelioration of life in this world, however desirable, could not prepare one for eternity in the next. Yet Carey also knew that every person he met was made in the image of God and precious in His sight. The New Testament, which he translated into so many languages, told of a Christ who had fed the hungry, healed the sick, and raised the dead. Carey's goal as a missionary was to make this Christ known to the people of India as Saviour, Redeemer, Son of God, Lord of all life. Yet, as Daniel Potts has observed, the route to this goal was "often stony, strewn with suffering and misery." Thus Carey and the others who served with him found it necessary "to become doctors, teachers, botanists, translators, printers, agriculturalists—all to the greater glory of their God and the ultimate conversion to Christianity of the people of the Indian subcontinent."[49]

PRAY for us that we may be faithful to the end.

Carey to John Williams, 1801

10

Faithful to the End

O N August 17, 1831, Carey wrote the following lines to his son Jabez.

I am this day seventy years old, a monument of Divine mercy and goodness, though on a review of my life I find much, very much, for which I ought to be humbled in the dust; my direct and positive sins are innumerable, my negligence in the Lord's work has been great, I have not promoted his cause, nor sought his glory and honour as I ought, notwithstanding all this, I am spared till now, and am still retained in his Work, and I trust I am received into the divine favour through him. I wish to be more entirely devoted to his service, more compleatly sanctified and more habitually exercising all the Christian Graces, and bringing forth the fruits of righteousness to the praise and honour of that Saviour who gave his life a sacrifice for sin.[1]

Throughout his more than 40 years as a missionary in India, Carey used the occasion of his birthday to look back over his life and take stock of his spiritual progress. His birthday letters all carry the same theme: his sense of unworthiness, gratitude for God's sustaining presence amidst numerous trials, and a determination to be "more entirely devoted" to Christ.

We may think Carey was overly scrupulous and unduly hard on himself. For example, writing to Jabez on his birthday in 1819, he confessed, "I am this day 58, but how little I have done for God."[2] This from the man who had translated the Bible into dozens of languages, founded schools and mission stations all over India, preached and evangelized and worked to reform a society in which the flagrant abuse of human rights was accepted as a normal course of affairs. If Carey had done so little for God, what might lesser mortals claim? Yet Carey never allowed such comparisons for he knew how ultimately meaning-less they were. He also knew the difference between self-exami-nation and mere introspection. The former is based upon the objective standard of God's written Word ("My eyes stay open through the watches of the night, that I may meditate on your promises" [Psalm 119:148 NIV]), while the latter leads to an unbiblical, self-centered spirituality. Carey did not disparage the evidence of God's blessing in his life and ministry. But he real-ized he had not yet "arrived." Like Paul he pressed onward toward the goal, straining forward for the prize of the heavenly call of God in Christ Jesus (Phil. 3:13-14).

The Three Mrs. Careys

On June 13, 1525, Martin Luther (a former monk) and Katharina von Bora (a runaway nun) were united in holy matri-mony, bequeathing to the Protestant tradition a model of mar-riage sanctified to the benefit of man's natural and spiritual life. Thomas Becon spoke for the Puritan adaptation of this tradition when he defined marriage as a "high, holy and blessed order of life, ordained not of man, but of God, . . . wherein one man and one woman are coupled and knit together in one flesh and body in the fear and love of God, . . . and spend their lives in equal partaking of all such things as God shall send them with thanks-giving."[3]

In their more than 25 years of married life, William and Dorothy Carey never attained the blissful ideal of conjugal part-nership envisioned by Becon. When the two exchanged vows of love in the village church of Piddington in 1781, neither real-ized how drastically their lives would change in the years ahead. The daughter of a devout Puritan family, Dorothy was illiterate, a homebody, and several years Carey's senior.

Dorothy Carey has not come off well in the many biogra-phies of her famous husband. She is remembered as a nagging, embittered shrew of a wife. In the words of George Smith, "Never had minister, missionary, or scholar a less sympathetic mate," all the while Carey "showed her loving reverence" and bore with patience her "reproachful tongue."[4]

While there is much evidence to support this view, there is another side to it as well. Dorothy stood by Carey during their early years of abject poverty. She did learn to read and write, no doubt at her husband's urging and perhaps with his help. She bore him seven children, three of whom (Ann, Lucy, and Peter) died in childhood. The four surviving sons all became missionaries and supporters of Carey's vision in India. As a young pastor's wife, Dorothy abandoned the denominational tradition of her parents and submitted to believer's baptism at the hands of her husband. While she regarded Carey's desire to go as a missionary to India as foolish and impractical (as did many others, including his father), she *did* finally agree to go with him, although she was still nursing their infant son.

Ruth A. Tucker has described Dorothy Carey, along with Mary Livingstone, as "reluctant missionaries," those who were drawn to the missions field without ever experiencing the compelling call to overseas service or making the kind of decisive surrender which constrained their husbands to forsake all in obedience to God's claim on their lives.[5] Clearly Carey believed that missionary teams should be comprised of families, married men with their wives and children who would both work together to procure the necessities of life in a strange land and also model Christian community to their unbelieving neighbors there. Before Dorothy yielded to the last-minute importunities of John Thomas and agreed to sail with the whole family to India, Carey had planned to make the journey with Felix; but only with the idea that he would return in a year or so to bring over Dorothy and the other children to their new home.

It should be noted that not everyone agreed with Carey's policy of combining marriage and missions. Melville Horne went to Sierra Leone in Africa in hopes of establishing a missionary post there, but had returned frustrated to England when he realized he could not settle his family there. "I could not persuade myself to take a sickly, delicate woman and young children, and place them in an African wood, where I must leave them for one-half of my time, while I engaged in rambling from village to village."[6] He came to the conclusion that an essential component of a genuine call to missions was freedom from domestic responsibilities. He recognized, of course, that there were exceptions to this rule. If the minister's wife is willing to share the perils and labors of her husband, and if he himself is prepared to see his family risk life and limb, then "let them go, and give an example to Christendom, which we so greatly want."

On the other hand, should the prospective missionary wife be unwilling to go of her own accord, then "Christianity will not justify a divorce by leaving her behind him, and good sense will not justify him to take her abroad into circumstances of distress and danger, where all her passions will be armed to war against his peace and to discredit himself in his ministry."[7]

When those words were first published, the Careys had already been in India for more than a year. It is doubtful whether they would have made any difference in Carey's attitude toward his family's role in the mission since he saw clearly God's hand in the decision of his wife to go with him. Having once set his hand to the plow, there was no turning back.

Unlike William and the children, Dorothy never adjusted to the "distress and danger" of life in India. The years took their toll—enforced exile from her native land and close-knit family (Kitty's marriage to Charles meant separation from her beloved sister, her one remaining bond with home); poor housing; a subsistence diet; sickly children; oppressive heat; and, finally, the loss of little Peter carried away by the fever—all these forces conspired to render Dorothy unable to cope with reality.

Dorothy's mental breakdown and gradual deterioration can be traced in the letters Carey wrote back home during the last ten years of her life. Over and over he refers to "poor Mrs. Carey." To his sisters from Mudnabatty he writes in 1798: "Poor Mrs. Carey is as wretched as insanity can make her almost, and often makes all the family so too, but we are supported by a gracious God."[8] To his father from Serampore in 1800: "Poor Mrs. Carey is totally deranged in her intellect."[9] And two years later: "Poor Mrs. Carey . . . is obliged to be confined or closely watched continually. There is, I fear, no reason to hope that she will ever recover."[10]

In her unstable condition, Dorothy vented wild accusations about Carey and tried on more than one occasion to kill him. "Her misery and rage is extreme," he confided to his sisters. "Bless God all the dirt which she throws is such as cannot stick, but it is the ruin of my children to hear such continual accusations."[11] While many advised Carey to commit Dorothy to the care of an asylum, he refused to take this step, knowing full well how patients with mental illness were treated in such places in his day. Hannah Marshman was a godsend. She washed Dorothy and cared for her needs and provided a mothering presence to her four sons when they needed it most.

How did Carey cope? Partly by devoting himself to the children ("The children are well, very fine growing lads," he reported to his sisters. "Felix is a printer and William a bookbinder."); partly by immersing himself in his work ("I am laboring with all my might to get the translation finished."). Through it all Carey continued to wait upon God; to seek His face in the midst of circumstances which he himself could not change; and which God, for His own reasons, would not, or at least did not, change for many years. "We may be sure," Carey advised his sisters, speaking as much to himself as to them no doubt, "that God does not willingly afflict nor grieve the children of men, and that some important purpose is always to be answered thereby."[12] And again this truth burnished on the anvil of experience, "look not only on the dark side, but take a peep on the other side; see what God hath wrought, what He has promised to do; reflect on His power, and on this: that He knows all you have to conflict with—the omniscience of God is a sweet theme to a genuine praying Christian."[13]

Mercifully for Dorothy her 12 years of anguished suffering came to an end on December 8, 1807, when she died of a fever. William Ward recorded the event in his journal.

> This evening Mrs. Carey died of the fever under which she has languished some time. Her death was a very easy one; but there was no appearance of returning reason, nor any thing that could cast a dawn of hope or light on her state.[14]

Dorothy would have been 52 had she lived a few more weeks. Undoubtedly her death brought both grief and relief to Carey and the Serampore Mission. John Clark Marshman, who remembered the Carey household as a young boy, later observed that it was a mark of Carey's character that he was able to accomplish his arduous biblical and literary labors with an insane wife, frequently disturbed to the point of frenzy, in the next room to his study.[15] Carey realized his wife was not responsible for her sad condition. To the end he provided, with the invaluable help of the missionary sisters, affectionate attention and constant care. As her death approached, he was deeply touched by the loving support which their sons also gave both to their afflicted mother and to him as well.

A mere six weeks after Dorothy's death, Carey wrote to his sisters of his intention to marry again.

> I am well aware that there is a degree of indelicacy in mentioning so early my design to marry again after a proper time, but as I shall not be able to write to you very often, . . . I shall tell you that after some months I intend to marry Mrs. Rumohr. I have proposed the matter to her and she has testified her agreement thereto. She is one of the most pious and conscientious persons with whom I am acquainted, and is two or three months older than myself.[16]

When news of Carey's proposed remarriage leaked out, it precipitated the closest thing to a scandal in all of his life. A petition protesting the wedding circulated among the missionary families. However, convinced that he knew better than others how to discern God's will in marital decisions, Carey proceeded with his plans and married Charlotte von Rumohr on May 9, 1808. Her sterling character and willingness to get involved in every aspect of the mission soon won over the naysayers who had questioned the propriety of Carey's choice and timing.

Charlotte, the daughter of a wealthy Danish count, had come to Serampore seeking a healthy climate for the debilitating illness she had contracted as a child. Unlike Dorothy, Charlotte was fluent in several languages and well read in the best literature of the day. She was devoted to Carey and contributed large sums to the support of the mission out of her private estate. She and Carey were able to share a common vision of their life together which blossomed into deep and lasting love. Her letters to him, written during brief periods of separation, reveal the closeness of their relationship.

> My dearest love—I feel very much in parting with thee, and feel much in being so far from thee. . . . I hope you will not think I am writing too often. . . . I cannot help longing for you. . . . I thank thee most affectionately, my dearest love, for thy kind letter. . . . I am much with you in my thoughts.[17]

Charlotte took a special interest in the Carey children, who spoke with great affection of her tenderness and motherly care for them. Even before their marriage, Carey tutored her in English, welcomed her to the Bible classes in the mission church, and finally baptized her in the Ganges River.[18] Their marriage was blessed by a mutual commitment to Christ which, in turn, strengthened their love for one another.

During the final years of their married life, Charlotte was a complete invalid and had to be carried to the garden, the church, and even the table where the community shared common meals. When she died in 1821 at the age of 60, Carey was heartbroken. He broke the sad news to his old friend John Ryland in this way: "We had been married thirteen years and three weeks, during all which season, I believe, we had as great a share of conjugal happiness as ever was enjoyed by mortals."[19] In his 1821 birthday letter to Jabez, Carey confessed, "I am exceedingly lonely; my house is to be a wilderness and I am often very low in my spirits. I hope you never will fail to pray for me."[20]

There was yet to be a third Mrs. Carey. She was Grace Hughes, herself married twice before and a widow for 10 years before she and Carey were united in matrimony in the summer of 1822. Carey had the joy of baptizing Grace, as he had Dorothy and Charlotte before. She too became an enthusiastic supporter of the mission. She cared for Carey during the remaining years of his life, nursing him through illness and bereavement. Concerning their marriage, Carey confided to Jabez, "We live in great happiness."[21] Doubtless this was true, although one hardly needs to read between the lines to surmise that Charlotte remained the indelible love of his life. In his last will and testament he left to Grace her choice of whatever English books in his library she should desire—a bequest of considerable monetary value. But he instructed his executors to make sure he was "buried by the side of my second wife, Charlotte Emilia Carey."[22]

"It is a mercy to have a faithful friend that loveth you entirely," wrote Richard Baxter, one "to whom you may open your mind and communicate your affairs."[23] Only with Charlotte did Carey enjoy this kind of marital intimacy. His own ideal of a Christian marriage was best expressed in the advice he offered Jabez shortly after the latter's marriage to a young woman named Eliza. As the two were about to embark on their first missionary assignment, Carey wrote to his sons these words of wisdom garnered from the sorrows and joys of his own life experience.

You are now a married man. Be not satisfied with conducting yourself towards your wife with propriety. Let love to her be the spring of your conduct towards her. Esteem her highly and so act that she may be induced thereby to esteem you highly. The first impressions of love arising from form or beauty will soon wear off, but the esteem arising from excellency of disposition and substance of character will endure and increase. Her honour is now yours and she cannot be insulted without your being degraded.

I hope as soon as you get on board and are settled in your cabin you will begin and end each day in uniting together to pray and praise God. Let religion always have a place in your house. If the Lord blesses you with children, bring them up in the fear of God and be always an example to others of the power of Godliness. This advice I also give to Eliza; and, if followed, you will be happy.[24]

No Other Gospel

"What is there in all this world worth living for, but the presence and service of God?" Carey asked. "I feel a burning desire that all the world may know this God, and serve Him."[25] These words, written shortly after Carey's arrival in India, reveal the consuming passion of his life: to know the true and living God and to make known the way of salvation through His Son Jesus Christ. This missionary concern led Carey to forge channels of cooperation with other Christians who were committed to the same goal. At the same time it also made him wary of others, even some nominal Christians and erstwhile Baptists, whose betrayal of the gospel seemed to undermine the very purpose of the mission.

Carey and the Serampore missionaries pursued a deliberate policy of friendship and mutual support with other evangelical believers in India. Their stated goal, with respect to Christians of other denominations, was "to cherish a catholic spirit toward them, and engage in a ready cooperation with them in everything which did not require a sacrifice of religious principle."[26]

While Carey was sure God led him to India, his vision for evangelizing all the unreached peoples of earth remained as constant as it had been when he devised his homemade map of the world in the cobbler shop at Moulton. In 1803 he was anxious to hear from his friend John Williams in America how the missionary societies were flourishing in that land. "Is anything done toward translating the Bible into the different Indian languages?" he wondered. "I hope the glorious work in the Western and Southern states is still continuing and will continue."[27] He encouraged Marshman's efforts to translate the Scriptures into Chinese, so the gospel could be preached in that vast land. One of his sons, Felix, was a missionary to Burma; while another, Jabez, went to Amboyna in the Dutch East Indies.

When the London Missionary Society sent Nathaniel Forsyth, their first missionary to India, Carey and his Serampore colleagues welcomed him warmly and provided copies of their own school texts for him to use in his first mission school. We have seen how two Anglican chaplains, Claudius Buchanan and David Brown, sponsored Carey's appointment as a professor at Fort William College. Later Carey cooperated with these men and other evangelical Anglicans in launching the British and Foreign Bible Society. Despite some early tensions between the Baptists and this organization, they found a way to work together and raise funds for the translation and printing of the Scriptures.

In 1806 Carey surveyed the growing missionary efforts of the various denominational societies which had sprung up since the founding of the Baptist Missionary Society 14 years earlier. Considering the need for a coordinated strategy for world evangelization, he set forth what has been called the "most startling missionary proposal of all time."[28] In a letter to Fuller he asked:

> Would it not be possible to have a general association of all denominations of Christians, from the four quarters of the world, held there once in about ten years? I earnestly recommend this plan, let the first meeting be in the year 1810, or 1812 at furthest. I have no doubt but it would be attended with many important effects. We could understand one another better, and more entirely enter into one another's views by two hours' conversation than by two or three years epistolary correspondence.[29]

Fuller admired Carey's "pleasing dream" as he called it, but did not encourage its implementation. Such a meeting, he felt, could as easily be a seedbed for further dissension as a catalyst for the kind of united missionary action which Carey envisaged. Precisely 100 years after Carey had proposed such a gathering, the first International Mission Conference convened in Edinburgh in 1910.[30]

Despite their best efforts to maintain a united front against the pagan culture they had come to evangelize, missionaries of the various denominations were not entirely successful in steering clear of the hurtful disharmonies which had marred their common witness back in England. Baptists in particular felt put upon and discriminated against by establishment-minded Anglicans. Carey was a staunch advocate of the separation of church and state and the consequent abolition of "every political establishment of religion." Thus while he rejoiced in the revision of the charter of the East India Company because it allowed the legal admission of missionaries, he opposed the official appointment of an Anglican bishop at Calcutta and the setting up of a state-sponsored religious establishment there. The tension between this group is illustrated by a comment made by John Chamberlain, a Baptist missionary, after meeting with an Anglican official named Daniel Corrie. He felt that Corrie was filled with prejudice against him and his fellow missionaries. "We are Dissenters and worse, Baptists, and as we do not support the church we of course . . . are Democrats, demagogues, and enemies to the state!"[31]

As for the Baptists of Serampore, they refused to admit paedo-Baptists to the Lord's Supper. William Ward never approved of this strict policy, holding that "to partake of the Lord's Supper worthily, it requires only that a man's heart be right towards God."[32] This topic was a matter of discussion at many of the Saturday evening community gatherings as the brothers and sisters of Serampore debated the merits of open and closed communion. In the end Carey agreed with Fuller, who contributed several weighty epistles to the debated, and the more exclusive practice prevailed.[33]

An ominous event in the history of the Serampore Mission occurred on May 7, 1815, when Andrew Fuller died at age 61. He had been the chief spokesman, fund-raiser, and arbitrator for Carey and his associates since the founding of the society in 1792. Without his steadying presence, the delicate relationship between the missionaries on the field and the sponsors back home began to unravel. Carey, Marshman, and Ward were falsely accused of building up personal fortunes at the expense of the mission. At one point Carey replied that were he to die on the spot, his wife would hardly have enough money to pay for his coffin![34] True, the Serampore schools and publishing ventures had brought in large sums—far more than the paltry gifts they had received from England—but these resources, along with Carey's Fort William salary, had been plowed back into the mission.

Carey resented the arrogant tone which the new home secretary, John Dyer, used in his correspondence. "I cannot write to Mr. Dyer," he said. "All his communications are like those of a secretary of state, and not, as was formerly the case, with dear Dr. Fuller, those of a Christian friend."[35] To make matters worse, a team of younger missionaries, led by Carey's own nephew Eustace, set up a rival church and mission station in Calcutta quite independently of the Serampore leaders. The society backed the younger men and continued to press Carey and the Serampore Mission to surrender all property rights and strategic decision making to them. Eventually this dispute led to an open schism between Carey and the society his vision had first called into being.

Carey lamented this breach, for he knew squabbling among Christians could only hurt the cause of missions. "I am extremely grieved," he wrote to Jabez in 1828, "at the spirit of contention which has broken out among the churches of every denomination." The Congregationalists and Anglicans were in the same predicament as the Baptists. "This is a most distressing circumstance and has contributed greatly to injure the cause of God in the heathen world. I hope a better spirit and a better understanding may soon take place."[36]

While Carey felt such quarreling among fellow believers did great damage to the cause of Christ, he was even more distraught by the open denial of the gospel itself which he encountered among some fellow missionaries. Since his extensive discussions with a French Deist on board the ship to India many years ago, Carey had been aware of certain currents of thought which ran counter to the biblical faith as understood by the historic Christian tradition.

William Adam came to Bengal as a Baptist missionary in 1817, just as the dispute between the Serampore Trio and the "younger men" was erupting into a full-blown split. He based himself in Calcutta and became identified with the dissident Baptist group there. More seriously, he came under the influence of a Hindu intellectual, a Brahmin scholar named Rammohun Roy.

Roy had been impressed with Carey and the Baptist missionaries who hoped that he, as other Brahmins before him, would be converted to Christ. He, as much as they, abhorred such inhumane practices as infanticide and *sati* and joined in their protest against the evils of Hindu idolatry. However, he could never accept their basic theology and became involved in a major theological controversy, especially with Marshman, over such doctrines as the Trinity, the person and work of Jesus Christ, the Atonement, and the nature of biblical authority.[37]

Adam was attracted to Roy's "enlightened" view and soon joined in the attack on what he called "speculative doctrines and creeds" and "metaphysical arguments" about God. Writing to Ryland in 1821, Carey lamented, "Brother Adam now denies, or expresses doubts equal to a denial, of the proper deity of Christ. He is now engaged with Rammohun Roy in writing against the Trinity."[38] Adam soon organized a Unitarian church in Calcutta, which Roy attended. He also established a Unitarian Press as a counterfoil to the publishing enterprise of his former colleagues at Serampore.

Carey and the others were chagrined at the defection of the "second fallen Adam," as they called him after his lapse into Unitarianism. Ward spoke for them all when he exclaimed, "The heathen Rammohun Roy converting a missionary! How we are fallen! O Lord, help, or we perish!"[39]

What was so decisively at stake in this controversy was not a difference of opinion over minor matters of doctrine or church polity, but rather the very heart of the Christian gospel itself. As Marshman pointed out, Adam and Roy were opposing those essential doctrines "held by the mass of real Christians in every age."[40] If Jesus was only a great human teacher and not also the very Son of God, at one with the Father in His eternal deity, then He is neither worthy of our worship nor able to rescue us from the terrible plight of sin. Moreover, it was not possible to divorce the teaching of Jesus from the historical events of His life, death, and Resurrection which the Bible interprets as God's decisive salvific act on behalf of fallen humanity. Among the nonnegotiables of New Testament Christianity were these two doctrinal affirmations.

> That God views all sin as so abominable that the death of Jesus Christ alone can expiate its guilt; and that the human heart is so corrupt that it must be renewed by the Divine Spirit before a man

can enter heaven. . . . Without these two dogmas, what is the gospel?[41]

The central missiological significance of this episode can be reduced to the claim made again and again by Carey and his encounters with Hindu and Muslim believers, namely, that Jesus Christ is "the *only medium* through which man can approach God."[42] The problem of pluralism, as we have come to call it, was faced squarely by Carey as indeed it had been faced by the Reformers, the Schoolmen, the Fathers, and the apostles before him. His answer was identical to theirs. "Neither is there salvation in any other: for there is none other name under heaven given among men, whereby we must be saved" (Acts 4:12).

On Thy Kind Arms I Fall

On December 16, 1831, Carey wrote to his beloved sisters back in England, "The repeated attacks I have had, namely, eight or nine within the last twelve months, have much enfeebled me, and warn me to look forward to a change. This change, through the mercy of God, I do not fear. . . . The atoning sacrifice made by our Lord on the cross is the ground of my hope of acceptance, pardon, justification, sanctification, and endless glory."[43] Two years later he was still alive, though growing more and more infirm. To his sisters again he wrote what he described as "the last letter you are at all likely to receive from me. . . . The will of the Lord be done. Adieu, till I meet you in a better world."[44]

In 1832 Carey completed the eighth revision of his Bengali New Testament. He declared his work was done. He had nothing to do but wait upon the will of the Lord. Although the Serampore Mission had severed ties with the Baptist Missionary Society in 1828, the work continued to flourish. By the year of Carey's death there were 50 missionaries serving in 18 mission stations throughout India.

Carey spent the last month of his life writing, preaching (as he was able), receiving visitors, and walking through his lovely garden. On one occasion, he complained, with a twinkle in his eyes, "After I am gone, Brother Marshman will turn the cows into my garden!" The garden was his favorite place of prayer. Here too he could behold the beautiful flowers sent to him by friends and admirers from all over the world.

As the end drew near his surviving sons gathered around his bedside. Carey still bore the grief of Felix's death 12 years before. But Jabez and William, both missionaries themselves, were there as was Jonathan, whose conversion Carey had prayed for and finally witnessed.

Just at the crack of dawn, 5:30 A.M., on June 9, 1834, Carey died in his 73d year. Throughout his long life he had taken great comfort in the hymns of Isaac Watts. One of his last requests was that a couplet from one of his favorite Watts hymns, and nothing more, be inscribed on the stone slab which would mark his grave.

A wretched, poor, and helpless worm,
 On thy kind arms I fall.

One of those who witnessed his burial was a young missionary from Scotland, John Leechman. Carey would doubtless have approved of his description of the real meaning of that event.

And now what shall we do? God has taken up our Elijah to heaven. He has taken our master from our head to-day. But we must not be discouraged. The God of missions lives forever. His Cause must go on. The gates of death, the removal of the most eminent, will not impede its progress, nor prevent its success. Come: we have something also to do than mourn and be dispirited. With our departed leader all is well. He has finished his course gloriously. But the work now descends on us. Oh, for a double portion of the divine Spirit![45]

ALL changes, successes, disappointments—all that is memorable in the annals of history, all the risings and falls of empires, all the turns in human life—take place according to God's plan. In vain men contrive and combine to accomplish their own counsels. Unless they are parts of his counsel likewise, the efforts of their utmost strength and wisdom are crossed and reversed by the feeblest and most unthought-of circumstances. But when He has a work to accomplish and his time is come, however inadequate and weak that means He employs may seem to a carnal eye, the success is infallibly secured: for all things serve Him, and are in his hands as clay in the hands of the potter. Great and marvelous are thy works, Lord God Almighty! Just and true are thy ways, thou King of saints!

John Newton, 1787

11

Carey Today

WHERE would a man like William Carey fit in today? Two centuries after the founding of the Baptist Missionary Society and Carey's mission to India, the Christian world stands again at a critical juncture in the fulfillment of the Great Commission. Mission strategists have called for the evangelization of the world by the year A.D. 2000. Yet there are still 1.3 billion persons on earth who have never heard the name of Jesus for the first time. Hunger, violence, epidemics on a massive scale, racial and ethnic conflicts, debilitating poverty, illiteracy, political repression, and social dislocation; all these, together with fragmentation and loss of vision within the Christian world itself, present enormous challenges to the task of missions in tomorrow's world. What can we learn from Carey as we seek to be faithful witnesses in a world like this?

1. *The sovereignty of God.* Carey knew that Christian missions was rooted in the gracious, eternal purpose of the Triune God, Father, Son, and Holy Spirit, to call unto Himself a redeemed people out of the fallen race of lost humankind. As a young pastor in England he confronted and overcame the resistance of those Hyper-Calvinistic theologians who used the sovereignty of God as a pretext for their do-nothing attitude toward missions. It was not in spite of, but rather because of, his belief in the greatness of God and His divine purpose in election that Carey was willing "to venture all" to proclaim the gospel in the far corners of the world.

Time and again Carey was forced to learn the lesson of trusting in God to bring His purpose of love to fulfillment. Carey wanted to go to Tahiti; he was sent to India. He set out alone, accompanied only by John Thomas and his son Felix; he was providentially sent back to take with him his entire family. When the mission needed a new base in India, the governor of Serampore offered a haven. When the printing house was destroyed in a disastrous fire and it seemed that the Bible translations would come to a halt, Christians all over the world contributed more to missions than ever before. The Serampore Press recovered with an increased schedule of publication! None of this was accomplished without a struggle, fervent prayer, and an earnest seeking of the divine will. But, at the end of the day, it was clear that the gospel had gone forth, in India as in the early church of the New Testament, "unhindered" by the ploys of Satan or the opposition of his minions on earth.

Today, more than a new program of missionary training or another strategy for world evangelization, the Church of Jesus Christ needs a fresh vision of a full-sized God—eternal, transcendent, holy, filled with compassion, sovereignly working by His Holy Spirit to call unto Himself a people out of every nation, kindred, tribe, and language group on earth. Only such a vision, born of repentance, prayer, and self-denial, can inspire a Carey-like faith in a new generation of Christian heralds.

2. *The finality of Jesus Christ*. William Carey and generations of missionaries who followed in his wake shared a common conviction concerning the message they had been commissioned to proclaim: Personal faith in Jesus Christ is the only way of salvation for all peoples everywhere, and those who die without this saving knowledge face eternal damnation. Hudson Taylor reflected this view when he spoke to students in 1894: "There is a great Niagara of souls passing into the dark in China," he exclaimed. "Every day, every week, every month they are passing away! A million a month in China they are dying without God."[1] In 1920 a Presbyterian statement echoed the same theme: "The supreme and controlling aim of foreign missions is to make Jesus Christ known to all men as their Divine Savior and Lord and to persuade them to become His disciples."[2]

More recently, however, the uniquely divine nature of Jesus Christ and the cruciality of Christian conversion have both been called into question. The task of the missionary, it is claimed by some, is to help adherents of other religions to discover what is best in their own traditions. "The aim should not be conversion. The ultimate aim . . . is the emergence of the various religions out of their isolation into a world fellowship in which each will find its appropriate place."[3]

As this view has come to dominate more and more in the old-line Protestant denominations, the sending of missionaries from these quarters has dwindled to a trickle. It is estimated that nine out of ten of today's career missionaries are evangelicals affiliated with conservative denominational boards or independent missions agencies.[4] Had Carey accepted the premise of much contemporary missiological thinking, he would never have gone to India in the first place; or, had he done so, he would have embraced there the indigenous Hindu belief that all religions are equally valid paths to the one unknowable god. His life and witness encourage us to resist the seductive power of syncretism and to remain faithful to the only gospel which can deliver lost men and women from the power of sin and death.

3. *The authority of the Holy Scriptures.* Nowhere is Carey's kinship with the Reformation tradition more clearly seen than in his role as a translator, publisher, and distributor of the Bible. Like Wycliffe, Luther, and Tyndale before him, Carey believed that everyone should be able to read the Scriptures in their own native language. Thus in an extraordinary labor of love he poured his life into mastering the difficult languages of India and the East until he had either translated or personally supervised the translation of the Bible into some 40 distinct tongues.

There were three bases in Carey's plan to evangelize India: Preach the gospel, translate the Bible, and establish schools. Proclamation, translation, education. This three-pronged strategy was itself an expression of Carey's confidence in the Reformation principle of *sola Scriptura*. Like Paul, Carey preached not himself but Christ Jesus the Lord. The mission schools taught a wide range of subjects, but Bible instruction was an integral part of their curriculum. Strange as it may seem, the task of translating the Scriptures into all the languages of the world remains incomplete 200 years after Carey's pioneering labors. Missions researchers estimate that there are some 10,000 language families who have yet to receive the Bible in their own tongue. The Wycliffe Bible Translators, among others, are dedicated to fulfilling Carey's vision of conveying God's written Word in all of the vernacular languages on earth.

Why was Carey so committed to a Bible-centered approach to missions? Because he knew that the Word of God was full of living power. Time and again he witnessed the transforming effect of the simple reading of the Scriptures on the people of India, steeped as they were in the fables and false theologies of their culture. Today, no less than then, missionary preaching must be true to the whole scope of the biblical revelation. Like Paul, we are charged to declare all the counsel of God, including the scriptural warnings about divine judgment and the reality of hell as well as the glad tidings of full Redemption through the sacrifice of Jesus Christ on the cross.

4. *Contextualization.* Carey may be best described as a horizonal figure in the history of Christianity. Like Augustine in the early church, Francis in the Middle Ages, and Luther in the Reformation, Carey lived at the intersection of two epochs. He witnessed the death throes of one age and the birth pangs of another. In three important missions trends, Carey anticipated by a century and more subsequent developments and still remains an important catalyst for contemporary thinking and mission strategy. These are contextualization, a holistic approach to missions, and the quest for Christian unity.

Contextualization refers to the need to communicate the gospel in such a way that it speaks to the total context of the people to whom it is addressed. From the beginning of his ministry in India, and even earlier in the *Enquiry,* Carey knew that he and other missionaries would have to take seriously the strange, non-Western setting of their work in such a faraway land. As a Dissenter in England, he was already sensitive to the countercultural posture of true New Testament Christianity. He would have agreed with Lesslie Newbigin, a twentieth-century missionary to India, that at the very heart of the biblical vision "is not an imperial power but the slain Lamb."[5]

The very act of engaging the vernacular languages as a vehicle for God's Word was itself a major departure from a kind of cultural imperialism which has shackled many efforts at world evangelization. For example, until quite recently Roman Catholic missionaries refused to translate the Bible into the languages of the peoples they encountered, holding to the near-sacred character of the Latin version approved at the Council of Trent. Carey believed that the miracle of Pentecost meant that the gospel was not limited to any one cultural or linguistic expression. In fulfillment of the prophecy of Joel, God's Spirit had been poured out "on all people. . . . And everyone who calls on the name of the Lord will be saved" (Acts 2:17,21 NIV).

Carey was a pioneer in what we have come to call cross-cultural communication. He was willing to experiment with new methods and to use hitherto untried approaches in reaching for Christ the people to whom he had been sent. The establishment of indigenous churches and the training of native pastors were two key elements in his plan for permeating India with the gospel. Realizing that male missionaries would have limited access to female hearers in the Hindu and Muslim cultures, he encouraged the cultivation of "Bible women" who were often able to break through the gender barrier to share a positive witness for Christ.

Carey was able to make these adaptations because he had gone to India not merely to convert the people there from one "religion" to another, much less to import an alien culture or civilization, but rather to proclaim the life-changing, culture-transforming message of salvation through repentance and faith in Jesus Christ. He did not aim to eradicate the positive values of Indian culture. He had great respect for the antiquity and beauty of the cultural legacy he encountered. Indeed, his translations and critical editions of the ancient Hindu classics contributed to what has been called an "Indian Renaissance." At the same time, he was quite sure that devotion to these writings and the religion they had spawned could never lead to eternal life, anymore than being born in England or America automatically made one a Christian. Carey's ability to contextualize the gospel without compromising the nonnegotiable essentials of Christian doctrine provides a balanced model for a truly evangelical missiology which seeks to be faithful in an age of social upheaval and cultural dissolution.

5. *Holistic missions.* Speaking to the International Congress on World Evangelization at Lausanne in 1974, Billy Graham outlined five concepts which may be taken as hallmarks of an evangelical approach to missions: (1) the authority of the Scriptures; (2) the lostness of human beings apart from Jesus Christ; (3) salvation in Jesus Christ alone; (4) a witness to the gospel in word and deed; (5) the necessity of evangelism.[6] The fourth principle, declaring the good news "in word and deed," points to the dual necessity of *both* a propositional *and* an incarnational dimension to the life and mission of the Church.

As we have seen throughout this study, Carey never shrank from understanding his mission to include both a social and an evangelistic responsibility. If he gave *priority* to the latter over the former, it was because he sensed so keenly the eternal destiny of every person he met and shuddered to think of the dire consequences of spurning Christ's invitation to eternal life.

Still, he refused to divorce conversion from discipleship. He knew that Jesus had given food to hungry people on the same occasion that he presented Himself to them as the Bread of life. He would have agreed with the statement of E. Stanley Jones: A soul without a body is a ghost; a body without a soul is a corpse. The gospel is addressed to living persons, soul and body, in all of their broken humanity and need for wholeness.

While Carey never lost sight of the individual, he saw clearly that the Christian message also applied to the sinful social structures of his day. He vigorously opposed slavery and rejoiced when the slave trade was abolished within the British Empire shortly before his death. He urged legislation to curb the inhumane practices of *sati* and infanticide. He detested the wanton destruction wrought by war and prayed for peace among the nations of the world. Without neglecting the transcendent dimension, so often attenuated in contemporary liberation theologies, Carey fully embraced the biblical concern for justice and reconciliation throughout human society. He prayed and worked to transform the structures of oppression in the light of the holistic gospel of Redemption and deliverance.

6. *Christian unity.* The modern quest for Christian unity was born on the missions field. Here again Carey pointed the way by working closely with non-Baptist evangelicals in India and by calling for an international conference of missionaries from various denominations around the world.

What would Carey think of contemporary ecumenical efforts today? He would likely be wary of an uncritical ecumenism which would sacrifice the distinctiveness of the gospel in the interests of a bland togetherness. And, in the context of competing worldviews, he would doubtless warn us against confusing the fact of plurality with the ideology of pluralism and its corollaries of relativism and syncretism. At the same time, he would surely rejoice in the coalescence of "Great Commission Christians" of evangelical persuasion in the task of world evangelization. While Carey was intensely loyal to his Baptist identity, to the point of advocating a policy of closed communion, he also knew how to distinguish minor and secondary matters of doctrine from the evangelical essentials to which all Bible-believing Christians are committed.

The burden of Christian unity in his day, as in ours, was not denominational differences among Baptists, Presbyterians, Methodists, Anglicans, and others; but rather the great divide between those who are committed to the great principles of historic Christian orthodoxy and others whose accommodation to the reigning ideologies of the contemporary world has resulted in "a God without wrath who brings men without sin into a kingdom without judgment through the ministrations of a Christ without a cross." Carey is a corrective to this kind of ecumenism by dilution, even as he is a model for another approach to cooperation among Christian believers, one rooted in the Reformation maxim: In essentials, unity; in nonessentials, liberty; in all things, charity.

7. *Faithfulness.* Carey's mission to India was a catalyst for a great missionary awakening throughout the Church. During the past two centuries, thousands of individuals and hundreds of denominations, societies, and mission boards have responded to Jesus' command to "go into all the world, making disciples." Although his support from the Baptist Missionary Society in England was sometimes tenuous and meager, Carey knew that he was no Lone Ranger. He had been called, commissioned, and sent forth by a company of believers who vowed to pray faithfully and give sacrificially that the work of the mission would go forward. Those who "held the ropes," the Fullers, Rylands, Sutcliffs, Pearces, and many worthy saints of lesser fame, contributed much to the furtherance of the gospel through the life and mission of William Carey. Today, as we stand on the brink of a new millennium with the mandate for world evangelization still looming before us, the best lesson we can learn from Carey is the principle by which he lived and died: "You should think of us as Christ's servants, who have been put in charge of God's secret truths. The one thing required of such a servant is that he be faithful to his master" (1 Cor. 4:1-2 TEV).

ABBREVIATIONS USED IN NOTES

CMW	John Clark Marshman, *The Life and Times of Carey, Marshman, and Ward: Embracing the History of the Serampore Mission,* 2 vols. (London: Longman, Brown, Green, Longmans, and Roberts, 1859).
Memoir	Eustace Carey, *Memoir of William Carey* (1836; Hartford: Robins and Smith, 1844).
Fuller	*The Complete Works of the Rev. Andrew Fuller,* 3 vols. (Philadelphia: American Baptist Publication Society, 1845; reprinted from the 3d London ed., rev. Joseph Belcher).
Edwards	*The Works of Jonathan Edwards,* 2 vols. Rev. and corr. Edward Hickman (1834; Edinburgh: Banner of Truth Trust, 1974).
Carey	S. Pearce Carey, *William Carey, D.D., Fellow of Linnaean Society* (New York: George H. Doran Company, 1923).
BMS	F. A. Cox, *History of the Baptist Missionary Society from 1792 to 1842,* 2 vols. (London: T. Ward and Co., 1842).
LMS	Richard Lovett, *The History of the London Missionary Society, 1795-1895,* 2 vols. (London: Henry Frowde, 1899).
BQ	*Baptist Quarterly*
CMS	Eugene Stock, *The History of the Church Missionary Society, Its Environment, Its Men, and Its Work,* 3 vols. (London: Church Missionary Society, 1899).

NOTES

Chapter 1

[1] *CMW* 2:35.

[2] George Smith, *The Life of William Carey, Shoemaker and Missionary* (London: John Murray, 1887), 306, 308. These disparaging remarks were published by Sydney Smith, a former canon of St. Paul's Cathedral, in an 1808 issue of the *Edinburgh Review.* They elicited a response from Robert Southey who pointed out that "in fourteen years these low-born, low-bred mechanics have done more towards spreading the knowledge of the Scriptures among the heathen than has been accomplished, or even attempted, by all the princes and potentates of this world—and all the universities and establishments into the bargain." Ibid., 309.

[3]*Memoir*, 28.

[4]Ibid., 38.

[5]Smith, *Life of William Carey*, 365.

[6]*Memoir*, 38.

[7]Ibid., 40. Is there a hint of suicide in the comment of Carey's sister Mary that her grandfather was so smitten by the death of his son "that he never got over it; and, in about a fortnight after, he was removed by death also"? See also *Carey*, 17-18.

[8]M. A. Laird, *Missionaries and Education in Bengal, 1793-1837* (Oxford: Clarendon Press, 1972), 3. The charity schools were products of the Society for Promoting Christian Knowledge (SPCK), a reform movement founded by Thomas Bray in 1699. By 1723 the SPCK reported 1,329 schools which offered instruction to 23,421 students.

[9]*Memoir*, 29.

[10]Carey to Jabez Carey, Calcutta, February 1, 1815.

[11]*Carey*, 44.

[12]William E. Winks, *Lives of Illustrious Shoemakers* (New York: Funk and Wagnall, 1883), 131-32.

[13]Courtney Anderson, *To the Golden Shore: The Life of Adoniram Judson* (Boston: Little, Brown, and Company, 1956), 28.

[14]*Memoir*, 19.

[15]Ibid., 31.

[16]Ibid., 30.

[17]John Bunyan, *Grace Abounding to the Chief of Sinners* (Grand Rapids, MI: Baker Book House, 1978), 11.

[18]*Carey*, 29.

[19]*Memoir*, 33.

[20]Ibid., 34.

[21]Ibid., 43.

[22]Ibid., 44.

[23]Carey to his parents, Moulton, March 3, 1787.

[24]J. L. Nickalls, ed., *The Journal of George Fox* (Cambridge: Cambridge University Press, 1952), 484, 491.

[25]Henry Sacheverell, *The Perils of False Brethren* (London, 1709), 36.

[26]Michael Watts, *The Dissenters* (Oxford: Clarendon Press, 1978), 266. On this period, see also Gerald R. Cragg, *The Church and the Age of Reason, 1648-1789* (Baltimore: Penguin Books, 1960), 117-40.

[27]*Memoir*, 33.

[28]Ibid., 36.

[29]*Carey*, 38.

Chapter 2

[1]*Carey*, 37.

[2]*Memoir*, 45.

[3]John Allen Moore, "Carey, the Plodder," *Commission* (May 1979): 46; *Memoir*, xv.

[4]Ibid., 36

[5]*Carey*, 33.

[6]F. Deaville Walker, *William Carey: Missionary Pioneer and Statesman* (Chicago: Moody Press, 1960), 47.

[7]*Carey,* 51.

[8]Ibid., 50.

[9]*Biographical and Literary Notices of William Carey* (Northampton: Taylor and Son, 1886), 2.

[10]Ibid., 79-80. Also published in the *Baptist Reporter* (July 1844).

[11]*Carey,* 48.

[12]Carey to his sisters, Tanquan River, December 22, 1796.

[13]*Memoir,* 37.

[14]William Benham, ed., *The Poetical Works of William Cowper* (London: Macmillan and Co., 1874), 117. On the role of Cook in the expanding world consciousness of the age, see P. J. Marshall and Glyndwr Williams, *The Great Map of Mankind: Perceptions of New Worlds in the Age of Enlightenment* (Cambridge: Harvard University Press, 1982).

[15]Walker, *William Carey,* 50.

[16]Sir Harry Verelst to the Council of Fort William, December 1769. Quoted in Constance Padwick, *Henry Martyn: Confessor of the Faith* (London: Inter-Varsity Fellowship, 1953), 17.

[17]*Carey,* 51.

[18]Ibid.

[19]*CMW* 1:9

[20]*Memoir,* 51.

[21]William Carey, *An Enquiry into the Obligations of Christians to Use Means for the Conversion of the Heathens* (1792; reprint, Dallas: Criswell Publications, 1988), 49. The *Enquiry* has appeared in various editions since it was first published at Leicester in 1792. In 1907 it was included in an anthology of discourses on missions edited by T. B. Ray, *The Highway of Mission Thought* (Nashville: Sunday School Board, 1907), 9-35.

[22]*Carey,* 52.

[23]*Periodical Accounts Relative to the Baptist Missionary Society,* 1:112-13.

[24]Will Durant and Ariel Durant, *Rousseau and Revolution* (New York: Simon and Schuster, 1967), 732.

[25]Carey, *Enquiry,* 7. Cf. also his comment that "a noble effort has been made to abolish the inhuman Slave Trade, and though at present it has not been so successful as might be wished, yet it is to be hoped it will be persevered in till it is accomplished." Ibid., 60-61. See also J. B. Middlebrook, *William Carey* (London: Carey Press, 1961), 82.

[26]Carey, *Enquiry,* 57.

[27]Basil Miller, *William Carey* (Minneapolis: Bethany House Publishers, 1952), 32.

[28]*Biographical and Literary Notices,* 3.

[29]*Memoir,* 61.

[30]Carey to his father, Moulton, January 12, 1788.

[31]Marion A. Habig, ed., *St. Francis of Assisi: Omnibus of Sources* (Chicago: Franciscan Herald Press, 1983), 807. The quotation is from the "Minor Life of St. Francis" by St. Bonaventure.

[32]*Carey,* 61.

[33]Carey to his father, Leicester, November 12, 1790.

[34]*Carey*, 56.

[35]Ibid., 59.

[36]W. L. Lumpkin, ed., *Baptist Confessions of Faith* (Valley Forge: Judson Press, 1959), 168.

[37]*Memoir*, 74-75.

[38]Ibid., 74.

[39]Carey to his father, Moulton, January 12, 1788.

[40]Carey to his father, Leicester, September 4, 1792.

[41]Carey to his father, Leicester, November 27, 1792.

[42]S. P. Carey, *Samuel Pearce, the Baptist Brainerd* (London: Carey Press, n.d.), 58.

[43]Ibid., 104.

[44]*Fuller* 1:147-48.

[45]*Memoir*, 76.

[46]George Smith, *The Life of William Carey, Shoemaker and Missionary* (London: John Murray, 1887), 35.

[47]John Ryland, *The Work of Faith, the Labour of Love, and the Patience of Hope Illustrated in the Life and Death of the Reverend Andrew Fuller* (Bristol, 1815), 241-42.

[48]See the very convincing case made by A. Christopher Smith, "The Spirit and the Letter of Carey's Catalytic Watchword: A Study in the Transmission of Baptist Tradition," *BQ* 33 (1990): 201-37.

[49]*Carey*, 83.

[50]Ryland, *Work of Faith*, 241.

[51]Andrew Fuller to John Fawcett, Kettering, August 30, 1793.

[52]*CMW* 1:15.

[53]Smith, "Carey's Catalytic Watchword," 227.

Chapter 3

[1]Eusebius of Caesarea, *Ecclesiastical History* 3:37, 2-3.

[2]For a classic exposition of early Christian missions, see Adolf von Harnack, *The Mission and Expansion of Christianity in the First Three Centuries* (New York: Harper and Row, 1961). Cf. also the survey article by Timothy George, "The Challenge of Evangelism in the History of the Church," in *Evangelism in the Twenty-first Century*, ed. Thom S. Rainer (Wheaton, IL: Harold Shaw Publishers, 1989), 9-20. Some of the material in this section is adapted from this essay.

[3]Justin Martyr, *Dialogue with Trypho, a Jew*, 117; Alexander Roberts et al., eds., *Ante-Nicene Fathers* (Grand Rapids, MI: William B. Eerdmans Publishing Company, 1981ff.), 1:258.

[4]Stephen Neill, *A History of Christian Missions* (Grand Rapids, MI: William B. Eerdmans Publishing Company, 1964), 47.

[5]William Carey, *An Enquiry into the Obligations of Christians to Use Means for the Conversion of the Heathens* (1792; reprint, Dallas: Criswell Publications, 1988), 22.

[6]This statement is from chapter 1 of the Second Helvetic Confession of 1566 of which Bullinger was the principal author. Cf. John H. Leith, ed., *Creeds of the Churches* (Atlanta: John Knox Press, 1982), 133.

[7]In the Smalcald Articles of 1537 Luther wrote: "Nothing in this article can

be given up or compromised, even if heaven and earth and things temporal should be destroyed." D. Martin Luthers Werke, *Kritische Gesamtansgabe (WA)*, 58 vols. (Weimar: Bohlan, 1833-), 50:1191. See also *WA* 25:375.

[8]For a comparative study of the nuanced differences in soteriology among the major Reformers, see Timothy George, *Theology of the Reformers* (Nashville: Broadman Press, 1988).

[9]Cf. R. Pierce Beaver, "The Genevan Mission to Brazil," in *The Heritage of John Calvin*, ed. John H. Bratt (Grand Rapids, MI: William B. Eerdmans Publishing Company, 1973), 55-73.

[10]D. W. Torrance and T. F. Torrance, eds., *Calvin's New Testament Commentaries* (Grand Rapids, MI: William B. Eerdmans Publishing Company, 1972), 251.

[11]Robert Bellarmine, *Controversiae*, book 4; quoted in Neill, *History of Christian Missions*, 221.

[12]This statement is by A. C. Thompson; quoted in Eugene Stock, *The History of the Church Missionary Society, Its Environment, Its Men, and Its Work*, 3 vols. (London: Church Missionary Society, 1899), 1:16.

[13]See Neill, *History of Christian Missions*, 229-31. For a fuller account of the Tranquebar Mission, see Stephen Neill, *A History of Christianity in India, 1707-1858* (Cambridge: Cambridge University Press, 1985), 28-58.

[14]Ernest A. Payne, *The Church Awakes* (London: Carey Press, 1942), 97.

[15]Carey, *Enquiry*, 7.

[16]*CMS* 1:25.

[17]William Bradford, *Of Plymouth Plantation* (New York: Alfred A. Knopf, Inc., 1952), 27.

[18]Edward Johnson, *Wonder-Working Providence of Sions Saviour: A History of New England* (London: Hath. Brooke, 1654), 26.

[19]Bradford, *Plymouth*, 374-75.

[20]Cotton Mather, *Magnalia Christi Americana* (New York: Russell and Russell, 1852), 532.

[21]Quoted, Samuel Eliot Morison, *Builders of the Bay Colony* (Boston: Houghton Mifflin Company, 1930), 316-17.

[22]Nevill B. Cryer, "Biography of John Eliot," in *Five Pioneer Missionaries* (London: Banner of Truth Trust, 1965), 221.

[23]Neill, *History of Christian Missions*, 226.

[24]Payne, *Church Awakes*, 85.

[25]Ibid., 85-86.

[26]See the excellent biographical sketch of Brainerd by John Thornbury in *Five Pioneer Missionaries* (London: Banner of Truth Trust, 1965),15-91. Cf. also the popular biography by David Wynbeek, *Beloved Yankee: A Biography of David Brainerd* (Grand Rapids, MI: William B. Eerdmans Publishing Company, 1961).

[27]Quoted, Iain H. Murray, *Jonathan Edwards: A New Biography* (Edinburgh: Banner of Truth Trust, 1987), 307.

[28]Constance E. Padwick, *Henry Martyn: Confessor of the Faith* (London: Inter-Varsity Fellowship, 1953), 49.

[29]William W. Sweet, *The Story of Religion in America* (New York: Harper and Brothers, 1930), 162.

[30]Quoted, Trevor Douglas, "Wanted! More Single Men," *Evangelical Missions Quarterly* 24 (1988): 66. On the importance of Brainerd as a model for

Carey, see A. de M. Chesterman, "The Journals of David Brainerd and William Carey," *BQ* 19 (1961): 147-56.

Chapter 4

[1]John Thornbury, "Biography of David Brainerd," in *Five Pioneer Missionaries* (London: Banner of Truth Trust, 1965), 16.

[2]E. A. Payne, "The Prayer Call of 1784," in *Ter-Jubilee Celebrations* (London: Baptist Missionary Society, 1945), 21.

[3]Ibid., 24; *Fuller* 1:35-47.

[4]William Carey, *An Enquiry into the Obligations of Christians to Use Means for the Conversion of the Heathens* (1792; reprint, Dallas: Criswell Publications, 1988), 59-60.

[5]Iain H. Murray, *Jonathan Edwards: A New Biography* (Edinburgh: Banner of Truth Trust, 1987), 299.

[6]*Edwards* 2:291.

[7]Ibid., 292.

[8]Ibid., 306.

[9]Ibid. To be fair to Edwards, he did not predict this precise ordering of events related to the spread of the gospel, but cited these various stages of world evangelization to show what an extensive and difficult process it involved. For a summary of Edwards's millennial views, see J. A. DeJong, *As the Waters Cover the Sea* (Kampen: J. H. Kok, 1970), 124-37.

[10]*Edwards* 2:278.

[11]Murray, *Edwards*, 299. Around the turn of the century prophetic speculations greatly increased. In a sermon delivered in Edinburgh in 1799, Fuller is reported to have said, "The last branch of the last of the four beasts is now in its dying agonies. No sooner will it be proclaimed, Babylon is fallen! than the marriage of the Lamb will come." *Missionary Magazine* 4:551. It would be fascinating to know how closely Fuller's sermons on the Apocalypse preached at Kettering around 1810 tracked those of Carey delivered at Leicester during his last years in England. Fuller's "Expository Discourses on the Apocalypse" are printed in *Fuller* 3:201-307.

[12]*Edwards* 2:295.

[13]Ibid., 279.

[14]*CMW* 1:10. See also the reconstructions of this event in *Carey*, 50 and *Memoir*, 62. Ryland, Jr., denied that his father ever hurled such an epithet at Carey. However, another minister who was present on the occasion, Webster Morris, gave evidence to the contrary. Carey himself verified the substance of the remark, if not the precise wording as reported by Morris.

[15]Raymond Brown, *The English Baptists of the Eighteenth Century* (London: Baptist Historical Society, 1986), 23.

[16]These five points of Calvinism, as they are sometimes called, were set forth at the Dutch Reformed Synod of Dort (1618-19). The Canons of Dort are printed in Philip Schaff, *Creeds of Christendom* (New York: Harper and Brothers, 1877), 3:550-97.

[17]See Peter Toon, *The Emergence of Hyper-Calvinism in English Nonconformity, 1689-1765* (London: Olive Tree, 1967), 70-89.

[18]G. F. Nuttall, "Northamptonshire and *The Modern Question*," *Journal of Theological Studies* 16 (1965): 110.

[19]Quoted, Brown, *English Baptists*, 76. Actually, Fuller distinguished three

kinds of Calvinists: High, Moderate (followers of Richard Baxter's system), and Strict. The Strict Calvinist he identified as the one who really holds to the teaching of Calvin. "I do not believe everything that Calvin taught," wrote Fuller, "nor anything because he taught it; but I reckon Strict Calvinism to be my own system." John Ryland, *The Work of Faith, the Labour of Love, and the Patience of Hope Illustrated in the Life and Death of the Reverend Andrew Fuller* (Bristol, 1816), 566-67.

[20]*Fuller* 1:42-43.

[21]*Fuller* 2:343-66. For this last point Fuller is indebted to John Owen's *Display of Arminianism,* chapter 10.

[22]Cf. O. C. Robison, "Particular Baptists in England, 1760-1820" (PhD diss., Oxford University, 1967), 57.

[23]*Memoir,* 36.

[24]*Biographical and Literary Notices of William Carey* (Northampton: Taylor and Son, 1886), 34.

[25]John Bunyan, *The Pilgrim's Progress* (New York: Penguin Books, 1968), 41. Shortly before his death Fuller recalled the influence which Edwards had had on him and his colleagues in the missionary movement. In his farewell letter to Ryland, he wrote: "We have some, who have been giving out of late, that if Sutcliff and some others had preached more of Christ, and less of Jonathan Edwards, they would have been more useful! If those who talk thus, preached Christ half as much as Jonathan Edwards did, and were half as useful as he was, their usefulness would be double what it is. It is very singular that the Mission to the East should have originated with me of these [Calvinistic] principles; and without pretending to be a prophet, I may say, if ever it falls into the hands of men who talk in this strain it will come to nothing." Fuller to John Ryland, Kettering, April 28, 1815. Cf. E. A. Payne, "The Evangelical Revival and the Beginnings of the Modern Missionary Movement," *Congregational Quarterly* 21 (1943): 223-36.

[26]Carey, *Enquiry,* 1.

[27]Ibid., 8.

[28]Ibid., 16.

[29]Ibid., 22-23.

[30]Ibid., 52-53.

[31]Ibid., 53.

[32]Ibid., 56-57.

[33]Ibid., 63-64.

[34]Ibid., 65.

Chapter 5

[1]*Fuller* 1:60-61; cf. Gilbert Laws, *Andrew Fuller: Pastor, Theologian, Ropeholder* (London: Carey Press, 1942), 61.

[2]Ibid., 60.

[3]*Carey,* 90.

[4]*BMS* 1:18.

[5]*Carey,* 91.

[6]S. P. Carey, *Samuel Pearce, the Baptist Brainerd* (London: Carey Press, n.d.), 135; cf. S. W. Lynd, *Memoir of the Rev. William Staughton* (Boston: Lincoln, Edmands, and Company, 1834), 170-91.

[7]Carey to his father, Leicester, November 27, 1792.

[8]*LMS* 1:11-12; *CMS* 1:47, 94-95; cf. Melville Horne's commendation of Carey: "I beg leave to present my tribute of the general approbation due to the Rev. Mr. Carey, a Minister of the Particular Baptists, for publishing two years ago, *An Enquiry into the Obligations of Christians to Use Means for the Conversion of the Heathens.* I recommend the perusal of this treatise to my readers; and, if it may operate as an inducement with them to comply with my request, I have the pleasure to assure them, that gentleman has given to his precepts the force of example, by actually embarking in a mission to India." *Letters on Missions Addressed to the Protestant Ministers of the British Churches* (1794; reprint, Andover: Flagg and Gould, 1815), xvi.

[9]This Baptist mission to Sierra Leone was also short-lived. See Basil Amey, "Baptist Missionary Society Radicals," *BQ* 26 (1976): 363-76.

[10]*Carey,* 96.

[11]C. B. Lewis, *The Life of John Thomas* (London: Macmillan and Company, 1873), 9.

[12]Ibid., 48.

[13]Constance Padwick, *Henry Martyn: Confessor of the Faith* (London: Inter-Varsity Fellowship, 1953), 21-22; cf. *CMS* 1:52-54.

[14]Lewis, *Thomas,* 53.

[15]Ibid., 62.

[16]It is worth noting that Carey, who had his own problems with Thomas, took his side in the dispute with Grant. In a letter of June 17, 1796, he wrote: "Mr. Grant's opposition to the work, I think abominable. The fact is . . . that Mr. Thomas left a much more lucrative employment, and the society of his family, at Mr. Grant's desire, to preach the gospel among the natives; who afterwards, because he would not conform to his peremptory dictates, in matters which he could not conscientiously do, cut off all his supplies, and left him to shift for himself in a foreign land." Ibid., 157, 160.

[17]Ibid., 218.

[18]*The Baptist Mission in India* (Philadelphia: Hellings and Aitken, 1811), 20.

[19]*CMW* 1:52.

[20]*BMS* 1:20. S. Pearce Carey has suggested that the image of rope holding originated with Fuller who later projected it back onto Carey. In support of this hypothesis, he cites a statement Fuller made to Christopher Anderson: "We had no one to guide us; and, whilst we were thus deliberating, Carey, *as it* were, said, 'Well, I will go down, if you will hold the rope.' But, before he descended, he *as it seemed to me* took an oath from each of us at the mouth of the pit, to this effect that 'whilst we lived we should never let go the rope.'" *Carey,* 115; *Fuller* 1:68.

[21]Lewis, *Thomas,* 220.

[22]Carey to his father, Leicester, January 17, 1793.

[23]*BMS* 1:23.

[24]Carey, *Pearce,* 144.

[25]Ibid. Fuller, whose solicitations for the missions would increase in the years to come, was torn between this responsibility and the needs of his church at home. On October 27, 1794, he entered this confession in his diary: "Of late I have been greatly employed in journeying and preaching, and endeavoring to collect for the East India Mission. . . . I feel weary of journeys on account of their interfering so much with my work at home. I long to visit my congrega-

tion, that I may know more of their spiritual concerns, and be able to preach to their cases." *Fuller* 1:66.

[26] *BMS* 1:21-22; *Carey*, 112.

[27] *Carey*, 113-14.

[28] Carey, *Pearce*, 142.

[29] Lewis, *Thomas*, 224.

[30] Ibid., 229.

[31] Leighton Williams and Mornay Williams, eds., *Serampore Letters* (New York: G. P. Putnam's Sons, 1892), 12.

[32] Ibid., 13.

Chapter 6

[1] George Smith, *The Life of William Carey, Shoemaker and Missionary* (London: John Murray, 1887), 47.

[2] Ibid., 51; *Carey*, 119.

[3] *Carey*, 234; *Memoir*, 84-85. Newton along with his fellow London pastors Thomas Scott (whose preaching had influenced Carey as a young man) and Richard Cecil were leading figures in the formation of the Church Missionary Society. See *CMS* 1:57-67.

[4] *Carey*, 120-21.

[5] C. B. Lewis, *The Life of John Thomas* (London: Macmillan and Company, 1873), 234-35.

[6] *Memoir*, 87.

[7] Ibid.

[8] Lewis, *Thomas*, 238.

[9] Ibid., 241.

[10] *Carey*, 129.

[11] Lewis, *Thomas*, 242.

[12] *Memoir*, 101.

[13] Ibid., 102.

[14] Ibid.

[15] Lewis, *Thomas*, 244.

[16] Courtney Anderson, *To the Golden Shore: The Life of Adoniram Judson* (Boston: Little, Brown, and Company, 1956), 110.

[17] *Memoir*, 107.

[18] Anderson, *Golden Shore*, 110.

[19] *Memoir*, 109.

[20] Ibid., iii; cf. the initial impression another missionary had of the natives: "They appeared active, talkative, and as though capable of acquiring a knowledge of the Christian religion, if instructed." Anderson, *Golden Shore*, 131.

[21] *Carey*, 143.

[22] Percival Spear, *The Nabobs: A Study of the Social Life of the English in Eighteenth-Century India* (London: Oxford University Press, 1932), 95.

[23] Ibid., 59.

[24] *Memoir*, iii; Carey to the Baptist Missionary Society, Calcutta, November 25, 1793.

Chapter 7

[1] John Robinson, *A Justification of Separation from the Church of England* (Amsterdam, 1610), 62.

[2]Iain H. Murray, *Jonathan Edwards: A New Biography* (Edinburgh: Banner of Truth Trust, 1987), 352.

[3]Carey to his father, Calcutta, November 25, 1793: "The greatest evil is the mosquitoes."

[4]*Memoir*, 121.

[5]Ibid., 122.

[6]Ibid., 126.

[7]Ibid., 123.

[8]Ibid., 122.

[9]Ibid., 123-26.

[10]Ibid., 129.

[11]Ibid., 126.

[12]William Carey, *An Enquiry into the Obligations of Christians to Use Means for the Conversion of the Heathens* (1792; reprint, Dallas: Criswell Publications, 1988), 54-57.

[13]*Carey*, 148.

[14]*Memoir*, 131.

[15]Ibid., 109.

[16]*Carey*, 167.

[17]*The Baptist Mission in India* (Philadelphia: Hellings and Aitken, 1811), 306-7; cf. *Ye Are My Witnesses, 1792-1942: One Hundred and Fiftieth Anniversary of the Baptist Missionary Society in India* (Calcutta: Baptist Mission Press, 1942), 2.

[18]*Memoir*, 135.

[19]Ibid., 138.

[20]Ibid., 143.

[21]Ibid., 135-36, 147.

[22]For an analysis of Puritan spirituality, see J. I. Packer, *A Quest for Godliness: The Puritan Vision of the Christian Life* (Wheaton, IL: Crossway Books, 1990). Cf. also the introduction to David Lyle Jeffrey, ed., *A Burning and a Shining Light: English Spirituality in the Age of Wesley* (Grand Rapids, MI: William B. Eerdmans Publishing Company, 1987), 1-52.

[23]*Memoir*, 142.

[24]Ibid., 143-44.

[25]Ibid., 144, 140.

[26]Ibid., 137, 146-47.

[27]Ibid., 143.

[28]Ibid., 149.

[29]Ibid., 155.

[30]Ibid., 161.

[31]Ibid., 177.

[32]Ibid., 205.

[33]Ibid. Thomas too was stung by these accusations and wrote to Fuller: "If I thought it was the will of God, I had rather be a fugitive and a vagabond tomorrow, and go and translate all the rest of my days in Calcutta jail, than be an indigo planter." C. B. Lewis, *The Life of John Thomas* (London: Macmillan and Company, 1873), 282.

[34]*Baptist Mission in India*, 228.

[35]Ibid., 222.

[36]Ibid., 226.

[37]*Memoir,* 156, 162.

[38]Ibid., 157. Years later Carey's son Jabez recalled the anguish his father must have felt when he was faced with a similar dilemma following the tragic death of his own little daughter.

> I have for once felt that anguish which you must have felt, my dear father, when you had to bury my brother at Mudnabatty. I was told by the people on board our boat that no one would dig the grave, and I had determined to do it myself, when our cook and bearer came forward and offered to do it, and to carry the little one to burial. I assure you I could not help shedding tears of gratitude for this their kindness towards us. How bitter would it have been to us, if we had had to do everything ourselves! None of the others refused to eat or smoke with them, but all tried every way they could to help us.

Carey, 161.

[39]Carey to his sisters, Mudnabatty, April 10, 1796.

[40]*Memoir,* 184.

[41]Ibid., 178.

[42]Ibid., 152.

[43]Ibid., 190.

[44]Carey to the society, Mudnabatty, March 18, 1795.

[45]Carey to his sisters, Mudnabatty, March 11, 1795.

[46]William Carey, *Dialogues Intended to Facilitate the Acquiring of the Bengalese Language* (1801; reprint, Serampore: Mission Press, 1806), 13-15.

[47]*Memoir,* 173.

[48]Carey to "My very dear Brethren," Mudnabatty, March 18, 1795.

[49]*Circular Letters Relative to the Mission in India* (Serampore: Mission Press, 1807), 9-10.

[50]*Memoir,* 202.

[51]Lewis, *Thomas,* 389.

[52]Ibid., 398.

[53]Ibid., 392.

[54]Carey to Samuel Pearce, Mudnabatty, October 2, 1795.

[55]Carey to the society, Malda, December 1795.

[56]Carey to son William.

[57]Carey to Andrew Fuller, Mudnabatty, November 16, 1796.

[58]Ibid.

[59]John Fountain to Andrew Fuller, Mudnabatty, November 8, 1796.

[60]*CMW* 1:75.

[61]See Basil Amey, "Baptist Missionary Radicals," *BQ* 26 (1976): 370.

[62]Carey to the society, Hooghly River, near Plassey, January 10, 1799.

[63]*Memoir,* 317.

[64]Carey to Jabez Carey, Serampore, June 12, 1819.

[65]Carey to his sisters, Mudnabatty, April 10, 1796.

Chapter 8

[1]S. P. Carey, *Samuel Pearce, the Baptist Brainerd* (London: Carey Press, n.d.), 202.

[2]Ibid., 202-3.

[3] *William Ward's Missionary Journal, 1799-1811,* May 26, 1799.

[4] Ibid.

[5] Ibid.

[6] Ibid., December 1, 1799.

[7] Ibid., December 2, 1799.

[8] Ibid., January 18, 1800.

[9] *Carey,* 186.

[10] Ibid., 248-49.

[11] *BMS* 1:61-62.

[12] *Carey,* 187.

[13] Ibid., 256.

[14] *CMW* 1:118.

[15] Hannah Marshman to a friend in Bristol, Serampore, October 13, 1804. Quoted, Mary Drewery, *William Carey: A Biography* (Grand Rapids, MI: Zondervan Publishing House, 1978), 117.

[16] Carey to John Dyer, Calcutta, April 27, 1826; cf. Kenneth Ingham, *Reformers in India, 1793-1833* (New York: Octagon Books, 1973), 90-95. See also *Essays Relative to the Habits, Climate, and Moral Improvement of the Hindoos* (London: Kingsbury, Parbury and Allen, 1823).

[17] Drewery, *Carey,* 116.

[18] E. Daniel Potts, *British Baptist Missionaries in India, 1793-1837* (Cambridge: Cambridge University Press, 1967), 17; *CMW* 1:106.

[19] Carey to John Ryland, Serampore, January 17, 1800.

[20] *The Baptist Mission in India* (Philadelphia: Hellings and Aitken, 1811), 135.

[21] Carey to Andrew Fuller, Serampore, October 22, 1800.

[22] Carey to John Ryland, May 24, 1810.

[23] Drewery, *Carey,* 114.

[24] Carey to Andrew Fuller, Serampore, November 23, 1800.

[25] Drewery, *Carey,* 139.

[26] *BMS* 1:98.

[27] *Baptist Mission in India,* 309-10. The translation was made by John Fountain.

[28] Quoted, J. B. Middlebrook, *William Carey* (London: Carey Press, 1961), 56-57.

[29] Carey to John Sutcliff, Serampore, December 18, 1800.

[30] Leighton Williams and Mornay Williams, eds., *Serampore Letters* (New York: G. P. Putnam's Sons, 1892), 62.

[31] *Ward's Missionary Journal,* December 22, 1800.

[32] Andrew Fuller to William Ward, Kettering, August 1, 1801.

[33] *Ward's Missionary Journal,* December 28, 1800.

[34] Quoted, George Smith, *The Life of William Carey, Shoemaker and Missionary* (London: John Murray, 1887), 118.

Chapter 9

[1] *LMS* 1:19.

[2] Ibid., 129.

[3] *CMS* 1:81-91.

[4] *Carey,* 131; cf. Carl Hunker, "The Influence of William Carey on the Prin-

ciples of Subsequent Missions" (ThD diss., Southern Baptist Theological Seminary, 1946), 55-134.

[5]Carey to the Mission House, Serampore, October 10, 1800.

[6]*Memoir,* 319.

[7]Joshua Marshman, *Divine Grace the Source of All Human Excellence* (Serampore: Mission Press, 1823), 22.

[8]*Luther's Works* 36:107.

[9]George Smith, *The Life of William Carey, Shoemaker and Missionary* (London: John Murray, 1887), 211.

[10]Ibid.; cf. Jerry H. Bentley, *Humanists and Holy Writ: New Testament Scholarship in the Renaissance* (Princeton: Princeton University Press, 1983), 112-93.

[11]*Circular Letters Relative to the Mission in India* (Serampore: Mission Press, 1807), 8.

[12]Carey to Samuel Pearce, Mudnabatty, October 2, 1795.

[13]Smith, *Life of William Carey,* 224.

[14]Ibid., 226.

[15]*Second Report of Native Schools* (Serampore: Mission Press, 1818), 23-24.

[16]Cf. Nemai Sadhan Bose, *The Indian Awakening and Bengal* (Calcutta, 1920). See also A. K. Priolkar, *The Printing Press in India* (Bombay: Marathi Samshodhana Mandala, 1958).

[17]Brynmor F. Price, "Carey and Serampore—Then and Now," *BQ* 19 (1961): 103.

[18]Carey to John Ryland, Serampore, December 14, 1803.

[19]Cf. Fuller's comment that "by aiming at too much we may accomplish the less." Quoted, E. Daniel Potts, *British Baptist Missionaries in India, 1793-1837* (Cambridge: Cambridge University Press, 1967), 81 n. 4.

[20]Francis Wayland, *A Memoir of the Life and Labor of Reverend Adoniram Judson* (Boston: Phillips, Sampson, and Company, 1853, 45. See also *Massachusetts Baptist Missionary Magazine* 1:289-91, 293-94.

[21]Carey to Andrew Fuller, Serampore, April 20, 1808.

[22][Carey, Marshman, and Ward], *Memoir Relative to the Translation of the Sacred Scriptures to the B.M.S. in England* (Dunstable: J. W. Morris, 1808), 11.

[23]G. E. Smith, "Patterns of Missionary Education: The Baptist India Mission, 1794-1824," *BQ* 20 (1964): 294.

[24]Carey to Jabez Carey, Serampore, August 20, 1815.

[25]Carey to Jabez Carey, Calcutta, November 16, 1819.

[26]Quoted, Roland Bainton, *Here I Stand: A Life of Martin Luther* (Nashville: Abingdon Press, 1950), 335.

[27]Smith, "Patterns of Missionary Education," 296.

[28]Carey to the Baptist Missionary Society, Hooghly River, January 10, 1799.

[29]Smith, "Patterns of Missionary Education," 302-3; cf. the excellent study of M. A. Laird, *Missionaries and Education in Bengal, 1793-1837* (Oxford: Clarendon Press, 1972, esp. 63-100.

[30]*Institution for the Encouragement of Native Schools in India* (Serampore: Mission Press, 1817), 12.

[31]*William Ward's Missionary Journal, 1799-1811,* October 8, 1800; Potts, *British Baptist Missionaries,* 122.

[32]Potts, *British Baptist Missionaries,* 124. Ward believed that if women were taught to read the Bible, they would become pious and faithful wives and moth-

ers. This in turn would ameliorate the horrible abuses of infanticide, child marriage, *sati*, etc.

[33] *Carey*, 205.

[34] Ibid.

[35] Carey to John Ryland, Serampore, June 14, 1801.

[36] Smith, *Life of William Carey*, 140.

[37] *Carey*, 208.

[38] Carey to John Ryland, Calcutta, June 12, 1806.

[39] Smith, *Life of William Carey*, 333.

[40] *The Story of Serampore and Its College* (Serampore: Council of Serampore College, 1965), 121.

[41] Leighton Williams and Mornay Williams, eds., *Serampore Letters* (New York: G. P. Putnam's Sons, 1892), 87-88.

[42] *Memoir*, 157.

[43] Cf. the claim that Carey's "exertions first led to the prevention of infanticide at Gunga Saugor," *Englishman* (June 1834). Quoted, Potts, *British Baptist Missionaries*, 141.

[44] C. B. Lewis, *The Life of John Thomas* (London: Macmillan and Company, 1873), 294-95.

[45] *Friend of India* 3:265; cf. Potts, *British Baptist Missionaries*, 143.

[46] Carey to John Ryland, Mudnabatty, April 1, 1799.

[47] *CMW* 1:221-23.

[48] Potts, *British Baptist Missionaries*, 167; cf. Kanti Prasanna Sen Gupta, *The Christian Missionaries in Bengal, 1793-1833* (Calcutta: K. L. Mukhopadhyay, 1971).

[49] Potts, *British Baptist Missionaries*, 245.

Chapter 10

[1] Carey to Jabez Carey, Serampore, August 17, 1831.

[2] Carey to Jabez Carey, Serampore, August 17, 1819.

[3] From Becon's *Book of Matrimony;* quoted in Leland Ryken, *Worldly Saints: The Puritans as They Really Were* (Grand Rapids, MI: Zondervan Publishing House, 1986), 49. On Luther's marriage, see Heiko A. Oberman, *Luther: Between God and the Devil* (New Haven: Yale University Press, 1982), 272-97.

[4] George Smith, *The Life of William Carey, Shoemaker and Missionary* (London: John Murray, 1887), 20. Among recent biographers of Carey, Mary Drewery presents a somewhat more sympathetic perspective on Dorothy.

[5] Ruth A. Tucker, *Guardians of the Great Commission: The Story of Women in Modern Missions* (Grand Rapids, MI: Zondervan Publishing House, 1988), 13-20.

[6] Melville Horne, *Letters on Missions* (Andover: Flagg and Gould, 1815), vii.

[7] Ibid., 127-29.

[8] Carey to his sisters, Mudnabatty, January 18, 1798.

[9] Carey to his father, Serampore, October 6, 1800.

[10] Carey to his father, Calcutta, December 1, 1802.

[11] Carey to his sisters, Mudnabatty, October 5, 1795.

[12] Carey to his sisters, Serampore, July 17, 1805.

[13] Carey to his sisters, Tanquan River, December 22, 1796.

[14] *William Ward's Missionary Journal, 1799-1811,* December 8, 1807.

[15] *CMW* 1:397.

[16]Carey to his sisters, Serampore, January 20, 1808.

[17]Quoted, Mary Drewery, *William Carey: A Biography* (Grand Rapids, MI: Zondervan Publishing House, 1978), 147-48.

[18]Ibid., 147. The governor general, referring to Carey's wedding, noted that he had married a Danish countess "whom he had converted from a Christian to a Baptist" by "very near drowning her in the ceremony of Baptism . . . performed in that sect."

[19]Carey to John Ryland, Serampore, June 15, 1821.

[20]Carey to Jabez Carey, Serampore, August 18, 1821.

[21]*Carey*, 359.

[22]Smith, *Life of William Carey*, 374.

[23]Ryken, *Worldly Saints*, 43.

[24]Carey to Jabez Carey, Calcutta, January 24, 1814.

[25]*Brief Narrative of the Baptist Mission in India* (London: Button and Son, 1819), 10.

[26]Ibid., 3.

[27]Leighton Williams and Mornay Williams, eds., *Serampore Letters* (New York: G. P. Putnam's Sons, 1892), 87.

[28]Ruth Rowse, "William Carey's 'Pleasing Dream'," *International Review of Missions* 38 (1949): 181.

[29]Carey to Andrew Fuller, Calcutta, May 15, 1806.

[30]Cf. E. Glenn Hinson, "William Carey and Ecumenical Pragmatism," in *Baptists and Ecumenism*, ed. W. J. Boney and Glenn A. Igleheart (Valley Forge: Judson Press, 1980), 73-83.

[31]John Chamberlain to Andrew Fuller, Serampore, May 3, 1815. Quoted, E. Daniel Potts, *British Baptist Missionaries in India, 1793-1837* (Cambridge: Cambridge University Press, 1967), 58.

[32]*CMW* 1:215.

[33]Andrew Fuller to William Ward, September 21, 1800. A part of Fuller's reasoning, which Carey accepted, read like this: "To disperse with baptism as a term of visible communion is to connive at either a total neglect of an ordinance which is binding by the authority of Christ to the end of the world, or at a gross corruption of that ordinance, and in many cases at both. . . . To connive at a known omission of the will of God must be wrong, and render us partakers of other men's sins."

[34]Carey to John Ryland, Calcutta, April 22, 1817.

[35]Carey to John Ryland, Serampore, June 14, 1821.

[36]Carey to Jabez Carey, Serampore, December 16, 1828.

[37]The best account of the controversy is found in M. M. Thomas, *The Acknowledged Christ of the Indian Renaissance* (London: SCM Press, 1969), 1-37.

[38]Carey to John Ryland, Serampore, June 14, 1821.

[39]William Ward to Samuel Hope, Serampore, November 7, 1821; quoted, Potts, *British Baptist Missionaries*, 234.

[40]Thomas, *Acknowledged Christ*, 5.

[41]Ibid., 13.

[42]Ibid., 25.

[43]Carey to his sisters, Serampore, December 16, 1831.

[44]Carey to his sisters, Serampore, July 27, 1833.

[45]*Carey*, 385.

Chapter 11

[1]Quoted, Paul A. Varg, "Motives in Protestant Missions, 1890-1917," *Church History* 23 (1954): 71.

[2]James Alan Patterson, "The Loss of a Protestant Missionary Consensus: Foreign Missions and the Fundamentalist-Modernist Conflict," in *Earthen Vessels: American Evangelicals and Foreign Missions, 1880-1980,* ed. Joel A. Carpenter and Wilbert R. Shenk (Grand Rapids, MI: William B. Eerdmans Publishing Company, 1990), 74.

[3]Quoted, Jaroslav Pelikan, *Jesus Through the Centuries* (New York: Harper and Row, 1985), 229.

[4]Carpenter and Shenk, *Earthen Vessels,* xii.

[5]Lesslie Newbigin, *The Gospel in a Pluralist Society* (Grand Rapids, MI: William B. Eerdmans Publishing Company, 1989), 159.

[6]Billy Graham, "Why Lausanne?" in *Let the Earth Hear His Voice,* ed. J. D. Douglas (Minneapolis: World Wide Publications, 1975), 29-30.

It was at a meeting in Hackleton that Carey chose to become a Dissenter.

The Moulton church as seen from Carey house and shop.

This pulpit now in Carey's workshop was used by Carey in his Moulton church.

Carey's home and workshop during Moulton days were housed here.

Carey delivered shoes here to Thomas Gotch until the latter freed him
from these duties by financing his studies.

The Baptist Missionary Society was called into being in the back parlor
of the Wallis house.

This window in Fuller Memorial Baptist Church, Kettering, depicts
Andrew Fuller, Carey's friend and supporter.

This snuffbox was used to collect the first offering for the Baptist
Missionary Society when it met in the home of Widow Wallis.

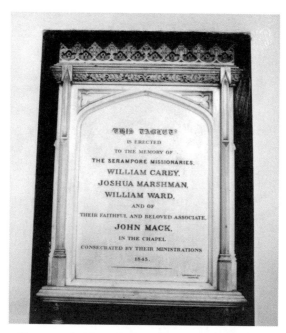

Plaque on inside wall of Serampore Baptist Church.

Administration and library building of Serampore College, which Carey helped found.

William Carey's desk at the William Carey Museum, Serampore College.

Carey Baptist Church in Calcutta, founded by Carey.

AN ENQUIRY INTO THE OBLIGATIONS OF
CHRISTIANS, TO USE MEANS FOR THE CONVERSION
OF THE HEATHENS. IN WHICH THE RELIGIOUS
STATE OF THE DIFFERENT NATIONS OF THE WORLD,
THE SUCCESS OF FORMER UNDERTAKINGS, AND
THE PRACTICABILITY OF FURTHER UNDERTAKINGS,
ARE CONSIDERED, BY WILLIAM CAREY.

For there is no Difference between the Jew and the Greek;
for the same Lord over all, is rich unto all that call upon him.
For whosoever shall call on the name of the Lord shall be saved.
How then shall they call on him, in whom they have not believed? and how shall they believe in him of whom they have
not heard? and how shall they hear without a Preacher? and
how shall they preach except they be sent?

Paul.

LEICESTER:
Printed and sold by ANN IRELAND, and the other Booksellers
in *Leicester;* J. JOHNSON, St. Paul's Church yard; T. KNOTT,
Lombard Street; R. DILLY, in the Poultry, *London;* and
SMITH, at *Sheffield.*
[Price One Shilling and Six-pence.]
MDCCXCII.

CONTENTS

INTRODUCTION

As our blessed Lord has required us to pray that his kingdom may come, and his will be done on earth as it is in heaven, it becomes us not only to express our desires of that event by words, but to use every lawful method to spread the knowledge of his name. In order to do this, it is necessary that we should become in some measure acquainted with the religious state of the world; and as this is an object we should be prompted to pursue, not only by the gospel of our Redeemer, but even by the feelings of humanity, so an inclination to conscientious activity therein would form one of the strongest proofs that we are the subjects of grace, and partakers of that spirit of universal benevolence and genuine philanthropy which appear so evident in the character of God himself.

Sin was introduced amongst the children of men by the fall of Adam, and has ever since been spreading its baneful influence. By changing its appearances to suit the circumstances of the times, it has grown up in ten thousand forms, and constantly counteracted the will and designs of God. One would have supposed that the remembrance of the deluge would have been transmitted from father to son, and have perpetually deterred mankind from transgressing the will of their Maker; but so blinded were they, that in the time of Abraham, gross wickedness prevailed wherever colonies were planted, and the iniquity of the Amorites was great, though not yet full. After this, idolatry spread more and more, till the seven devoted nations were cut off with the most signal marks of divine displeasure. Still, however, the progress of evil was not stopped, but the Israelites themselves too often joined with the rest of mankind against the God of Israel. In one period the grossest ignorance and barbarism prevailed in the world; and afterwards, in a more enlightened age, the most daring infidelity, and contempt of God; so that the world which was once overrun with ignorance, now "by wisdom knew not God, but changed the glory of the incorruptible God" as much as in the most barbarous ages, "into an image made like to corruptible man, and to birds, and four-footed beasts, and creeping things" (1 Cor.

1:21; Rom. 1:23). Nay, as they increased in science and politeness, they ran into more abundant and extravagant idolatries.

Yet God repeatedly made known his intention to prevail finally over all the power of the devil, and to destroy all his works, and set up his own kingdom and interest among men, and extend it as universally as Satan had extended his. It was for this purpose that the Messiah came and died, that God might be just, and the justifier of all that should believe in him. When he had laid down his life, and taken it up again, he sent forth his disciples to preach the good tidings to every creature, and to endeavour by all possible methods to bring over a lost world to God. They went forth according to their divine commission, and wonderful success attended their labours; the civilized greeks, and uncivilized barbarians, each yielded to the cross of Christ, and embraced it as the only way of salvation. Since the apostolic age many other attempts to spread the gospel have been made, which have been considerably successful, notwithstanding which a very considerable part of mankind is still involved in all the darkness of heathenism. Some attempts are still being made, but they are inconsiderable in comparison with what might be done if the whole body of Christians entered heartily into the spirit of the divine command on this subject. Some think little about it, others are unacquainted with the state of the world, and others love their wealth better than the souls of their fellow-creatures.

In order that the subject may be taken into more serious consideration, I shall (1) enquire, whether the commission given by our Lord to his disciples be not still binding on us, (2) take a short view of former undertakings, (3) give some account of the present state of the world, (4) consider the practicability of doing something more than is done, and (5) the duty of Christians in general in this matter.

SECTION ONE
An Enquiry whether the Commission given by our Lord to his Disciples be not still binding on us.

Our Lord Jesus Christ, a little before his departure, commissioned his apostles to "Go," and "teach all nations" (Matt. 28:19); or, as another evangelist expresses it, "Go into all the world, and preach the gospel to every creature" (Mark 16:15). This commission was as extensive as possible, and laid them under obligation to disperse themselves into every country to the habitable globe, and preach to all the inhabitants, without exception, or limitation. They accordingly went forth in obedience to the command, and the power of God evidently wrought with them. Many attempts of the same kind have been made since their day, and which have been attended with various success; but the work has not been taken up, or prosecuted of late years (except by a few individuals) with that zeal and perseverance with which the primitive Christians went about it. It seems as if many thought the commission was sufficiently put in execution by what the apostles and others have done; that we have enough to do to attend to the salvation of our own countrymen; and that, if God intends the salvation of the heathen, he will some way or other bring them to the gospel, or the gospel to them. It is thus that multitudes sit at ease, and give themselves no concern about the far greater part of their fellow sinners, who to this day, are lost in ignorance and idolatry. There seems also to be an opinion existing in the minds of some, that because the apostles were extraordinary officers and have no proper successors, and because many things which were right for them to do would be unwarrantable for us, therefore it may not be immediately binding on us to execute the commission, though it was so upon them. To the consideration of such persons I would offer the following observations.

First, if the command of Christ to teach all nations be restricted to the apostles, or those under the immediate inspiration of the Holy Ghost, then that of baptizing should be so too; and every denomination of Christians, except the Quakers, do wrong in baptizing with water at all.

Secondly, if the command of Christ to teach all nations be confined to the apostles, then all such ordinary ministers who have endeavoured to carry the gospel to the heathens, have acted without a warrant, and run before they were sent. Yea, and though God has promised the most glorious things to the heathen world by sending his gospel to them, yet whoever goes first, or indeed at all, with that message, unless he have a new and special commission from heaven, must go without any authority for so doing.

Thirdly, if the command of Christ to teach all nations extend only to the apostles, then, doubtless, the promise of the divine presence in this world must be so limited; but this is worded in such a manner as expressly precludes such an idea. "Lo, I am with you always, to the end of the world" (Matt. 28:20).

That there are cases in which even a divine command may cease to be binding is admitted. As for instance, if it be repealed, as the ceremonial commandments of the Jewish law; or if there be no subjects in the world for the commanded act to be exercised upon, as in the law of septennial release, which might be dispensed with when there should be no poor in the land to have their debts forgiven (Deut. 15:4); or if, in any particular instance, we can produce a counter-revelation, of equal authority with the original command, as when Paul and Silas were forbidden of the Holy Ghost to preach the word in Bythinia (Acts 16:6,7); or if, in any case, there would be a natural impossibility of putting it in execution. It was not the duty of Paul to preach Christ to the inhabitants of Otaheite, because no such place was then discovered, nor had he any means of coming at them. But none of these things can be alleged by us in behalf of the neglect of the commission given by Christ. We cannot say that it is repealed, like the commands of the ceremonial law; nor can we plead that there are no objects for the command to be exercised upon. Alas! the far greater part of the world, as we shall see presently, is still covered with heathen darkness! Nor can we produce a counter-revelation, concerning any particular nation, like that to Paul and Silas, concerning Bythinia; and, if we could, it would not warrant our sitting still and neglecting all the other parts of the world; for Paul and Silas, when forbidden to preach to those heathens, went elsewhere, and preached to others. Neither can we allege a natural impossibility in the case. It has been said that we ought not to force our way, but to wait for the openings, and leadings of Providence; but it might with equal propriety be answered in this case, neither ought we to neglect embracing those openings in providence which daily present themselves to us. What openings of providence do we wait for? We can neither expect to be transported into the heathen world without ordinary means, nor to be endowed with the gift of tongues, etc., when we arrive there. These would not be providential interpositions, but miraculous ones. Where a command exists nothing can be necessary to render it binding but a removal of those obstacles which render obedience impossible, and these are removed already. Natural impossibility can never be pleaded so long as facts exist to prove the contrary. Have not the popish missionaries surmounted all those difficulties which we have generally thought to be insuperable? Have not the missionaries of the Unitas Fratrum, or Moravian Brethren, encountered the scorching heat of Abyssinia, and the frozen climes of Greenland, and Labrador, their difficult languages, and savage manners? Or have not English traders, for the sake of gain, surmounted all those things which have generally been counted insurmountable obstacles in the way of preaching the gospel? Witness the trade to Persia, the East Indies, China, and Greenland, yea even the accursed Slave-Trade on the coasts of Africa. Men can insinuate themselves into the favour of the most barbarous clans, and uncultivated tribes, for the sake of gain; and however different the circumstances of trading and preaching are, yet this will prove the possibility of ministers being introduced there; and if this is but thought a sufficient reason to make the experiment, my point is gained.

It has been said that some learned divines have proved from Scripture that the time is not yet come that the heathen should be converted; and that first the "witnesses" must be slain (Rev. 11:1-13), and many other prophecies fulfilled. But admitting this to be the case (which I much doubt*) yet if any objection is made from this against preaching to them immediately, it must be founded on one of these things; either that the secret purpose of God is the rule of our duty, and then it must be as bad to pray for them, as to preach to them; or else that none shall be converted in the heathen world till the universal down-pouring of the Spirit in the last days. But this objection comes too late; for the success of the gospel has been very considerable in many places already.

It has been objected that there are multitudes in our own nation, and within our immediate spheres of action, who are as ignorant as the South-Sea savages, and that therefore we have work enough at home, without going into other countries. That there are thousands in our own land as far from God as possible, I readily grant, and that this ought to excite us to ten-fold diligence in our work, and in attempts to spread divine knowledge among them is a certain fact; but that it ought to supercede all attempts to spread the gospel in foreign parts seems to want

---

*See Edwards on Prayer, on this subject, lately reprinted by Mr. Sutcliffe.

proof. Our own countrymen have the means of grace, and may attend on the word preached if they choose it. They have the means of knowing the truth, and faithful ministers are placed in almost every part of the land, whose spheres of action might be extended if their congregations were but more hearty and active in the cause: but with them the case is widely different, who have no Bible, no written language (which many of them have not), no ministers, no good civil government, nor any of those advantages which we have. Pity therefore, humanity, and much more Christianity, call loudly for every possible exertion to introduce the gospel amongst them.

SECTION TWO
Containing a short Review of former Undertakings for the Conversion of the Heathen.

Before the coming of our Lord Jesus Christ the whole world were either heathens, or Jews; and both, as to the body of them, were enemies to the gospel. After the resurrection the disciples continued in Jerusalem till Pentecost. Being daily engaged in prayer and supplication, and having chosen Matthias to supply the place of Judas in the apostolic office, on that solemn day, when they were assembled together, a most remarkable effusion of the Holy Spirit took place, and a capacity of speaking in all foreign languages was bestowed upon them. This opportunity was embraced by Peter for preaching the gospel to a great congregation of Jews and proselytes, who were from Parthia, Media, Elam, Mesopotamia, Judea, Cappadocia, the proconsular Asia, Phrygia, Pamphilia, Egypt, Lybia, Crete, Arabia, Rome, etc., and at the first effort God wrought so powerfully that three thousand were converted, who immediately after were baptized, and added to the church. Before this great addition they consisted of but about "an hundred and twenty persons" (Acts 1:15), but from that time they constantly increased. (Acts 2.) It was but a little after this that Peter and John, going up to the temple, healed the lame man; this miracle drew a great multitude together, and Peter took occasion while they stood wondering at the event to preach Jesus Christ to them. (Acts 3.) The consequence was that five thousand more believed (Acts 4:4).

This was not done without opposition; the priests and Sadducees tried all the methods they could invent to prevent them from preaching the gospel. The apostles, however, asserted their divine warrant, and as soon as they were set at liberty addressed God, and prayed that a divine power might attend their labours, which petition was heard, and their future ministry was very successful. On account of the needs of those who were engaged in this good work, those amongst them who had possessions, or goods, sold them, and devoted the money to pious uses. (Acts 4.)

About this time a man and his wife, out of great pretence of piety, sold an estate, and brought part of the money to the apostles, pretending it to be the whole; for which dissimulation both he and his wife were struck dead by the hand of God. This awful catastrophe however was the occasion of many more men and women being added to the church. The miracles wrought by the apostles, and the success attending their ministry, stirred up greater envy in the priests and Sadducees, who imprisoned them; from which confinement they were soon liberated by an angel; upon which they went immediately as they were commanded and preached in the temple: here they were seized, and brought before the council, where Gamaliel spake in their favour, and they were dismissed. After this they continued to prosecute their work, rejoicing that they were counted worthy to suffer shame for the name of Christ. (Acts 5.)

By this time the church at Jerusalem was so increased that the multiplicity of its temporal concerns was the occasion of some neglects, which produced a dissatisfaction. The apostles, therefore, recommended to the church to choose seven pious men, whose office it should be to attend upon its temporal affairs; that "they might give themselves to prayer, and the ministry of the word" (Acts 6:4). Seven were accordingly chosen, over whom the apostles prayed, and ordained them to the office of Deacons by imposition of hands: and, these things being settled, the church increased more and more. (Acts 6.) One of these Deacons, whose name was Stephen, being a person of eminent knowledge and holiness, wrought many miracles, and disputed with great evidence and energy for the truth of Christianity, which raised him up a number of opponents. These soon procured his death, and carried their resentment so far as to stir up such a persecution that the church, which till now had been confined to Jerusalem, was dispersed, and all the preachers except the apostles were driven thence, and went everywhere preaching the word. (Acts 7:1-8:4.)

A young man whose name was Saul was very active in this persecution; he had been educated under Gamaliel, a member of the Sanhedrin, was a person of promising genius, by profession a Pharisee, and much attached to the Jewish ceremonies. When Stephen was stoned he appeared much pleased with it, and had the custody of the clothes of his executioners; and from that time was fired with such a spirit of persecution himself, that he went about dragging some to prison, and compelling others to blaspheme the name of the Lord Jesus. Neither was he contented with exercising his rage at Jerusalem, but went to the chief priests and obtained testimonials of authority to carry on the same work at Damascus. But on his way, as he was almost ready to enter into the city, the Lord changed his heart in a very wonderful manner; so that instead of entering the town to persecute, he began to preach the gospel as soon as he was able. This presently brought upon him the same persecution which he had designed to exercise upon others, and even endangered his life, so that the brethren found it necessary to let him down the city wall in a basket by night, and so he escaped the hands of his enemies. From thence he went to Jerusalem where he preached the word, but being persecuted there he went to Cesarea, and from thence to Tarsus. (Acts 9:1-30.)

In the time of this trouble in the church, Philip went and preached at Samaria with great success, nay so great was the work that an impostor, who had deceived the people with legerdemain tricks for a long time, was so amazed, and even convinced, as to profess himself a Christian, and was baptized; but was afterwards detected, and appeared to be an hypocrite. Besides him a great number believed in reality, and being baptized a church was formed there. Soon after this the Lord commanded Philip to go the way which led from Jerusalem to Gaza, which he did, and there found a eunuch of great authority in the court of Ethiopia, to whom he preached Christ, who believed, and was baptized; after which Philip preached at Ashdod, or Azotus. (Acts 8.)

About the same time Peter went to Lydda, or Diospolis, and cured Eneas of a palsy, which was the means of conversion not only of the inhabitants of that town, but also of the neighbouring country, called Saron, the capital of which was Lasharon; and while he was there, a circumstance turned up which tended much to the spread of the truth. A woman of Joppa, a sea-port town in the neighbourhood, died and they sent to Lydda for Peter, who went over, and when he had prayed she was raised to life again; which was an occasion of the conversion of many in that town. Peter continued preaching there for some time, and lodged at the house of a tanner. (Acts 9:32-43.)

Now another circumstance also tended to the further propagation of Christianity, for a Roman military officer who had some acquaintance with the Old Testament Scriptures, but was not circumcised, was one day engaged in prayer in his house at Cesarea, when an angel appeared to him, and bid him send for Peter from Joppa to preach in his house. Before this the work of God had been wholly confined to the Jews, and Jewish proselytes, and even the apostles appeared to have had very contracted ideas of the Christian dispensation; but now God by a vision revealed to Peter that Christianity was to be spread into all nations. He accordingly went and preached at the house of Cornelius, at Cesarea, when several were converted, and baptized, and the foundation of a church laid in that city. (Acts 10.)

Some of the dispersed ministers, having fled to Antioch in Syria, began to preach to the Greeks in that city about the same time, and had good success; upon which the apostles sent Paul and Barnabas, who instructed and strengthened them, and a church was formed in that city also, which in a little time sent out several eminent preachers. (Acts 11:19-26.)

In the Acts of the Apostles we have an account of four of the principal journeys which Paul and his companions undertook. The first, in which he was accompanied by Barnabas, is recorded in the thirteenth and fourteenth chapters, and was the first attack on the heathen world. It was a journey into Asia Minor. On their way they passed over the land of Cyprus. No sooner had they entered on their undertaking than they met with great difficulty; for Mark, whom they had taken as their minister, deserted them, and returned to Jerusalem, where, it seems, he thought he should enjoy the greatest quiet. Paul and Barnabas however went forward; in every city they preached the word of the Lord, entering into the Jewish synagogues and first preaching Christ to them, and then to the Gentiles. They were heard with great eagerness and candour by some, and rejected by others with obstinacy and wrath, and cruel persecution. On one occasion they had enough to do to restrain the people from worshipping them as gods, and soon after that Paul was stoned, dragged out of the city, and left for dead. Having penetrated as far as Derbe, they thought it proper to return by the way that they came, calling at every city where they had sown the good seed. They found in most, if not all these places, some who had embraced the gospel, and exhorted and strengthened them in the faith. They formed them into churches, and ordained them elders, and fasted and prayed with them; and so having commended them to the Lord on whom they had believed, returned to Antioch in Syria, from whence they first set out, and rehearsed to the church all that God had done with them, and how He had opened the door of faith to the Gentiles. (Acts 13, 14.)

About this time a dispute arose in the churches concerning circumcision, and Paul and Barnabas were deputed to go up to Jerusalem, to consult the apostles and elders on the subject. The business being completed, they, accompanied with Judas and Silas, returned to Antioch with the general resolution, and continued there for a season, teaching and preaching the word of the Lord. (Acts 15:1-35.)

Paul now proposed to Barnabas, his fellow-labourer, that they might visit their brethren in the places where they had been already, and see how they did. To this Barnabas readily agreed, but a difference arising between them about taking with them John Mark, who had deserted them before, these two eminent servants of God were parted asunder, and never appear to have travelled together any more. They continued however each to serve in the cause of Christ, though they could not walk together. Barnabas took John, and sailed to Cyprus, his native island, and Paul took Silas, and went through Syria and Cilicia, to Derbe and Lystra, cities where he and Barnabas had preached in their first excursion. (Acts 15:36-41.)

Here they found Timothy, a promising young man, whom they encouraged to engage in the ministry.

Paul being now at Lystra, which was the boundary of his first excursion, and having visited the churches already planted, and delivered to them the decrees of the apostles and elders relating to circumcision, seems to have felt his heart enlarged, and attempted to carry on the glorious work of preaching the gospel to the heathen to a greater extent. With Silas and Timothy in his second journey he took a western direction, passing through Phrygia, and the region of Galatia. Having preaching the word with considerable success (Acts 18:23), he and his companions wished to have gone into the proconsular Asia, and afterwards tried to go into Bythinia; but being forbidden of the Holy Ghost, who seems to have had a special design of employing them elsewhere, passing by Mysia they came down to Troas on the sea-coast. Here a vision appeared to Paul, in which he was invited to go over to Macedonia. Obedient to the heavenly vision, and greatly encouraged by it, they with all speed crossed the Aegean Sea, and passing through the island of Samothracia, landed at Neapolis, and went from thence to Philippi, the chief city of that part of Macedonia. It was here that Paul preached on a Sabbath day to a few women by a river side, and Lydia, a woman of Thyatira, was converted and baptized, and her household with her. It was here that a poor girl, who brought her employers considerable profit by foretelling future events, followed the apostles, had her spirit of divination ejected, on which account her masters were much irritated, and raised a tumult, the effect of which was that Paul and Silas were imprisoned. But even this was over-ruled for the success of the gospel, in that the keeper of the prison, and all his house, were thereby brought to believe in the Lord Jesus Christ, and were baptized. (Acts 16.)

From Philippi they passed through Amphipolis, Apollonia, Thessalonica (now Salonichi), Berea, Athens, and Corinth, preaching the gospel wherever they went. From hence Paul took ship and sailed to Syria, only giving a short call at Ephesus, determining to be at Jerusalem at the feast of the passover; and having saluted the church, he came to Cesarea, and from thence to Antioch. (Acts 17:1-18:22.)

Here ended Paul's second journey, which was very extensive, and took up some years of his time. He and his companions met with their difficulties in it, but had likewise their encouragements. They were persecuted at Philippi, as already noticed, and generally found the Jews to be their most inveterate enemies. These would raise tumults, inflame the minds of the gentiles against them and follow them from place to place, doing them all the mischief in their power. This was the case especially at Thessalonica, Berea, and Corinth. But amidst all their persecutions God was with them, and strengthened them in various ways. At Berea they were candidly received, and their doctrine fairly tried by the Holy Scriptures; and "therefore," it is said, "many of them believed" (Acts 17:12). At other places, though they affected to despise the apostle, yet some clave unto him. At Corinth opposition rose to a great height; but the Lord appeared to his servant in a vision, saying, "Be not afraid, but speak, and hold not thy peace, for I am with thee, and no man shall set on thee to hurt thee; for I have much people in this city" (Acts 18:9,10). And the promise was made abundantly good in the spirit displayed by Gallio, the proconsul, who turned a deaf ear to the accusations of the Jews, and nobly declined interfering in matters beside his province. Upon the whole a number of churches were planted during this journey, which for ages after shone as lights in the world.

When Paul had visited Antioch, and spent some time there, he prepared for a third journey into heathen countries, the account of which begins at Acts 18:23 and ends at Acts 21:17. At his first setting out he went over the whole country of Galatia and Phrygia in order, strengthening all the disciples; and passing through the upper coasts come to Ephesus. There for the space of three months he boldly preached in the Jewish synagogue, disputing, and persuading the things concerning the kingdom of God. But when the hardened Jews had openly rejected the gospel, and spake evil of that way before the multitude, Paul openly separated the disciples from them, and assembled in the school of one Tyrannus. This, it is said, continued for the space of two years, "so that all who dwelt in" the proconsular "Asia heard the word of the Lord Jesus, both Jews and Greeks" (Acts 19:10). Certain magicians about this time were exposed, and others were converted, who burnt their books and confessed their deeds. So mightily grew the word of the Lord, and prevailed.

After this, an uproar having been raised by Demetrius the silversmith, Paul went into Macedonia, visited the churches planted in his former journey, and from thence passed into Greece. Having preached up and down for three months, he thought of sailing from thence directly to Syria; but in order to avoid the Jews, who laid wait for him near the sea coast, he took another course through Macedonia, and from thence to Troas, by the way of Philippi. There is no mention made in his former journey of his having preached at Troas; yet it seems he did, and a church was gathered, with whom the apostle at this time united in "breaking of bread" (Acts 20:7). It was here that he preached all night and raised Eutychus, who being overcome with sleep had fallen down and was taken up dead. From thence they set sail for Syria, and on their way called at Miletus, where Paul sent for the elders of the church at Ephesus, and delivered that most solemn and affectionate farewell, recorded in the twentieth chapter of the Acts of the Apostles. From hence they sailed for Tyre, where they tarried seven days and from thence proceeded to Jerusalem.

Paul's fourth and last journey (or rather voyage) was to Rome, where he went in the character of a prisoner. For while being at Jerusalem he was quickly apprehended by the Jews; but being rescued by Lysias, the chief captain, he was sent to Cesarea to take his trial. Here he made his defence before Felix and Drusilla, in such a way that the judge, instead of the prisoner, was made to tremble. Here also he made his defence before Festus, Agrippa, and Bernice, with such force of evidence that Agrippa was almost persuaded to be a Christian. But the malice of the Jews being insatiable, and Paul finding himself in danger of being delivered into their hands, was constrained to appeal unto Caesar. This was the occasion of his being sent to Rome, where he arrived after a long and dangerous voyage, and being shipwrecked on the island of Melita, where he wrought miracles, and Publius, the governor, was converted. (Acts 21:17-28:10)

When he arrived at Rome he addressed his countrymen the Jews, some of whom believed; but when others rejected the gospel, he turned from them to the Gentiles, and for two whole years dwelt in his own hired house preaching the kingdom of God, and teaching those things which concern the Lord Jesus Christ, with all confidence, no man forbidding him. (Acts 28:16-31.)

Thus far the history of the Acts of the Apostles informs us of the success of the word in the primitive times; and history informs us of its being preached about this time in many other places. Peter speaks of a church at Babylon (1 Pet. 5:13); Paul proposed a journey to Spain (Rom. 15:24), and it is generally believed he went there and likewise came to France and Britain. Andrew preached to the Scythians, north of the Black Sea. John is said to have preached in India, and we know that he was at the Isle of Patmos, in the Archipelago. Philip is reported to have preached in upper Asia, Scythia, and Phrygia; Bartholomew in India, on this side of the Ganges, Phrygia, and Armenia; Matthew in Arabia, or Asiatic Ethiopia, and Parthia; Thomas in India, as far as the coast of Coromandel, and some say in the island of Ceylon; Simon, the Canaanite, in Egypt, Cyrene, Mauritania, Lybia, and other parts of Africa, and from thence to have come to Britain; and Jude is said to have been principally engaged in the lesser Asia and Greece. Their labours were evidently very extensive, and very successful; so that Pliny the Younger, who lived soon after the death of the apostles, in a letter to the emperor Trajan, observed that Christianity had spread not only through towns and cities but also through whole countries. Indeed before this, in the time of Nero, it was so prevalent that it was necessary to oppose it by an Imperial Edict, and accordingly the proconsuls, and other governors, were commissioned to destroy it.

Justin Martyr, who lived about the middle of the second century, in his dialogue with Trypho, observed that there was no part of mankind, whether Greeks or barbarians, or any others, by whatever name they were called, whether Sarmatians, or the Scenites of Arabia Petrea, who lived in tents among their cattle, where supplications and thanksgivings are not offered up to the Father, and maker of all things, through the name of Jesus Christ. Irenaeus, who lived about the year 170, speaks of churches that were founded in Germany, Spain, France, the eastern countries, Lybia, and the middle of the world. Tertullian, who lived and wrote at Carthage in Africa, about twenty years afterwards, enumerating the countries where Christianity had penetrated, makes mention of the Parthians, Medes, Elamites, Mesopotamians, Armenians, Phrygians, Cappadocians, the inhabitants of Pontus, Asia, Pamphylia, Egypt, and the regions of Africa beyond Cyrene, the Romans, and Jews, formerly of Jerusalem, many of the Getuli, many borders of the Mauri, or Moors, in Mauritania; now Barbary, Morocco, etc., all the borders of Spain, many nations of the Gauls, and the places in Britain which were inaccessible to the Romans; the Dacians, Sarmatians, Germans, Scythians, and the inhabitants of many hidden nations and provinces, and of many islands unknown to him, and which he could not enumerate. The labors of the ministers of the gospel in this early period were so remarkably blessed of God that the last-mentioned writer observed, in a letter to Scapula, that if he began a persecution the city of Carthage itself must be decimated thereby. Yes, and so abundant were they in the three first centuries, that ten years constant and almost universal persecution under Diocletian could neither root out the Christians nor prejudice their cause.

After this they had great encouragement under several emperors, particularly Constantine and Theodosius, and a very great work of God was carried on; but the ease and affluence which in these times attended the church served to introduce a flood of corruption, which brought on by degrees the whole system of Popery, by means of which all appeared to be lost again; and Satan set up his kingdom of darkness, deceit, and human authority over conscience, through all the Christian world.

In the time of Constantine one Frumentius was sent to preach to the Indians, and met with great success. A young woman who was a Christian, being taken captive by the Iberians, or Giorgians, near the Caspian Sea, informed them of the truths of Christianity, and was so much regarded that they sent to Constantine for ministers to come and preach the word to them. About the same time some barbarous nations, having made irruptions into Thrace, carried away several Christians captive, who preached the gospel; by which means the inhabitants upon the Rhine, and the Danube, the Celtae, and some other parts of Gaul, were brought to embrace Christianity. About this time also James of Nisbia went into Persia to strengthen the Christians and preach to the heathens; and his success was so great that Adiabene was almost entirely Christian. About the year 372 one Moses, a Monk, went to preach to the Saracens, who then lived in Arabia, where he had great success; and at this time the Goths, and other northern nations, had the kingdom of Christ further extended amongst them, but they were very soon corrupted with Arianism.

Soon after this the kingdom of Christ was further extended among the Scythian Nomades, beyond the Danube, and about the year 430 a people called the Burgundians received the gospel. Four years after that Palladius was sent to preach in Scotland, and the next year Patrick was sent from Scotland to preach to the Irish, who before his time were totally uncivilized and, some say, cannibals; he however was useful, and laid the foundations of several churches in Ireland. Soon after this, truth spread further among the Saracens, and in 522 Zathus king of the Colchians encouraged it, and many of that nation were converted to Christianity. About this time also the work was extended in Ireland by Finian, and in Scotland by Constantine and Columbia; the latter of whom preached also to the Picts, and Brudaeus, their king, with several others, was converted. About 541 Adad, the king of Ethiopia, was converted by the preaching of Mansionarius; the Heruli beyond the Danube were now made obedient to the faith, and so were the Abfagi near the Caucasian Mountains.

But now popery, especially the compulsive part of it, was risen to such a height that the usual method of propagating the gospel, or rather what was so called, was to conquer pagan nations by force of arms, and then oblige them to submit to Christianity, after which bishoprics were erected and persons were sent to instruct the people. I shall just mention some of those who are said to have laboured thus.

In 596, Austin, the monk, Melitus, Justus, Paulinus, and Ruffinian, laboured in England, and in their way were very successful. Paulinus, who appears to have been one of the best of them, had great success in Northumberland; Birinnius preached to the West Saxons, and Felix to the East Angles. In 589 Amandus Gallus laboured in Ghent, Chelenus in Artois, and Gallus and Columbanus in Suabia. In 648, Egidius Gallus in Flanders, and the two Evaldi in Westphalia. In 684, Willifred, in the Isle of Wight. In 688, Chilianus, in upper Franconia. In 698, Boniface, or Winifred, among the Thuringians, near Erford, in Saxony, and Willibroad in West Friesland. Charlemagne conquered Hungary in the year 800, and obliged the inhabitants to profess Christianity, while Modestus likewise preached to the Venedi, at the source of the Save and Drave. In 833 Anigarius preached in Denmark, Gaudibert in Sweden, and about 861 Methodius and Cyril in Bohemia.

About the year 500, the Scythians overran Bulgaria, and Christianity was wiped out, but about 870 they were reconverted. Poland began to be brought over about the same time, and afterwards, about 960 or 990, the work was further extended amongst the Poles and Prussians. The work was begun in Norway in 960, and in Muscovy in 989, the Swedes propagated Christianity in Finland in 1168, Lithuania became Christian in 1386, Samitoga in 1439. The Spaniards forced popery upon the inhabitants of South America, and the Portuguese did the same in Asia. The Jesuits were sent into China 1552. Xavier, whom they call the apostle of the Indians, laboured in the East Indies and Japan from 1541 to 1552, and several missions of Capauchins were sent to Africa in the seventeenth century. But blind zeal, gross superstition, and infamous cruelties, so marked the appearances of religion all this time, that the professors of Christianity needed conversion as much as the heathen world.

A few pious people had fled from the general corruption, and lived obscurely in the valleys of Piedmont and Savoy. They were like the seed of the church. Some of them now and then needed to travel into other parts, where they faithfully testified against the corruptions of the times. About 1369 Wickliffe began to preach the faith in England, and his preaching and writings were the means of the conversion of great numbers, many of whom became excellent preachers; and a work was begun which afterwards spread in England, Hungary, Bohemia, Germany, Switzerland, and many other places. John Huss and Jerome of Prague preached boldly and successfully in Bohemia and the adjacent parts. In the following century Luther, Calvin, Melancthon, Bucer, Martyr, and many others stood up against all the rest of the world; they preached, and prayed, and wrote; and nations agreed one after another to cast off the yoke of popery, and to embrace the doctrine of the gospel.

In England popish cruelty was followed by episcopal tyranny, which in the year 1620 obliged many pious people to leave their native land and settle in America; these were followed by others in 1629, who laid the foundations of several gospel churches which have increased amazingly since that time, and the Redeemer has fixed his throne in that country where but a little time ago Satan had universal dominion.

In 1632 Mr. Elliott of New England, a very pious and zealous minister, began to preach to the Indians, among whom he had great success; several churches of Indians were planted, and some preachers and schoolmasters were raised up amongst them; since which time others have laboured amongst them with some good encouragement. About the year 1743 Mr. David Brainerd was sent as a missionary to some more Indians, where he preached, and prayed, and after some time an extraordinary work of conversion was wrought, and wonderful success attended his ministry. At this present time Mr. Kirkland and Mr. Sargeant are employed in the same good work, and God has considerably blessed their labours.

In 1706 the king of Denmark sent a Mr. Ziegenbalg and some others to Tranquebar, on the Coromandel coast in the East Indies. They were useful to the natives, so that many of the heathens were turned to the Lord. The Dutch East India Company likewise having extended their commerce built the city of Batavia, and a Church was opened there; and the Lord's Supper was administered for the first time on the 3rd of January, 1621, by their minister James Hulzibos; from hence some ministers were sent to Amboyna, who were very successful. A seminary of learning was erected at Leyden, in which ministers and assistants were educated under the renowned Walaeus, and for some years a great number were sent to the East, at the Company's expense, so that in a little time many thousands at Formosa, Malabar, Ternate, Jaffanapatnam, in the town of Columba, at Amboyna, Java, Banda, Macassar, and Malabar, embraced the religion of our Lord Jesus Christ. The work had decayed in some places, but they now have churches in Ceylon, Sumatra, Java, Amboyna, and some other of the spice islands, and at the Cape of Good Hope in Africa.

But none of the moderns have equalled the Moravian Brethren in this good work; they have sent missions to Greenland, Labrador, and several of the islands of the West Indies, which have been blessed for good. They have likewise sent to Abyssinia in Africa, but what success they have had I cannot tell.

The late Mr. Wesley lately made an effort in the West Indies, and some of their ministers are now labouring amongst the Caribbs and Negroes, and I have seen pleasing accounts of their success.

SECTION THREE
Containing a Survey of the present State of the World.

In this survey I shall consider the world as divided, according to its usual division, into four parts, Europe, Asia, Africa, and America, and take notice of the extent of the several countries, their population, civilization, and religion. The article of religion I shall divide into Christian, Jewish, Mahometan, and Pagan; and shall now and then hint at the particular sect of them that prevails in the places which I shall describe. The following Tables will exhibit a more comprehensive view of what I propose, than anything I can offer on the subject.

EUROPE

Countries.	EXTENT		Number of Inhabitants.	Religion.
	Length. Miles.	Breadth. Miles.		
Great Britain	680	300	12,000,000	Protestants, of many denominations.
Ireland	285	160	2,000,000	Protestants, and Papists.
France	600	500	24,000,000	Catholics, Deists, and Protestants.
Spain	700	500	9,500,000	Papists.
Portugal	300	100	2,000,000	Papists.
Sweden, *including*				
Sweden proper, Gothland, Shonen, Lapland, Bothnia, and Finland	800	500	3,500,000	The Swedes are serious Lutherans, but most of the Laplanders are Pagans, and very superstitious.
Isle of Gothland	80	23	5,000	
—Oefel	45	24	2,500	
—Oeland	84	9	1,000	
—Dago	26	23	1,000	

EUROPE

Countries.	EXTENT		Number of Inhabitants.	Religion.
	Length. Miles.	Breadth. Miles.		
Isle of Aland	24	20	800	Lutherans of the Helvetic Confession.
—Hogland	9	5	100	Ditto.
Denmark	240	114	360,000	Ditto.
Isle of Zeeland	60	60	284,000	Ditto.
—Funen	38	32	144,000	Ditto.
—Arroe	8	2	200	Ditto.
—Iceland	435	185	60,000	Ditto.
—Langeland	27	12	3,000	Ditto.
—Laland	38	30	148,000	Ditto.
—Falster	27	12	3,000	Ditto.
—Mona	14	5	600	Ditto.
—Alfen	15	6	600	Ditto.
—Femeren	13	8	1,000	Ditto.

EUROPE

Countries.	EXTENT		Number of Inhabitants.	Religion.
	Length. Miles.	Breadth. Miles.		
Isle of Bornholm..............	20	12	2,000	Lutherans.
Greenland.....................	Undiscovered		7,000	Pagans, and Moravian Christians.
Norway.......................	750	170	724,000	Lutherans.
24 Faro Isles			4,500	Ditto.
Danish Lapland...............	285	172	100,000	Ditto, and Pagans.
Poland	700	680	9,000,000	Papists, Lutherans, Calvinists, & Jews.
Prussia*	400	160	2,500,000	Calvinists, Catholics, & Lutherans.
Sardinia......................	135	57	600,000	Papists.
Sicily........................	180	92	1,000,000	Ditto.
Italy.........................	660	120	20,000,000	Ditto.
United Netherlands...........	150	150	2,000,000	Protestants of several denominations.
Austrian Netherlands.........	200	200	2,500,000	Papists and Protestants.

*The rest of Prussian dominions being scattered about in several countries, are counted to those countries where they lie.

EUROPE

Countries.	EXTENT		Number of Inhabitants.	Religion.
	Length. Miles.	Breadth. Miles.		
Switzerland...........	260	100	2,880,000	Papists and Protestants.
The Grisons	100	62	800,000	Lutherans and Papists.
The Abbacy of St. Gall........	24	10	50,000	Ditto.
Neufchatel...........	32	20	100,000	Calvinists.
Valais.................	80	30	440,000	Papists.
Piedmont.............	140	98	900,000	Ditto, and Protestants.
Savoy.................	87	60	720,000	Ditto.
Geneva, City...........			24,000	Calvinists.
Bohemia	478	322	2,100,000	Papists and Moravians.
Hungary	300	200	2,500,000	Papists.
Germany	600	500	20,000,000	Ditto, and Protestants.
Russia in Europe......	1,500	1,100	22,000,000	Greek Church.
Turkey in Europe......	1,000	900	18,000,000	Greek Christians, Jews, & Mahometans.

EUROPE

Countries.	EXTENT		Number of Inhabitants.	Religion.
	Length. Miles.	Breadth. Miles.		
Budziac Tartary	300	60	1,200,000	Greek Christians, Jews, & Mahometans.
Lesser Tartary	390	65	1,000,000	Ditto.
Crim Tartary	145	80	500,000	Ditto.
Isle of Tenedos	5	3	200	Mahometans.
—Negropont	90	25	25,000	Ditto.
—Lemnos	25	25	4,000	Ditto.
—Paros	36 in compass.		4,500	Greek Christians.
—Lesbos, or Mitylene	160 in compass.		30,000	Mahometans and Greeks.
—Naxia	100 in compass.		8,000	Greeks and Papists.
—Scio, or Chios	112 in compass.		113,000	Greek Christians, Papists, & Mahometans.
—Nio	40 in compass.		1,000	Ditto.
—Scyros	60 in compass.		1,000	Ditto.
—Mycone	36 in compass.		3,000	Ditto.

EUROPE

| Countries. | EXTENT | | Number of Inhabitants. | Religion. |
	Length. Miles.	Breadth. Miles.		
Isle of Samos............	30	15	12,000	Mahometans.
—Nicaria	70 in compass.		3,000	Greek Christians.
—Andros	120 in compass.		4,000	Ditto.
—Cyclades, *Delos the Chief.*			700	Ditto.
—Zia	40 in compass.		8,000	Ditto.
—Cerigo or Cytheraea	50 in compass.		1,000	Ditto.
—Santorin	36 in compass.		10,000	Ditto, and Papists.
—Policandra	8 in compass.		400	Ditto.
—Patmos	18 in compass.		600	Ditto.
—Sephanto	36 in compass.		5,000	Greeks.
—Claros..................	40 in compass.		1,700	Mahometans.
—Amorgo	36 in compass.		4,000	Greek Christians.
—Leros..................	18 in compass		800	Christians and Mahometans.

EUROPE

Countries.	EXTENT		Number of Inhabitants.	Religion.
	Length. Miles.	Breadth. Miles.		
Isle of Thermia............	40 in compass.		6,000	Greek Christians.
—Stampalia................	50 in compass.		3,000	Ditto.
—Salamis	50 in compass.		1,000	Ditto.
—Scarpanta...............	20 in compass.		2,000	Ditto.
—Cephalonia	130 in compass.		50,000	Ditto.
—Zant......................	50 in compass.		30,000	Greek Christians.
—Milo......................	60 in compass.		40,000	Ditto.
—Corfu	120 in compass.		60,000	Ditto.
—Candia, or Crete.......	200	60	400,000	Ditto, and Mahometans.
—Coos, or Stanchia	70 in compass.		12,800	Mahometans and Christians.
—Rhodes..................	60	25	120,000	Ditto.
—Cyprus...................	150	70	300,000	Mahometans.

ASIA

Countries.	EXTENT		Number of Inhabitants.	Religion.
	Length. Miles.	Breadth. Miles.		
Turkey in Asia *contains* ...... Anatolia, Syria, Palestine, Diabekr, Turcomania, and Georgia..............	1,000	800	20,000,000	Mahometanism is most prevalent, but there are many Greek, Latin, Eutychian, and Armenian Christians.
Arabia..............	1,300	1,200	16,000,000	Mahometans.
Persia..............	1,280	1,140	20,000,000	Ditto, of the Sect of Ali.
Great Tartary..............	4,000	1,200	40,000,000	Mahometans and Pagans.
Siberia..............	2,800	960	7,500,000	Greek Christians and Pagans.
Samojedia..............	2,000	370	1,900,000	Pagans.
Kamtscatcha..............	540	236	900,000	Ditto.
Nova Zembla..............	*Undiscovered*		thinly inhabit.	Ditto.
China	1,400	1,260	60,000,000	Ditto.
Japan *contains* Niphon Isl.	900	360	10,000,000	Ditto.

ASIA

| Countries. | EXTENT | | Number of Inhabitants. | Religion. |
	Length. Miles.	Breadth. Miles.		
Isle of Ximo..............	210	200	3,000,000	Pagans.
—Xicoco.................	117	104	1,800,000	Ditto.
—Tsussima	39	34	40,000	Ditto.
—Iki	20	17	6,000	Ditto.
—Kubitessima	30	26	8,000	Ditto.
—Matounsa	54	26	50,000	Ditto.
—Fastistia	36	34	30,000	Ditto.
—Firando	30	28	10,000	Ditto.
—Amacusa	27	24	6,000	Ditto.
—Awasi	30	18	5,000	Ditto.
India, *beyond the Ganges*........	2,000	1,000	50,000,000	Mahometans and Pagans.
Indostan	2,000	1,500	110,000,000	Ditto.
Tibet......................	1,200	480	10,000,000	Pagans.

ASIA

Countries.	EXTENT		Number of Inhabitants.	Religion.
	Length. Miles.	Breadth. Miles.		
Isle of Ceylon..............	250	200	2,000,000	Pagans, except the Dutch Christians.
—Maldives..................	1,000 in number.		100,000	Mahometans.
—Sumatra..................	1,000	100	2,100,000	Ditto, and Pagans.
—Java......................	580	100	2,700,000	Ditto.
—Timor....................	240	54	300,000	Ditto, and a few Christians.
—Borneo...................	800	700	8,000,000	Ditto.
—Celebes	510	240	2,000,000	Ditto.
—Boutam	75	30	80,000	Mahometans.
—Carpentyn	30	3	2,000	Christian Protestants.
—Ourature	18	6	3,000	Pagans.
—Pullo Lout...............	60	36	10,000	Ditto.

Besides the little Islands of Manaar, Aripen, Caradivia, Pengandiva, Analativa, Nainandiva, and Nindundiva, which are inhabited by Christian Protestants.

ASIA

Countries.	EXTENT		Number of Inhabitants.	Religion.
	Length. Miles.	Breadth. Miles.		
And Banca, Madura, Bally, Lambeck, Flores, Solor, Leolana, Pantera, Miscomby, and several others, inhabited by Pagans and Mahometans.				
The Moluccas are,				
—Banda	20	10	6,000	Pagans and Mahometans.
—Buro	25	10	7,000	Ditto.
—Amboyna	25	10	7,500	Christians;—the Dutch have 25 Ch.
—Ceram	210	45	250,000	Pagans and Mahometans.
—Gillola	190	110	650,000	Ditto.

And Pullo-way, Pullo-rin, Nera, Guamanapi, Guilliaien, Ternate, Motir, Machian, and Bachian, which are inhabited by Pagans and Mahometans.

ASIA

The Philippine Islands are supposed to be about 11,000;—some of the chief are,

| Countries. | EXTENT | | Number of Inhabitants. | Religion. |
	Length. Miles.	Breadth. Miles.		
Isle of Mindanao	60	40	18,000	Pagans and Mahometans.
—Bahol	24	12	6,000	Ditto.
—Layta	48	27	10,000	Ditto.
—Parragon	240	60	100,000	Ditto.
The Calamines are Sebu	60	24	10,000	Papists.
—Mindora	60	36	12,000	Pagans and Mahometans.
—Philippina	185	120	104,000	Ditto.
—Negroes Isle	150	60	80,000	Papists.
—Manilla			31,000	Ditto, and Pagans.

The Ladrone Islands are inhabited by most uncivilized Pagans.

ASIA

| Countries. | EXTENT | | Number of Inhabitants. | Religion. |
	Length. Miles.	Breadth. Miles.		
New Holland	2,500	2,000	12,000,000	Pagans;—1 or 2 Ministers are there.
New Zealand*	960	180	1,120,000	Ditto.
New Guinea	1,000	360	1,900,000	Ditto.
New Britain	180	120	900,000	Ditto.
New Ireland	180	60	700,000	Ditto.
Onrong Java	A Cluster of Isles.			Ditto.
New Caledonia	260	30	170,000	Ditto.
New Hebrides				Ditto.
Friendly Isles	20 in number.			Ditto.
Sandwich Isles	7 in number.		400,000	Ditto.
Society Isles	6 in number.		800,000	Ditto.
Kurile Isles	45 in number.		50,000	Ditto.

*Two Islands.

ASIA

Countries.	EXTENT		Number of Inhabitants.	Religion.
	Length. Miles.	Breadth. Miles.		
Pelew Isles				Pagans.
Oonalashaka Isle	40	20	3,000	Ditto.
The other South-Sea Islands.				Ditto.

AFRICA

Egypt................	600	250	2,200,000	Mahometans and Jews.
Nubia	940	600	3,000,000	Ditto.
Barbary..............	1,800	500	3,500,000	Mahometans, Jews, and Christians.

AFRICA

Countries.	EXTENT		Number of Inhabitants.	Religion.
	Length. Miles.	Breadth. Miles.		
Biledulgerid	2,500	350	3,500,000	Mahometans, Christians, and Jews.
Zaara, or the Desart	3,400	660	800,000	Ditto.
Abyssinia	900	800	5,800,000	Armenian Christians.
Abex	540	130	1,600,000	Christians and Pagans.
Negroland	2,200	840	18,000,000	Pagans.
Loango	410	300	1,500,000	Ditto.
Congo	540	220	2,000,000	Ditto.
Angola	360	250	1,400,000	Ditto.
Benguela	430	180	1,600,000	Ditto.
Mataman	450	240	1,500,000	Ditto.
Ajan	900	300	2,500,000	Ditto.
Zanguebar	1,400	350	3,000,000	Ditto.
Monoemugi	900	660	2,000,000	Ditto.

AFRICA

Countries.	EXTENT		Number of Inhabitants.	Religion.
	Length. Miles.	Breadth. Miles.		
Sofala..................	480	300	1,00,000	Pagans.
Terra de natal...........	600	350	2,000,000	Ditto.
Cassraria, or the Hottentots Country...............	708	660	2,000,000	Ditto, & a few Christians at the Cape.
Isle of Madagascar........	1,000	220	2,000,000	Pagans and Mahometans.
—St. Mary..............	54	9	5,000	French Papists.
—Mascarin.............	39	30	17,000	Ditto.
—St. Helena	21 *in compass.*		1,000	English and French Christians.
—Annabon	16	14	4,000	Portuguese Papists.
—St. Thomas..........	25	23	9,000	Pagans.
—Zocotora	80	54	10,000	Mahometans.
—Comora Isles	5 *in number.*		5,000	Ditto.
—Mauritius...........	150 *in compass.*		10,000	French Papists.

AFRICA

Countries.	EXTENT		Number of Inhabitants.	Religion.
	Length. Miles.	Breadth. Miles.		
Isle of Bourbon............	90 in compass.		15,000	French Papists.
—Madeiras	3 in number.		10,000	Papists.
—Cape Verd Isles	10 in number.		20,000	Ditto.
—Canaries................	12 in number.		30,000	Ditto.
—Azores..................	9 in number.		100,000	Ditto.
—Maltha..................	15	8	1,200	Ditto.

AMERICA

Brazil....................		2,900	900	14,000,000	Pagans and Papists.
Paraguay.................		1,140	460	10,000,000	Pagans.
Chile		1,200	500	2,000,000	Pagans and Papists.

AMERICA

| Countries. | EXTENT | | Number of Inhabitants. | Religion. |
	Length. Miles.	Breadth. Miles.		
Peru..........	1,800	600	10,000,000	Pagans and Papists.
Country of the Amazons........	1,200	900	8,000,000	Pagans.
Terra Firma........	1,400	700	10,000,000	Pagans and Papists.
Guiana..........	780	480	2,000,000	Ditto.
Terra Magellancia	1,400	460	9,000,000	Pagans.
Old Mexico	2,220	600	13,500,000	Ditto and Papists.
New Mexico	2,000	1,000	14,000,000	Ditto.
The States of America	1,000	600	3,700,000	Christians, of various denominations.
Terra de Labrador, Nova Scotia, Louisiana, Canada, and all the country inland from Mexico to Hudson's Bay.	1,680	600	8,000,000	Christians, of various denominations, but most of the North-American Indians are Pagans.

AMERICA

| Countries. | EXTENT | | Number of Inhabitants. | Religion. |
	Length. Miles.	Breadth. Miles.		
California, and from thence along the western coast to 70 degrees south latitude, and so far inland as to meet the above article.	2,820	1,380	9,000,000	Pagans.
All to the North of 70 degrees	unknown.			Pagans.
Cape Breton	400	110	20,000	Christians.
—Newfoundland	350	200	1,400	Protestants.
—Cumberland's Isle	780	300	10,000	Pagans.
—Madre de Dios	105	30	8,000	Ditto.
—Terra del Fuego..........	120	36	5,000	Ditto.

AMERICA

Countries.	EXTENT		Number of Inhabitants.	Religion.
	Length. Miles.	Breadth. Miles.		
All the Islands in the vicinity of Cape Horn				Pagans.
The Bermudas extend	16	5	20,000	Half English, and Half Slaves.
The Little Antilles are				
—Aruba	5	3	200	Dutch, and Pagan Negroes.
—Curassoa	30	10	11,000	Ditto.
—Bonaire	10	3	300	Ditto.
—Margaritta.........	40	24	18,000	Spaniards, and Pagan Negroes.
—St. Trinidad	90	60	100,000	Ditto.
The Bahamas are				
—Bahama..............	50	16	16,000	Pagans.
—Providence.........	28	11	6,000	Ditto.

AMERICA

Countries.	EXTENT		Number of Inhabitants.	Religion.
	Length. Miles.	Breadth. Miles.		
Besides Eluthera, Harbour, Lucayonegua, Andross, Cigateo, Guanaliana, Yumeta, Samana, Yuma, Mayaguana, Ynagua, Caieos, Triangula—Pagans.				
The Antilles are				
—Cuba..............	700	60	1,000,000	Papists.
—Jamaica	140	60	400,000	English, and Pagan Negroes.
—St. Domingo	450	150	1,000,000	French, Spaniards, and Negroes.
—Porto Rico	100	49	300,000	Spaniards and Negroes.
—Vache, or Cows I...	18	2	1,000	Ditto.

The Virgin Isles are 12 *in number*, of which Danes Island is the principal—Protestants.

AMERICA

Countries.	EXTENT		Number of Inhabitants.	Religion.
	Length. Miles.	Breadth. Miles.		
The Carribbees are				
—St. Cruz	30	10	13,500	Danish Protestants.
—Anguilla	30	9	6,000	Protestants, and Negroes.
—St. Martin............	21	12	7,500	Ditto.
—St. Bartholomew ...	6	4	720	Ditto.
—Barbuda	20	12	7,500	Ditto.
—Saba	5	4	1,500	Ditto.
—Guardulope..........	45	38	50,000	Catholics, and Pagan Negroes.
—Marigalante.........	15	12	5,400	Ditto.
—Tobago	32	9	2,400	Ditto.
—Desiada...............	12	6	1,500	Ditto.
—Granada	30	15	13,500	English, and Pagan Negroes.
—St. Lucia.............	23	12	5,000	Ditto, and Native Pagan Caribbs.

AMERICA

Countries.	EXTENT		Number of Inhabitants.		Religion.
	Length. Miles.	Breadth. Miles.	Whites.	Negroes.	
—St. Eustatia............	6	4	5,000	15,000	Dutch, English, &c.
—St. Christopher......	20	7	6,000	36,000	English.
—Nevis....................	6	4	5,000	10,000	Ditto.
—Antigua................	20	20	7,000	30,000	Ditto.
—Montserrat	6	6	5,000	10,000	Ditto.
—Martinico	60	30	20,000	50,000	French.
—St. Vincent's.........	24	18	8,000	5,000	The 8,000 are Native Caribbs.
—Barbadoes	21	14	50,000	100,000	English.
—Dominica..............	28	13		40,000	Ditto, 2,000 of them Native Caribbs.
—St. Thomas	15 in compass.			8,000	Danish Protestants.

This, as nearly as I can obtain information, is the state of the world; though in many countries, as Turkey, Arabia, Great Tartary, Africa, and America except the United States, and most of the Asiatic Islands, we have no accounts of the number of inhabitants that can be relied on. I have therefore only calculated the extent, and counted a certain number on an average per square mile; in some countries more, and in others less, according as circumstances determine. A few general remarks upon it will conclude this section.

First, the inhabitants of the world according to this calculation amount to about seven hundred and thirty-one millions; four hundred and twenty millions of whom are still in pagan darkness; an hundred and thirty millions of the followers of Mahomet; an hundred millions catholics; forty-four millions protestants; thirty millions of the Greek and Armenian churches, and perhaps seven millions of Jews. It must undoubtedly strike every thinking mind that a vast proportion of the sons of Adam remain in the most deplorable state of heathen darkness, without any means of knowing the true God, except what are afforded them by the works of nature; and utterly destitute of the knowledge of the gospel of Christ, or of any means of obtaining it. In many of these countries they have no written language, consequently no Bible, and are only led by the most childish customs and traditions. Such, for instance, are all the middle and back parts of North America, the inland parts of South America, the South Sea Islands, New Holland, New Zealand, New Guinea; and I may add Great Tartary, Siberia, Samojedia, and the other parts of Asia contiguous to the frozen sea; the greatest part of Africa, the island of Madagascar, and many places beside. In many of these parts also they are cannibals, feeding upon the flesh of their slain enemies with the greatest brutality and eagerness. The truth of this was ascertained beyond a doubt by the late eminent navigator, Cooke, of the New Zealanders and some of the inhabitants of the western coast of America. Human sacrifices are also very frequently offered, so that scarce a week elapses without instances of this kind. They are in general poor, barbarous, naked pagans, as destitute of civilization as they are of true religion.

Secondly, barbarous as these poor heathens are, they appear to be as capable of knowledge as we are; and in many places, at least, have displayed uncommon genius and teachability; and I greatly question whether most of the barbarities practiced by them have not originated in some real or supposed affront, and are therefore more properly acts of self-defence than proofs of inhuman and bloodthirsty dispositions.

Thirdly, in other parts where they have a written language, as in the East Indies, China, Japan, etc., they know nothing of the gospel. The Jesuits indeed once made many converts to popery among the Chinese; but their highest aim seemed to be to obtain their good opinion; for though the converts professed themselves Christians, yet they were allowed to honour the image of Confucius their great lawgiver; and at length their ambitious intrigues brought upon them the displeasure of the government, which terminated in the suppression of the mission and almost, if not entirely, of the Christian name. It is also a melancholy fact that the vices of Europeans have been communicated wherever they themselves have been; so that the religious state of even heathens has been rendered worse by dealings with them!

Fourthly, a very great proportion of Asia and Africa, with some parts of Europe, are Mahometans; and those in Persia who are of the sect of Hali, are the most inveterate enemies to the Turks; and they in return abhor the Persians. The Africans are some of the most ignorant of all the Mahometans; especially the Arabs, who are scattered through all the northern parts of Africa, and live upon the depredations which they are continually making upon their neighbours.

Fifthly, in respect of those who bear the Christian name, a very great degree of ignorance and immorality abounds amongst them. There are Christians, so called, of the Greek and Armenian churches, in all the Mahometan countries; but they are, if possible, more ignorant and vicious than the Mahometans themselves. The Georgian Christians, who are near the Caspian Sea, maintain themselves by selling their neighbours, relations, and children, for slaves to the Turks and Persians. And it is remarked that if any of the Greeks of Anatolia turn Muslim, the Turks never set store by them, on account of their being so much noted for dissimulation and hypocrisy. It is well known that most of the members of the Greek Church are very ignorant. Papists also are in general ignorant of divine things, and very vicious. Nor do the bulk of the Church of England much exceed them, either in knowledge or in holiness; and many errors, and much looseness of conduct, are to be found amongst dissenters of all denominations. The Lutherans of Denmark are much on a par with the churchmen in England; and the face of most Christian countries presents a dreadful scene of ignorance, hypocrisy, and profligacy. Various baneful and pernicious errors appear to gain ground in almost every part of Christendom; the truths of the gospel, and even the gospel itself, are attacked, and every method that the enemy can invent is employed to undermine the kingdom of our Lord Jesus Christ.

All these things are loud calls to Christians, and especially to ministers, to exert themselves to the utmost in their several spheres of action, and to try to enlarge them as much as possible.

SECTION FOUR
The Practicability of Something being done, more than what is done, for the Conversion of the Heathen.

The impediments in the way of carrying the gospel among the heathen must arise, I think, from one or other of the following things: either their distance from us, their barbarous and savage manner of living, the danger of being killed by them, the difficulty of procuring the necessities of life, or the unintelligibleness of their languages.

First, as to their distance from us, whatever objections might have been made on that account before the invention of the mariner's compass, nothing can be alleged for it with any colour of plausibility in the present age. Men can now sail with as much certainty through the Great South Sea as they can through the Mediterranean or any lesser sea. Yea, and Providence seems in a manner to invite us to the trial, as there are to our knowledge trading companies whose commerce lies in many of the places where these barbarians dwell. At one time or other ships are sent to visit places of more recent discovery, and to explore parts the most unknown; and every fresh account of their ignorance, or cruelty, should call forth our pity, and excite us to concur with Providence in seeking their eternal good. Scripture likewise seems to point out this method, "Surely the Isles shall wait for me; the ships of Tarshish first, to bring my sons from far, their silver, and their gold with them, unto the name of the Lord, thy God" (Isaiah 60:9). This seems to imply that in the time of the glorious increase of the church in the latter days, of which the whole chapter is undoubtedly a prophecy, commerce shall subserve the spread of the gospel. The ships of Tarshish were trading vessels which made voyages for goods to various parts; this much therefore must be meant by it, that navigation, especially that which is commercial, shall be one great means of carrying on the work of God; and perhaps it may imply that there shall be a very considerable appropriation of wealth to that purpose.

Secondly, as to their uncivilized and barbarous way of living, this can be no objection to any except those whose love of ease renders them unwilling to expose themselves to inconveniences for the good of others.

It was no objection to the apostles and their successors, who went among the barbarous Germans and Gauls, and still more barbarous Britons! They did not wait for the ancient inhabitants of these countries to be civilized before they could be christianized, but went simply with the doctrine of the cross; and Tertullian could boast that "those parts of Britain that were proof against the Roman armies were conquered by the gospel of Christ." It was no objection to an Elliott, or a Brainerd, in later times. They went forth, and encountered every difficulty of the kind, and found that a cordial reception of the gospel produced those happy effects which the longest intercourse with Europeans could never accomplish without the gospel. It now is no objection to commercial men. It only requires that we should have as much love for the souls of our fellow-creatures and fellow-sinners as they have for the profits arising from a few otter-skins, and all these difficulties would be easily surmounted.

After all, the uncivilized state of the heathen, instead of affording an objection against preaching the gospel to them, ought to furnish an argument for it. Can we as men, or as Christians, hear that ignorance and barbarism envelops a great part of our fellow creatures, whose souls are as immortal as ours and who are as capable as ourselves of adorning the gospel, and contributing by their preaching, writings, or practices to the glory of our Redeemer's name, and the good of the church? Can we hear that they are without the gospel, without government, without laws, and without arts and sciences, and not exert ourselves to introduce amongst them the sentiments of men, and of Christians? Would not the spread of the gospel be the most effectual means of their civilization? Would that not make them useful members of society? We know that such effects did in measure follow the afore-mentioned efforts of Elliott, Brainerd, and others amongst the American Indians; and if similar attempts were made in other parts of the world, and were followed with a divine blessing (which we have every reason to think they would) might we not expect to see able Divines, or read well-conducted treatises in the defence of the truth, even amongst those who at present seem to be scarcely human?

Thirdly, in respect to the danger of being killed by them, it is true that whoever goes must put his life in his hand, and not consult with flesh and blood; but do not the goodness of the cause, the duties incumbent on us as the creatures of God, and Christians, and the perishing state of our fellow men, loudly call upon us to venture all and use every warrantable exertion for their benefit? Paul and Barnabas, who "hazarded their lives for the name of the Lord Jesus Christ" (Acts 15:26), were not blamed as being rash but commended for so doing, while John Mark, who through timidity of mind deserted them in their perilous undertaking, was branded with censure. After all, as has been already observed, I greatly question whether most of the barbarities practiced by the savages upon those who have visited them have not originated in some real or supposed affront, and were therefore more properly acts of self-defence than proofs of ferocious dispositions. No wonder if the imprudence of sailors should prompt them to offend the simple savage, and the offence be resented; but Elliott, Brainerd, and the Moravian missionaries have been very seldom molested. Nay, in general the heathen have showed a willingness to hear the word; and have principally expressed their hatred of Christianity on account of the vices of nominal Christians.

Fourthly, as to the difficulty of procuring the necessities of life, this would not be so great as may appear at first sight; for though we could not procure European food, yet we might procure such as the natives of those countries which we visit subsist upon themselves. And this would only be passing through what we have virtually engaged in by entering on the ministerial office. A Christian minister is person who is "not his own" (1 Cor. 6:19); he is the "servant" of God, and therefore ought to be wholly devoted to him. By entering on that sacred office he solemnly undertakes to be always engaged as much as possible in the Lord's work, and not to choose his own pleasure or employment, or pursue the ministry as a something that is to subserve his own ends or interest, or as a kind of sideline. He engages to go where God pleases, and to do or endure what he sees fit to command or call him to in the exercise of his function. He virtually bids farewell to friends, pleasures, and comforts, and stands in readiness to endure the greatest sufferings in the work of the Lord, his Master. It is inconsistent for ministers to please themselves with thoughts of a numerous congregation, cordial friends, a civilized country, legal protection, affluence, splendour, or even an income that is sufficient. The slights and hatred of men, and even pretended friends, gloomy prisons, and tortures, the society of barbarians of uncouth speech, miserable accommodations in wretched wildernesses, hunger and thirst, nakedness, weariness, and diligence, hard work, and but little worldly encouragement, should rather be the objects of their expectation. Thus the apostles acted in primitive times and endured hardness as good soldiers of Jesus Christ; and though we live in a civilized country where Christianity is protected by law, and are not called to suffer these things while we continue here, yet I question whether all are justified in staying here, while so many are perishing without means of grace in other lands. I am sure that it is entirely contrary to the spirit of the gospel for its ministers to enter upon it from motives of self-interest or with great worldly expectations. On the contrary the commission is a sufficient call to them to venture all, and, like the primitive Christians, go everywhere preaching the gospel.

It might be necessary, however, for two, at least, to go together, and in general I should think it best that they should be married men. To prevent their time from being employed in procuring necessities, two or more other persons, with their wives and families, might also accompany them, who would be wholly employed in providing for them. In most countries it would be necessary for them to cultivate a little spot of ground just for their support, which would be a resource for them whenever their supplies failed. Not to mention the advantage they would reap from each other's company, it would take off the enormous expense which has always attended undertakings of this kind, for the first expense would be the whole; for though a large colony needs support for a considerable time, yet so small a number would, upon receiving the first crop, maintain themselves. They would have the advantage of choosing their situation, their wants would be few; the women, and even the children, would be necessary for domestic purposes; and a few articles of stock, as a cow or two, and a bull, and a few other cattle of both sexes, a very few utensils of husbandry, and some corn to sow their land, would be sufficient. Those who attend the missionaries should understand husbandry, fishing, fowling, etc., and be provided with the necessary implements for these purposes. Indeed a variety of methods may be thought of, and when once the work is undertaken, many things will suggest themselves to us, of which we at present can form no idea.

Fifthly, as to learning their languages, the same means would be found necessary here as in trade between different nations. In some cases interpreters might be obtained, who might be employed for a time; and where these were not to be found, the missionaries must have patience, and mingle with the people, till they have learned so much of the language as to be able to communicate their ideas to them in it. It is well known to require no very extraordinary talents to learn, in the space of a year, or two at most, the language of any people upon earth, so much of it, at least, as to be able to convey any sentiments we wish to their understandings.

The missionaries must be men of great piety, prudence, courage, and forbearance; of undoubted orthodoxy in their sentiments, and must enter with all their hearts into the spirit of their mission; they must be willing to leave all the comforts of life behind them, and to encounter all the hardships of a torrid or a frigid climate, an uncomfortable manner of living, and every other inconvenience that can attend this undertaking. Clothing, a few knives, powder and shot, fishing-tackle, and the articles of husbandry above-mentioned, must be provided for them; and when arrived at the place of their destination, their first business must be to gain some acquaintance with the language of the natives (for which purpose two would be better than one), and by all lawful means to endeavour to cultivate a friendship with them, and as soon as possible let them know the errand for which they were sent. They must endeavour to convince them that it was their good alone which induced them to forsake their friends and all the comforts of their native country.

They must be very careful not to resent injuries which may be offered to them, nor to think highly of themselves so as to despise the poor heathens, and by those means lay a foundation for their resentment or their rejection of the gospel. They must take every opportunity of doing them good, and labouring and travelling night and day they must instruct, exhort, and rebuke, with all long-suffering, and anxious desire for them, and, above all, must be instant in prayer for the outpouring of the Holy Spirit upon the people of their charge. Let but missionaries of the above description engage in the work and we shall see that it is not impracticable.

It might likewise be important, if God should bless their labours, for them to encourage any appearance of gifts amongst the people of their charge; if such should be raised up many advantages would be derived from their knowledge of the language and customs of their countrymen; and their change of conduct would give great weight to their ministrations.

SECTION FIVE
An Enquiry into the Duty of Christians in general, and what means ought to be used, in order to promote this work.

If the prophecies concerning the increase of Christ's kingdom be true, and if what has been argued concerning the commission given by him to his disciples being obligatory on us be just, it must be inferred that all Christians ought heartily to concur with God in promoting his glorious designs, for "he that is joined to the Lord is one Spirit" (1 Cor. 6:17).

One of the first and most important of those duties which are incumbent upon us is fervent and united prayer. However the influence of the Holy Spirit may be set at nought and run down by many, it will be found upon trial that all means which we can use will be ineffectual without it. If a temple is raised for God in the heathen world, it will not be "by might, nor by power," nor by the authority of the magistrate, or the eloquence of the orator; "but by my Spirit, saith the Lord of Hosts" (Zech. 4:6). We must therefore be in real earnest in supplicating his blessing upon our labours.

It is represented in the prophets that when there shall be "a great mourning in the land, as the mourning of Hadadrimmon in the valley of Megiddon, and every family shall mourn apart, and their wives apart," it shall all follow upon "a Spirit of grace, and supplication." And when these things shall take place it is promised that "there shall be a fountain opened for the house of David, and for the inhabitants of Jerusalem, for sin, and for uncleanness," and that "the idols shall be destroyed," and "the false prophets ashamed" of their profession. (Zech. 12:10-13:4.) This prophecy seems to teach that when there shall be a universal joining in fervent prayer, and all shall esteem Zion's welfare as their own, then upon the churches shall be shed copious influences of the Spirit, which like a purifying "fountain" shall cleanse the servants of the Lord. Nor shall this cleansing influence stop here; all old idolatrous prejudices shall be rooted out, and truth prevail so gloriously that false teachers shall be so ashamed as rather to wish to be classed with obscure herdsmen, or the meanest peasants, than bear the ignominy attendant upon their detection.

The most glorious works of grace that have ever taken place have been in answer to prayer; and it is in this way, we have the greatest reason to suppose, that the glorious outpouring of the Spirit, which we expect at last, will be bestowed.

With respect to our own immediate connections, we have within these few years been favoured with some tokens for good, granted in answer to prayer, which should encourage us to persist and increase in that important duty. I trust our monthly prayer-meetings for the success of the gospel have not been in vain. It is true a want of importunity generally attends our prayers; yet unimportunate and feeble as they have been, it is to be believed that God has heard, and in a measure answered them. The churches that have engaged in the practice have in general since that time been evidently on the increase; some controversies which have long perplexed and divided the church are more clearly stated than ever; there are calls to preach the gospel in many places where it has not been usually published; yea, a glorious door is opened, and is likely to be opened wider and wider, by the spread of civil and religious liberty, accompanied also by a diminution of the spirit of popery; a noble effort has been made to abolish the inhuman Slave Trade, and though at present it has not been so successful as might be wished, yet it is to be hoped it will be persevered in till it is accomplished. In the meantime it is a satisfaction to consider that the late defeat of the abolition of the Slave Trade has proved the occasion of a praiseworthy effort to introduce a free settlement, at Sierra Leone on the coast of Africa; an effort which, if followed with a divine blessing, not only promises to open a way for honourable commerce with that extensive country, and for the civilization of its inhabitants, but may prove the happy means of introducing amongst them the gospel of our Lord Jesus Christ.

These are events that ought not to be overlooked; they are not to be reckoned small things; and yet perhaps they are small compared with what might have been expected, if all had cordially entered into the spirit of the proposal, so as to have made the cause of Christ their own, or in other words to have been so solicitous about it as if their own advantage depended upon its success. If an holy solicitude had prevailed in all the assemblies of Christians on behalf of their Redeemer's kingdom, we might probably have seen before now not only an "open door" (2 Cor. 2:12) for the gospel, but "many running to and fro, and knowledge increased" (Dan. 12:4); or a diligent use of those means which Providence has put in our power accompanied with a greater than ordinary blessing from heaven.

Many can do nothing but pray, and prayer is perhaps the only thing in which Christians of all denominations can cordially and unreservedly unite; but in this we may all be one, and in this the strictest unanimity ought to prevail. Were the whole body thus animated by one soul, with what pleasure would Christians thus attend on all the duties of religion, and with what delight would their ministers attend on all the business of their calling.

We must not be contented however with praying without exerting ourselves in the use of means for the obtaining of those things we pray for. Were "the children of light" but "as wise in their generation as the children of this world" (Luke 16:8), they would stretch every nerve to gain so glorious a prize, nor ever imagine it was to be obtained in any other way.

When a trading company have obtained their charter they usually go to its utmost limits; and their stocks, their ships, their officers and men are so chosen and regulated as to be likely to answer their purpose; but they do not stop here, for encouraged by the prospect of success they use every effort, cast their bread upon the waters, cultivate friendship with everyone from whose information they expect the least advantage. They cross the widest and most tempestuous seas and encounter the most unfavourable climates; they introduce themselves into the most barbarous nations, and sometimes undergo the most affecting hardships; their minds continue in a state of anxiety, and suspense, and a longer delay than usual in the arrival of a vessel agitates them with a thousand changeful thoughts and foreboding apprehensions which continue till the rich returns are safe arrived in port. But why these fears? Whence all these disquietudes, and this labour? Is it not because their souls enter into the spirit of the project, and their happiness in a way depends on its success? Christians are a body whose truest interest lies in the exaltation of the Messiah's kingdom. Their charter is very extensive, their encouragements exceeding great, and the returns promised infinitely superior to all the gains of the most lucrative company. Let then everyone in his station consider himself as bound to act with all his might and in every possible way for God.

Suppose a company of serious Christians, ministers and private persons, were to form themselves into a society, and make a number of rules respecting the regulation of the plan, and the persons who are to be employed as missionaries, the means of defraying the expense, etc., etc. This society must consist of persons whose hearts are in the work, men of serious religion, and possessing a spirit of perseverance; there must be a determination not to admit any person who is not of this description, or to retain him longer than he answers to it.

From such a society a committee might be appointed, whose business it should be to procure all the information they could upon the subject, to receive contributions, to enquire into the characters, tempers, abilities and religious views of the missionaries, and also to provide them with the necessities for their undertakings.

They must also pay a great attention to the views of those who undertake this work; for want of this the missions to the Spice Islands, sent by the Dutch East India Company, were soon corrupted, many going more for the sake of settling in a place where temporal gain invited them, than of preaching to the poor Indians. This soon introduced a number of indolent or profligate persons, whose lives were a scandal to the doctrines which they preached; and by means of whom the gospel was ejected from Ternate in 1694, and Christianity fell into great disrepute in other places.

If there is any reason for me to hope that I shall have any influence upon any of my brethren and fellow Christians, probably it may be more especially amongst them of my own denomination. I would therefore propose that such a society and committee should be formed amongst the particular baptist denomination.

I do not mean by this in any way to confine it to one denomination of Christians. I wish with all my heart that everyone who loves our Lord Jesus Christ in sincerity would in some way or other engage in it. But in the present divided state of Christendom it would be more likely for good to be done by each denomination engaging separately in the work than if they were to embark in it together. There is room enough for us all, without interfering with each other; and if no unfriendly interference took place, each denomination would bear good will to the other, and wish and pray for its success, considering it as upon the whole friendly to the great cause of true religion; but if all were intermingled, it is likely their private discords might throw a damp upon their spirits, and much retard their public usefulness.

In respect to contributions for defraying the expenses, money will doubtless be wanting; and suppose the rich were to use in this important undertaking a portion of that wealth over which God has made them stewards, perhaps there are few ways that would turn to a better account at last. Nor ought it to be confined to the rich; if persons of more moderate circumstances were to devote a portion, suppose a tenth, of their annual increase to the Lord, it would not only correspond with the practice of the Israelites, who lived under the Mosaic economy, but of the patriarchs Abraham, Isaac, and Jacob, before that dispensation commenced. Many of our most eminent forefathers amongst the Puritans followed that practice; and if that were but attended to now, there would not only be enough to support the ministry of the gospel at home, and to encourage village preaching in our respective neighbourhoods, but to defray the expenses of carrying the gospel into the heathen world.

If congregations were to open subscriptions of one penny or more per week, according to their circumstances, and deposit it as a fund for the propagation of the gospel, much might be raised in this way. By such simple means they might soon have it in their power to introduce the preaching of the gospel into most of the villages in England; where, though men are placed whose business it should be to give light to those who sit in darkness, it is well known that they have it not. Where there was no person to open his house for the reception of the gospel, some other building might be procured for a small sum, and even then something considerable might be spared for the baptist or other committees for propagating the gospel amongst the heathen.

Many persons have of late left off the use of West India sugar on account of the iniquitous manner in which it is obtained. Those families which have done so, and have not substituted anything else in its place, have not only cleansed their hands of blood, but have made a saving to their families, some of sixpence, and some of a shilling a week. If this or a part of this were appropriated to the uses previously mentioned, it would abundantly suffice. We have only to keep the end in view, and have our hearts thoroughly engaged in the pursuit of it, and means will not be very difficult.

We are exhorted "to lay up treasure in heaven, where neither moth nor rust doth corrupt, nor thieves break through and steal" (Matt. 6:19). It is also declared that "whatsoever a man soweth, that shall he also reap" (Gal. 6:7). These Scriptures teach us that the enjoyments of the life to come bear a near relation to that which now is; a relation similar to that of the harvest, and the seed. It is true all the reward is of mere grace, but it is nevertheless encouraging; what a "treasure," what a "harvest" must wait such characters as Paul, and Elliott, and Brainerd, and others, who have given themselves wholly to the work of the Lord. What a heaven will it be to see the many myriads of poor heathens, of Britons among the rest, who by their labours have been brought to the knowledge of God. Surely a "crown of rejoicing" (1 Thess. 2:19) like this is worth aspiring to. Surely it is worth while to lay ourselves out with all our might in promoting the cause and kingdom of Christ.

INDEX